The Social Dimensions
of Learning Disabilities

Essays in Honor of Tanis Bryan

The LEA Series of Special Education and Disability
John Wills Lloyd, Series Editor

The Social Dimensions of Learning Disabilities

Essays in Honor of Tanis Bryan

Edited by

Bernice Y. L. Wong
Simon Fraser University

Mavis L. Donahue
University of Illinois at Chicago

2002

LAWRENCE ERLBAUM ASSOCIATES, PUBLISHERS
Mahwah, New Jersey   London

Lawrence Erlbaum Associates, Inc., Publishers
10 Industrial Avenue
Mahwah, New Jersey 07430

Cover design by Kathryn Houghtaling Lacey

Library of Congress Cataloging-in-Publication Data

The social dimensions of learning disabilities : essays in honor of Tanis Bryan / edited
by Bernice Y. L. Wong, Mavis L. Donahue.
    p. cm.
  Includes bibliographical references and index.
  ISBN 0-8058-3918-6 (cloth : alk. paper)
    1.   Learning disabled children—Education. 2. Learning disabilities—Social aspects. I.
Bryan, Tanis H., 1937- II. Wong, Bernice Y. L. III. Donahue, Mavis L.

  LC4704.5 .S63 2002
  371.9—dc21

                  2002016371

Books published by Lawrence Erlbaum Associates are printed on acid-free paper,
and their bindings are chosen for strength and durability.

Printed in the United States of America
10   9   8   7   6   5   4   3   2   1

Contents

v

Preface

Teachers and parents have always recognized the central role of social development in the lives of students with learning disabilities (LD). The pioneers of the field of learning disabilities, Kirk, Johnson and Mykelbust, Orton, also acknowledged social skills as a significant challenge for many of these students. Yet it was not until 1974 that two research articles were published that made the quality of these children's social lives impossible to ignore. Tanis Bryan (1974a) reported that mainstreamed children identified as LD were not only less popular than other children, but that their communicative environment with typical non-LD peers was more hostile (Bryan, 1974b). These startling findings ignited an explosion of research on the social development of students with LD.

More than 200 studies in the past 25 years have replicated, extended, refined, and clarified these findings. These studies have varied widely in theoretical perspectives, methodological techniques, and their participants' individual and demographic characteristics, and histories of educational placements (see Gresham & MacMillan, 1997; Pearl & Bay, 1999, for excellent reviews). Moreover, a meta-analysis of 152 of these studies (Kavale & Forness, 1996) showed that 3 out of 4 students with LD had social skills characteristics that are significantly different from typical non-LD peers. This proportion held true across teacher, peer, and self-ratings, and across most aspects of social competence.

Tanis Bryan is the pioneer in research on social competence of children with LD. Together with her research associates: Ruth Pearl, Mavis Donahue, James Bryan, and Susanna Pflaum, Tanis Bryan systematically researched critical issues concerning the low social competence or unpopularity of children with LD. They developed an interactional framework to guide their investigations. This framework assumed that "characteristics of children interact in significant ways with characteristics of teachers, classrooms, and families" (Bryan et al., 1983, p. 1). At the Chicago Institute of Research on Learning Disabilities (1977–1983), Bryan and her research team conducted numerous studies that covered diverse topics related to the social worlds of students with LD, including communicative competence and causal attributions, as well as the perceptions of others (peers, teachers, parents, and even naive raters) about these students' social interactions.

Tanis Bryan (1998) provides an excellent summary of the Chicago Institute's research. It suffices for us to highlight some of the most instructive findings, findings that resonate to what researchers and teachers continue to observe in children and adolescents with LD. These are the quallitative differences in communication between students with LD and their normally achieving peers. Specifically, as speakers, children with LD were found to be less assertive, less able to persuade their normally achieving peers to agree with them, less able to maintain an interesting flow in conversation by posing more open-ended questions. As listeners, they tended to be passive and not ask clarifying questions when the task was ambiguous.

Additionally, Tanis and her associates found an intriguing attribution pattern among children with LD. When they met success, they tended to attribute it to luck or teacher favor. When they failed, they tended to attribute it to a lack of ability. This finding underscores possible reasons why students with LD do not expend effort at learning. Other researchers, such as John Borkowski at Notre Dame University, have always maintained that students with LD need to learn that academic learning involves effort. The maladaptive attribution pattern that was found by Bryan and her associates suggests that reattribution training for children with LD may well be in order. Otherwise, they may remain relectant to expend effort at learning. Borkowski too, promotes reattribution learning for children with LD.

The impact of Tanis Bryan's research at the Chicago Institute has had a profound impact on the learning disabilities field, establishing social competence as the major area of basic and applied research. Since their seminal work, other researchers have broadened and deepened the research questions into related reasons (e.g., families of children with LD who have poor social competence, and loneliness of children with LD who have social–relational problems). As well, the original pioneering research by Bryan and her associates spawned social skills intervention research which assumed prominence in the 1990s (see Vaughn & Sinagub, 1997). Thus, research on social dimensions of learning disabilities is a vibrant area that appears to hold consistent and strong interests among university–college instructors, researchers, undergraduate and graduate students, and professionals in the learning disabilties field and related fields such as psychology and social work.

Surprisingly, despite the important accumulation of 25 years of research on the social dimensions of learning disabilities, to date, there is no book devoted to this research topic. We think that such a book is needed. A book that summarizes research findings and their implictions in the various areas in social dimensions of LD will be: (a) an excellent text for a special topics course in graduate programs in learning disabilities, special education, psychology, social work, and (b) a highly important resource for university–college teachers, researchers, graduate and honors students, and professionals in learning disabilities, social psychology, and social work.

The table of contents shows the range of topics that reflects nicely on the richness of the research interests on social dimensions of LD. The opening chapter places in context the work of Tanis Bryan and the researchers that follow her lead, in terms of the prevailing theoretical frameworks and social–political influences that led to the enormous impact of the work. In chapter 2, Tur-Kaspa grounds her research on social–relational problems of children and adolescents with LD in social cognition. She shows the relevance and appropriateness of social cogniton to this area of research. Cosden, Brown, and Elliott (chap. 3) offer interesting research on self-understanding and self-esteem in children and adults with LD. Margalit and Al-Yagon explore the lonely plight of children with LD. Their research furthers our awareness of the consequences of low social competence in children with LD. Chapter 5 by Pearl focus on peer influence on students with LD. Wiener (chap. 6) complements the chapter by Pearl by elaborating on the friendship patterns of children with LD. She examines extant research findings on variables related to these patterns, such as the number of friends, the identity of friends, and the stability and quality of friendships. Elaborating on significant others in the school environment of students with LD, Bay (chap. 7) writes on how teachers can be equipped to help students with LD in their social and emotional worlds. Keeping the theme of significant others in the lives of children with LD, Stone, Bradley, and Kleiner (chap. 8) discuss parental understanding and how this understanding shapes their scaffolding of learning in their children with language and learning disabilities. Their chapter presents new research that extends Stone's interest on scaffolding.

Turning to intervention research, Sridhar and Vaughn (chap. 9) report a new intervention approach toward enhancing self-concept and reading comprehension in students with LD through bibliotherapy. In chapter 10, Hutchinson, Freeman, and Steiner Bell provide important and timely information on interventions targeting enhancing peer relations and preventing school drop-out in adolescents with LD. The volume concludes with Keogh's chapter on models in longitudinal research with implications for research on social dimensions of learning disabilities.

REFERENCES

Bryan, T. (1974a). An observational analysis of classroom behaviors of children with learning disabilities. *Journal of Learning Disabilities, 7,* 26-34.

Bryan, T. (1947b). Peer popularity of learning disabled children. *Journal of Learning Disabilities, 7,* 621-625.

Bryan, T. (1983). Learning disabled children and youth's social competence. *Thalamus, 2,* 125.

Bryan, T. (1998). Social competence and learning disabled students. In B. Y. L. Wong (Ed.), *Learning about learning disabilities* (2nd ed., pp. 237-267). San Diego, CA: Academic Press.

Gresham, F. M., & MacMillan, D. L. (1997). Social competence and affective characteristics of students with mild disabilities. *Review of Educational Research, 67,* 377-415.

Kavale, K., & Forness, S. (1996). Social skill deficits and learning disabilities: A meta-analysis. *Journal of Learning Disabilities, 29,* 226-237.

Pearl, R., & Bay, M. (1999). Psychosocial correlates of learning disabilities. In V. L. Schwean & D. H. Saklofske (Eds.), *Handbook of psychosocial characteristics of exceptional children.* New York: Plenum Press.

Vaughn, S., & Sinagub, J. M. (1997). Social assessment of at-risk populations: Implications for students with learning disabilities. In S. M. Clancy Dollinger & L. DiLalla (Eds.), *Assessment and intervention issues across the lifespan* (pp. 159-180). Mahwah, NJ: Lawrence Erlbaum Associates.

Chapter 1

How to Start a Revolution

Mavis L. Donahue
University of Illinois at Chicago

Bernice Y. L. Wong
Simon Fraser University

How can a five-page research article start a revolution? In December of 1974 an article succinctly titled "Peer Popularity of Learning Disabled Children" appeared in the *Journal of Learning Disabilities*. Sandwiched between "The Organic Psychosyndrome of Early Childhood and its Effects on Learning" and "The Relation of Subclinical Lead Level to Cognitive and Sensorimotor Impairment in Black Preschoolers," Tanis Bryan's article was the "study read 'round the world." The notion that the social domain deserved significant attention was a radical departure from the focus on neurological/cognitive processing deficits typical of the 1960s and 1970s. For the first time the findings validated what families and teachers had long realized: that academic achievement was not the only challenge faced by children with learning disabilities (LD). Perhaps no other research topic in the field of learning disabilities has so resonated with the collective beliefs and values of those who care for and about these students.

In 2002, the claim that peer acceptance and positive social interaction is essential to children's development will likely receive the response "well, duh!" In fact, perhaps at no time in history have so many diverse theoretical perspectives converged on the importance of positive peer interaction to human development. Even medical models now acknowledge the benefits of peer support to physical and emotional well-being. One recent media frenzy centered on a book (Harris, 1998) that re-interpreted decades of research to support the claim that peers significantly outweigh parents in their influence on child development. In October of 2000 a federally funded conference was held at Temple University to address "The Other Side of the Report Card," focusing on the policy implications of research on how social and emotional factors influence academic and vocational success.

Of course, forefathers and foremothers of the learning disabilities field clearly recognized the central role of positive social interaction in the development of children with LD (e.g., Johnson & Myklebust, 1967; Orton, 1937). Yet as the emerging field struggled to establish learning disabilities as distinct from mental retardation and emotional disorders, early pioneers probably felt compelled to downplay the inter-relationships among social-emotional difficulties and learning disabilities. Instead, they initiated the tradition of research on learning disabilities as a search for the specific cognitive and neurological processes that underlie language and literacy disabilities. As a result, most definitions of learning disabilities specifically exclude students whose academic or language difficulties are primarily caused by problems in social interaction.

In 1974 two articles were published that made the quality of these children's social lives impossible to ignore. The first red flag suggested a less positive and less responsive classroom environment for mainstreamed children identified as LD than for their typical classmates (Bryan, 1974a). Using traditional sociometric methods, Bryan (1974b) confirmed these behavioral clues. She compared the peer ratings of 84 children with LD in 62 classrooms, across Grades 4, 5, and 6, with nondisabled children matched on gender, race, and classroom.

Typical of research on "individual differences," the findings were not straightforward. Although there was a main effect showing that students with LD received fewer nominations for positive social characteristics and more nominations for negative traits, the factors of race and gender made a difference. The groups most likely to be rated negatively by peers were girls with LD, and White students with LD. One year later, these group differences were replicated with 25 of the same White children with LD, even in classrooms where there was less than 25% overlap in peer raters across the 2 years (Bryan, 1976). This study represents one of the earliest research attempts to test the reliability of children's social characteristics across time, raters, and settings (cf. Keogh, chap. 11, this volume).

Like all revolutionary research, these findings raised more questions and speculations than were answered. Bryan (1974b) discussed three possible explanations for less positive peer ratings of the students with LD: lower intellectual and/or academic abilities, the potential stigma of the "learning disabilities" label, and differing expectations for academic achievement depending on race and gender. She then raised the issue that has perhaps sparked the most interest and controversy, that is, that whatever factors lead a child to have a learning disability might also affect a child's social learning. Deficits in attention, language, or perception might hinder the child in detecting critical cues or making inferences about people just as they appear to hinder the child in the acquisition of academic information. In short, the findings may support the premise that lack of peer popularity is not a question of intelligence, labeling, or expectancy, but rather another symptom of learning disabilities.

She makes an even bolder claim in 1976, when she affirms that "social status should be considered part of the child's learning disability (p. 311).

Given this stance, Bryan (1974b) then endorsed "educational programs which have social/affective components as well as cognitive/achievement goals" (p. 624), and affirmed "the need to think of social relationships much as we think about reading, writing, and spelling" (1976, p. 311). These claims must have seemed almost blasphemous in an era dominated by academic remediation models that focused on strengthening underlying information processing deficits (e.g., auditory sequential memory and visual motor integration). In the context of intervention activities that included naming colors, repeating digits, and copying shapes, a call for improving children's social relationships undoubtedly raised an enormous and collective sigh of relief and hope from the teachers and families of these students.

Perhaps no other study has had such an immediate and dramatic impact on research in the field of learning disabilities. These ideas begged to be tested. Within a decade the findings on peer acceptance had been theorized about, replicated, questioned, extended, critiqued, and clarified by dozens of researchers. For example, Swanson and Trahan (1986) identified the 33 most frequently cited articles in learning disabilities research published between 1976 to 1985. Remarkably, Bryan (1976), the follow-up study of Bryan (1974b), was the most frequently cited article (note that Bryan, 1974b was not in the Swanson and Trahan database). Five other articles authored or coauthored by Tanis Bryan also appeared on the list. In fact, Tanis Bryan was the most frequently cited author during that period. Of those 33 articles, the largest proportion focused on assessment practices (24%), followed closely by social interaction (22%). This contrasts with research published before 1970, which had a primary focus on perceptual processes. Surprisingly, research on reading, surely the hallmark of the LD category, comprised only 6% of these most frequently cited studies. Despite the fact that addressing reading difficulties is clearly the central endeavor of the learning disabilities field, social dimensions had become the top research priority within a decade of the publication of Bryan (1974b).

Even more impressive in a field known for its research fads and controversies is the *enduring* nature of this interest in social factors. An example is provided by a quick comparison of ERIC searches using the key terms "learning disabilities and reading instruction" vs. "learning disabilities and peer acceptance." In any given year in the past two decades, the ratio of published articles on the two topics is approximately 3:1. Twenty-eight years later, the chapters that comprise this book create a dramatic testimonial to the fact that a deep understanding of the social dimensions of learning disabilities can transform our assessment and intervention models. Equally important, these chapters convince us that the revolution begun by Bryan (1974b) is definitely not over. In fact, as social competence with typical peers increasingly becomes prerequisite to gaining full access to the academic curriculum, the potential for new theories and research on enhancing social–emotional development is even more compelling.

So how did Bryan (1974b) start a revolution? An understanding of this specific phenomenon of immediate and enduring impact may shed some light on the developmental pathways of all research ideas. Like any effective revolutions, the initial explosion of research on social dimensions has led to a period of evolution, a quieter time of reflection, theory-building, and methodological advances that is essential to sustaining a true paradigm shift. We will highlight three themes that emerged from Bryan (1974b) that help us understand why the field so immediately resonated to the topic. Not surprisingly, it is these same themes that foreshadowed the "burning questions" of the current research programs described in the chapters in this volume.

THEORY-FRIENDLY

One key to starting a revolution is to invite everyone to join the cause. There is no explicit reference to theoretical framework in Bryan's (1974b) introduction, and the stance that she took in her discussion of her findings is "theory-friendly." In essence, she invited the reader to speculate with her about the possible explanations for her findings: factors intrinsic to the child (language, attention or perceptual issues), the effects of the LD label, and/or cultural expectancies of peers and teachers. Although there are hints of social learning theory in her suggestion that "socialization of children occurs through observation, modeling and instructions," she did not stake a strong theoretical claim. Given the fragmented and "single-lens" nature of the theoretical frameworks in the field in 1974, this open-minded approach was notable. The implicit message was "solving the mystery of peer rejection is so important that we cannot afford to be dogmatic in our theoretical approaches." This message essentially gave an open invitation to all theorists to join the quest.

The hundreds of citations of Bryan's work in later studies, published in journals from many disciplines, confirm that researchers from diverse theoretical perspectives accepted her invitation. In the chapters that comprise this volume, authors invoke a variety of theoretical frameworks, often to explain similar findings, and sometimes in the same chapter. For example, they refer to frameworks from developmental psychology (e.g., Cosden, Brown, & Elliot; Keogh; Pearl), information processing (e.g., Tur-Kaspa; Sridhar & Vaughn; Wiener), social constructivism (e.g., Bay; Stone, Bradley, & Kleiner; Hutchinson, Freeman, & Steiner-Bell), family systems theory (Stone, Bradley, & Kleiner) and even attachment theory and psychodynamic models (Margalit & Al-Yagon; Sridhar & Vaughn). Even in 2002, none of these frameworks has been disqualified as having potential for how to collect and interpret data on the social–emotional lives of students with LD.

Even more compelling is the foreshadowing of transactional and risk–resilience models in Bryan (1974b) and (1976). In her speculations about possible influences on peer rejection, she assumed that data will be messy, and that child, attitudinal, and contextual factors will interact in complex ways. For example, she made a call for identifying the behavioral pathways to peer acceptance, even as she acknowledged that these attitude/behavior relationships "are neither simple, obvious, nor known" (1976, p. 310). In an uncanny foreshadowing of the unpredictable outcomes of the transactions of risk and protective factors, she recruits the notion of differing academic expectations to interpret her findings that African-American children with LD were just as popular as other children, noting that "it is then ironic that a lower expectancy for the Black children may have a positive social value."

The notion that multiple and transactional factors are essential to explaining social developmental outcomes in students with LD is implicit in every chapter of this volume. In particular, risk–resilience models appear to be especially valued, as 7 of the 10 chapters invoke these frameworks. The attractiveness of these models is that they move away from the typical "deficit" or "pathology" conclusions that emerge when students with LD are compared with their typical peers. Instead, it is argued that examination of the interactions of child and contextual factors *within* groups of students with and without LD will be more useful for understanding developmental outcomes and designing interventions that minimize risk factors and enhance protective factors.

For example, Keogh argues that various models of longitudinal research are critical for assessing how risk and protective factors play out across different samples and at different developmental points. Wiener's chapter describes a search for risk and protective influences on friendship and social adjustment that may be unique to students with LD. In two interesting findings, her data indicate that placement in self-contained special classrooms for the majority of the day is a risk factor for peer rejection, but receiving support each day in a resource room does *not* have adverse effects. Conversely, having high-quality friendships with children who do not attend their school is a protective factor that enhances emotional well-being for students with LD, but not for typical students. Similarly, Cosden, Brown and Elliot suggest that self-understanding of one's learning disability will serve as a protective factor in developing positive self-esteem and self-concepts. Hutchinson, Freeman, and Steiner-Bell use multiple case studies of students with LD who had successful or unsuccessful peer relationships to delineate personality, cognitive, classroom, or family predictors that may not emerge in group design research.

METHODOLOGY MATTERS

Another critical strategy for starting a revolution is to make clear that there are multiple methodologies to overthrow old regimes. However, anarchy should not be the result. Instead, reliable and valid methodology matters. For example, Bryan (1974b) selected well-established peer nomination techniques to assess peer popularity, yet she first confirmed the validity of the positive and negative items by asking a group of fourth-grade children to rate the desirability of each description. Because of student disagreement, 6 of the original 20 items were not used. Similarly, she then statistically confirmed that positive and negative items were indeed independent. Finally, she tested the effects of gender and race to identify the generalizability of the findings across subgroups. These findings predated the thorny issues around sample definitions and the subsequent move toward research on subtypes of children with LD.

This attention to methodology was critical given the difficulty of measuring social competence, an amorphous construct in 1974. The chapters in this volume attest to the dramatic progress that has been made on this front: re-conceptualizing the construct of social development, and designing reliable and valid ways to assess multiple dimensions of social competence. For example, Tur-Kaspa highlights the advances made in defining and measuring various dimensions of "social cognition." These refinements have revealed that not all students with LD differ from their peers on all phases of social information processing (e.g., encoding and interpreting social cues, clarifying interpersonal goals, generating and evaluating strategies, and then enacting a social response). In particular, some students with LD may be skilled at generating and evaluating effective solutions to social problems, but because of their social databases of past experiences with peers, or differing social goals, they may still select social strategies different from those of other children. Delineating these phases also enables researchers to identify those subgroups of students with LD who are most likely to have social interactional difficulties.

Similarly, other authors in this volume have gone far beyond socio-metric nominations to assess various aspects of peer relationships in children with LD. For example, typical measures now include the number of friends (or enemies) children name, whether these friendships are recip-rocal, child, parent, and teacher ratings of the quality and intimacy of these friendships, self-reports of feelings of loneliness, and perceptions of social support. And in one of the few findings that Bryan (1974b) did *not* foretell, Margalit and Al-Yagon report that having "e-friends" and "web-peers" predicts lower levels of loneliness in children with LD!

Chapters by Wiener and Pearl suggest that whether children with LD have friends is only one piece of the puzzle; it is equally important to know the social characteristics of those they "hang out with." For example, Wiener reports that children with LD are more likely to have friends who are younger, who have learning problems, and who are less likely to vali-date and sustain their friendships. Similarly, Pearl's research on social net-works indicates that most students with mild disabilities are members of a social group. However, they are overrepresented in groups character-ized by companions rated high in misconduct, and underrepresented in groups considered to be prosocial. These data raise the ironic concern that students with LD who have been successful in forming friendships may actually be more vulnerable to negative peer influences.

Despite (or perhaps because of) these major methodological advances in defining samples and subtypes, and in refining our measures of various aspects of social and emotional development, the fact remains that the sta-bility of Bryan's (1974b, 1976) findings is stunning. These chapters con-firm that difficulties in peer relationships begin in preschool children who have not yet been identified (Margalit & Al-Yagon), and persist through elementary and high school settings, and into adulthood (Hutchinson, Freeman, & Steiner-Bell). Differences in educational placement (ranging from full inclusion to self-contained classrooms) seem to have only small and inconsistent effects on peer acceptance. In one startling example, Margalit and Al-Yagon compared students raised in kibbutz environments with students raised with their families. Students with LD in both settings reported more loneliness and received lower peer ratings than typical classmates. Apparently, the central role of peers in the lives of kibbutz children was not sufficient to mitigate the effects of learning disabilities on successful social relationships.

The "stubborn" nature of these findings is particularly compelling in light of the measures that are used to actually identify learning disabilities.

It is likely that no *single* cognitive, language, or academic measure is sufficiently powerful to differentiate students with LD from typical peers. Even the vast literature confirming phonological processing as an important predictor of literacy development is not likely to rival the findings of the Kavale and Forness (1996) meta-analysis of 152 studies, showing that about 75% of students with LD had social skills characteristics that were significantly different from typical peers. These findings echo Bryan's (1976) claim that "social status should be considered part of the child's learning disability" (p. 311).

HOPE IS OUR MOST SIGNIFICANT VARIABLE

When Tanis Bryan received the Research Award from the Council for Exceptional Children in 1996, she made this comment: "I believe that **hope** is what research/science give to people with disabilities and special educators. Research lets us **hope** for a better understanding of disabilities. Research lets us **hope** that we will identify effective interventions. Research lets us track our **hope** that public policy will have a positive impact upon our constituents. **Hope** is our most significant variable."

Undoubtedly the one essential step in starting a revolution is to give stakeholders hope for a better future. This involves asking research questions that hold out promise that problems can be solved. Given the "minimal brain dysfunction" model of learning disabilities in 1974, neurological and information processing factors probably did not appear to be malleable, at least with the tools available to families and educators. In contrast, social dimensions appear to be within the sphere of influence of any individual in the child's life. Although parents may not know how to increase their child's visual memory, they certainly can arrange for amicable playmates to visit after school. General education teachers who are not convinced of their expertise in modifying a child's auditory attention may be talented in changing classroom structures so that peer interactions are more positive or less distracting. It is likely that the call for attention to children's social worlds expanded the ownership for peer interaction problems beyond the special education teacher, to include other educators, parents, siblings, peers, neighbors, and many significant others.

Several chapters address this important link between beliefs, especially the belief in one's ability to make an impact, and the potential for effective interventions. For example, Stone, Bradley, and Kleiner highlight the surprising gap in our understanding of parents' beliefs and their communicative interactions with their children with language and learning disabilities, especially beyond the preschool age. Although both parent beliefs and interactions had often been characterized in negative ways, as too pessimistic, controlling, or directive, a new transactional conceptualization and new data are used to reframe the potential for parents to provide scaffolds for their children's emerging abilities. Although enhancing parent–child communication may not be easy, especially if maladaptive parent beliefs are not addressed, it is likely to be a context in which parents and children feel some hope for change, especially compared to the challenge of modifying school-based intervention policies.

Clearly, special educators and teacher educators resonated to Bryan's (1974b) call for academic interventions to take into account children's social needs. As Bay points out, 8 of the 16 standards created by CEC for the preparation of special educators reflect the need for attention to the social dimensions of children's learning. For example, Sridhar and Vaughn take a new look at the familiar technique of bibliotherapy, recasting it as an intervention that holds promise for addressing the interdependent academic and social needs of students.

Both Bay and Hutchinson emphasize the critical role of teacher beliefs as they address the challenges of educating students with LD within the context of their peer relationships. In particular, Bay points out that prospective teachers are not "blank slates," but enter the profession with powerful ideas about good teaching, how learning occurs, and the role of peer interaction. Teacher education programs that do not enable these teacher candidates to confront and develop their beliefs and understandings are not likely to have an impact. In her series of case studies of teachers identified as exemplary in accommodating the range of social and academic needs in their classrooms, Hutchinson describes the motivation, optimism, and sense of empowerment that these teachers report as they make a difference in the quality of classroom life for children with LD.

How do you start a revolution? The lessons learned from this analysis of Bryan's (1974b, 1976) articles seem to be: enlist multiple theoretical perspectives in the quest, pay attention to methodology, and offer hope. As a case study of a remarkable phenomenon in social science, her work sustained a revolution whose impact is enacted in the quality of the social lives of children with learning disabilities and their families, all over the world. To those of you who know Tanis, this is not a surprise. She embodies the revolutionary spirit: in her strongly principled view of science and its role in improving our lives, her contagious passion for ideas, her insistence on good data, and her questioning soul. And she is the ultimate revolutionary in her tireless campaign for new recruits for her cause. The authors of these chapters represent a small proportion of those who have enlisted in her revolution!

REFERENCES

Bryan, T. (1974a). An observational analysis of classroom behaviors of children with learning disabilities. *Journal of Learning Disabilities, 7,* 26–34.

Bryan, T. (1974b). Peer popularity of learning disabled children. *Journal of Learning Disabilities, 7,* 621–625.

Bryan, T. (1976). Peer popularity of learning disabled children: A replication. *Journal of Learning Disabilities, 9,* 307–311.

Harris, J. R. (1998). *The nurture assumption: Why children turn out the way they do.* New York: Free Press.

Johnson, D., & Myklebust, H. (1967). *Learning disabilities: Educational principles and practices.* New York: Grune & Stratton.

Kavale, K., & Forness, S. (1996). Social skill deficits and learning disabilities: A meta-analysis. *Journal of Learning Disabilities, 29,* 226–237.

Orton, S. (1937). *Reading, writing, and speech problems in children.* New York: Norton & Company.

Swanson, H. L., & Trahan, M. (1986). Characteristics of frequently cited articles in learning disabilities. *Journal of Special Education, 20,* 167–182.

Chapter 2

Social Cognition in Learning Disabilities

Hana Tur-Kaspa
Tel Aviv University

During the last three decades, the social life of children with learning disabilities (LD) has drawn growing interest. This interest was primarily prompted by Tanis Bryan's early inquiries into these children's social status among their peers (Bryan, 1974, 1976). Bryan's and other researchers' studies have shown that children with LD exhibit difficulties in the establishment and maintenance of satisfying peer relationships (Bryan, 1997). Recent efforts to understand these children's social difficulties have demonstrated the utility of social–cognitive models of social adjustment (Tur-Kaspa & Bryan, 1993, 1994).

The study into children's social cognition has, for many years, been conducted by researchers working within diverse fields (for a review, see Shantz, 1983). Not surprisingly, many different aspects of children's social cognition have been emphasized by various researchers working at different points in time. In recent years, social information-processing models of children's social behavior have emerged that have significantly advanced our understanding of children's social adjustment (e.g., Crick & Dodge, 1994; Dodge, 1986). This chapter briefly reviews the research relevant to the social skills and social adjustment of children with LD as perceived by peers and significant adults (i.e., teachers and parents). Next, special attention is focused on these children's social–cognitive processing skills. This issue is reviewed by utilizing a model of social information processing as a conceptual framework (Crick & Dodge, 1994; Dodge, 1986). Finally, suggestions for future research are discussed.

SOCIAL SKILLS AND SOCIAL ADJUSTMENT
OF CHILDREN WITH LEARNING DISABILITIES

A host of studies have demonstrated that children with LD are more poorly accepted and more likely to be rejected or ignored by their classmates than are peers without LD (for a review and meta-analyses, see Kavale & Forness, 1996; Ochoa & Olivarez, 1995; and Swanson & Malone, 1992). Their relatively low social status has been found to be maintained across time (Bryan, 1976). Moreover, a recent study that examined the social experiences of children with LD over a period of one academic year, has indicated that second- to sixth-grade students with LD had more reciprocal rejections than did their non-LD (NLD) peers at the end of the year, although this group difference was not significant at the beginning of the year (Tur-Kaspa, Margalit, & Most, 1999).

Children with LD are also perceived less favorably by significant adults, that is, by teachers as well as parents. Extensive research has relied on teachers' ratings of children with LD and their NLD classmates on various measures of maladaptive behavior. By and large, these studies indicated that mainstream teachers, as well as resource-room teachers, perceive their students with LD as manifesting significantly more problems in school-appropriate behavior (e.g., poorer task orientation, independence, or reactivity) and in social functioning (e.g., acting-out, immaturity, internalizing or externalizing problem behaviors) than did their NLD peers (Baum, Duffelmeyer, & Geelan, 1988; Bender, 1985, 1986; Bender & Golden, 1988; Bursuck, 1989; Center & Wascom, 1986; Epstein, Bursuck, & Cullinan, 1985; Grolnick & Ryan, 1990; McKinney & Feagans, 1983; Perlmutter, Crocker, Cordray, & Garstecki, 1983; Pullis, 1985; Slate & Saudargas, 1986; Tur-Kaspa & Bryan, 1995).

Studies that included parents' ratings found that parents also view their children who have LD as exhibiting undesirable behaviors, when compared to their NLD siblings or to NLD peers (Gresham & Reschly, 1986; McConaughy, 1986; McConaughy & Ritter, 1986; Owen, Adams, Forrest, Stolz, & Fisher, 1971; Ritter, 1989).

Concern about these children's social experiences has been motivated in large part by research data indicating that peer acceptance plays an important role in children's social adjustment. Peer rejection has proved to be remarkably stable, and rejected children have been found to be at risk for a variety of social adjustment difficulties (Kupersmidt, Coie, & Dodge, 1990; Parker & Asher, 1987).

It should be noted that not all children with LD demonstrate social skill deficits. A considerable proportion of children classified as evidencing LD are as socially skilled and well accepted by peers as are NLD children (Baum et al., 1988; Gresham, 1989; Gresham & Reschly, 1986;

Kronick, 1981; Perlmutter et al., 1983). Nevertheless, the accumulating data suggest that children with LD are disproportionally represented in the low-accepted and socially rejected categories and, therefore, can be considered a population at heightened risk for the development of social relationship problems.

Most of the studies that evaluated social skills and adjustment of children with LD used peer sociometric assessment and teachers' and parents' ratings. These social assessment procedures are primarily useful for screening, identification, and classification (Gresham & Elliott, 1989). They are conducive to defining social skill deficits in terms of deviations from a normative sample. However, they offer little information about the underlying reasons for the child's social difficulties. What seems to be necessary is a way to identify the social–cognitive processes in which these children are engaged during social situations, and how these processes relate to their social behavior and adjustment.

SOCIAL–COGNITIVE SKILLS RESEARCH ON CHILDREN WITH LEARNING DISABILITIES

Although the social status and interactions of children with LD do appear to differ in some ways from those of their peers, the processes underlying these differences are less understood (Pearl, 1992). Thus, the focus within the field of LD has shifted toward identifying differences in various social cognition skills between children with and without LD in an attempt to explore possible explanations for these children's difficulties in the social realm (see Bryan, 1991, for a review). This kind of inquiry has been based on the premise that social cognitions constitute the mechanisms leading to social behaviors that, in turn, form the bases of social adjustment (e.g., Dodge, 1986; Ladd & Mize, 1983).

The results of a sizeable body of research have suggested that the difficulty in achieving social acceptance among students with LD may be accounted for by their deficient perception and interpretation of social and emotional cues in social situations (Pearl, 1987). This research trend suggests that social–cognitive skills mediate social behavior. It has been recognized that the appropriate deployment of behavior is, in part, a function of knowledge about the situation in which various behaviors are to be carried out (Chi, Feltovich, & Glazer, 1981).

Support for the hypothesis that deficits in social cognition may be a source of social problems for students with LD comes from several studies that compared students with LD and normally achieving students on various measures of social perception and social skills. The majority of investigations in the area of social perception among children with LD have focused on the interpretation of emotional displays and social situations through the presentation of schematic drawings, photographs, videotapes, recordings, and vignettes from television. Participants were required to select the dominant emotion(s) being displayed (Maheady & Sainato, 1986).

One of the earliest studies to examine how students with LD perceived nonverbal behavior was conducted by Wiig and Harris (1974). They found that adolescents with LD were significantly less accurate, both qualitatively and quantitatively, than adolescents without LD at labeling the emotion expressed by a young woman's videotaped nonverbal expressions of anger, embarrassment, fear, frustration, joy, and love. In a similar study, Bryan (1977) assessed third through fifth graders' ability to comprehend nonverbal cues on the Profile of Nonverbal Sensitivity measure (PONS; Rosenthal, Hall, Archer, DiMatteo, & Rogers, 1977). The PONS consisted of brief videotaped sequences in which a young woman expressed different affects. Following the presentation of each segment, the children were asked to choose one of two sentences that best matched the scene. Bryan found that children with LD were significantly less accurate in comprehending nonverbal cues compared to children without LD. However, Stone and La Greca (1984), who administered the PONS to 30 LD and 30 NLD boys (aged 9–12), adopted incentive procedures to control for possible attentional differences and found no significant differences between the two groups.

Several studies that used pictorial measures found students with LD to be less proficient at interpreting displayed emotions (Axelrod, 1982; Bachara, 1976; Emery, 1975; Gerber & Zinkgraf, 1982; Holder & Kirkpatrick, 1991; Jackson, Enright, & Murdock, 1987, and to make significantly more errors than their NLD peers in interpreting social situations and predicting consequences (Bruno, 1981; Saloner & Gettinger, 1985). Students with LD were also found to perceive both videotaped and verbal descriptions of social situations as more "unfriendly" than NLD students (Weiss, 1984). Additional evidence of poor social decoding ability among students with LD was presented by Pearl and Cosden (1982). They used vignettes from a television soap opera that were analogous in terms of content and complexity to many real-life interactions. This study found the LD group to be less accurate than the NLD group in their understanding of the social interactions they viewed.

Other studies attempted to examine the social perspective taking or role-taking ability (i.e., the individual's ability to understand another's thoughts and feelings) of students with LD. The results of these studies have been equivocal. For example, Dickstein and Warren (1980) examined the role-taking abilities of 5- through 9-year-olds. The study indicated that, at each age, the children with LD performed less skillfully than the NLD children who, by age 8, performed almost perfectly on the tasks. Two additional groups of 9- and 10-year-old children with LD were administered the tasks to see if they would reach the NLD students' level of performance. These older children with LD, however, showed no improvement in their role-taking ability beyond the scores achieved by the 8-year-old students with LD. Bruck and Hebert's (1982) study confirmed the poorer performance revealed by children with LD as compared to their age matched controls; whereas Wong and Wong (1980) found significant differences only for females with LD. Two other studies, however, found that children with LD did not differ significantly in cognitive and affective perspective taking from normal controls or from children with emotional disorders (Waterman, Sabesky, Silvern, Aoki, & McCaulay, 1981). Nor did children with LD differ significantly from normal peers in their social insight and role-taking skills (Horowitz, 1981), after controlling for general intelligence.

Several studies have explored differences between children with and without LD in social problem-solving skills, an important aspect of social competence (Spivack, Platt, & Shure, 1976). Carlson (1987) presented 48 second- through fifth-grade LD and NLD boys with four open-ended hypothetical, peer-related social situations, and interviews about their goals and strategies. She found boys with LD to be deficient in the quality and quantity of strategies spontaneously chosen in resolving two of the four situations that dealt with peer conflicts. In Oliva and La Greca's (1988) study, 8- to 9-year-old and 11- to 13-year-old boys with and without LD were interviewed regarding their strategies and goals in four hypothetical situations. They found that the goals of boys with LD were significantly less "sophisticated" than those provided by age-matched NLD peers, though the strategies they generated to achieve their social goals were just as "friendly" as those of NLD peers.

Three other studies (Berg, 1982; Schneider & Yoshida, 1988; Silver & Young, 1985) that used role-playing measures of social problem-solving skills (Platt & Spivack, 1975; Spivack et al., 1976) found children and adolescents with LD to be deficient in identifying a social problem, in generating alternative solutions to hypothetical social situations, and in offering the relevant means to accomplish desirable social outcomes. In a more recent study (Toro, Weissberg, Guare, & Liebenstein, 1990), students with LD (ages 7 to 11) were compared with matched NLD students on their social problem-solving skills using the Open Middle Interview (OMI; Polifka, Weissberg, Gesten, Flores de Apodaca, & Picolli, 1981). The OMI measure presented children with four different age-relevant social problem situations. The child's task was to generate as many different solutions as possible to each story. This study demonstrated that children with LD evidenced deficits in social problem-solving skills (i.e., generating alternative solutions) relative to children without LD. Together, these studies suggest that students with LD exhibit deficits in social problem-solving skills as compared to NLD students.

Finally, Swanson and Malone's (1992) meta-analytic synthesis of the literature regarding the social competence of students with LD showed that these students revealed poorer social problem-solving skills than 79% of NLD students, spent 80% less on-task time than did NLD students, and evidenced more interfering problem behaviors (i.e., internalizing and externalizing) than 78% of NLD students.

In sum, the majority of studies to date clearly demonstrate that children with LD have difficulties in various aspects of social cognition. Nevertheless, several studies failed to find deficits among children with LD on some measures of social knowledge. For example, Bryan, Sonnefeld, and Greenberg (1981) reported that children with LD were as aware as NLD children of the effectiveness of different ingratiation strategies. (However, they preferred ingratiation tactics that were judged by adults to be less socially desirable than those preferred by NLD youngsters.) In another study, Stone and La Greca (1984) did not find children with LD to differ from NLD on a "making friends" role-playing measure. However, their overall performance was rated by "blind" judges as significantly less socially skillful. The authors suggested that although the students with LD demonstrated a basic knowledge of what to say in a given social situation, the qualitative aspects of their verbal as well as nonverbal, behaviors may discriminate them from their NLD peers.

A SOCIAL INFORMATION PROCESSING MODEL

Studies of the social skills and competence of students with and without LD focused exclusively on only one or two aspects of the social-cognitive process, mainly on the processes of perception of social stimuli and on generating possible solutions to various hypothetical social situations. However, competent social skills and social behaviors are determined by more than one cognitive process, as suggested by these studies. Even when researchers discussed an awareness of the multiple processes involved, they rarely conducted assessments of multiple social–cognitive processes in a single study. This criticism led Dodge (1986) to develop a model that postulates a comprehensive assessment of multiple social–cognitive processes involved in a child's processing of social information. A major hypothesis of this model is that a comprehensive assessment of the multiple skills involved in social information processing, rather than an assessment of any single skill, will yield powerful predictions about the child's social behavior and adjustment.

The Model's Theoretical Background

Dodge's (1986) model of social competence is rooted in several theoretical models: Flavell's (1974) conception of the cognitive steps involved in making social inferences; Goldfried and d'Zurilla's (1969) behavioral–analytic model for the assessment of competence; Simon's (Newell & Simon, 1972) and Hayes' (1981) information-processing theories of cognitive problem solving, and McFall's (1982) model of social skills.

Flavell's (1974) model is grounded in cognitive developmental theory and, therefore, emphasizes the development of the child's inference-making abilities in interpersonal interactions. Flavell described a general model of interpersonal inferences, which consists of four sequential classes of knowledge and skills that may be brought into play when making inferences about other people's inner properties. According to this model, the person must first know or be aware of the existence of some psychological processes (percept, intention, feeling, etc.) of another individual. Second, the person must recognize the need for inferential activity about one or more of these properties. The person must then be able to actually carry out that inferential cognitive activity. Finally, the person must be capable of applying the resulting information about others as a means to some situationally appropriate interpersonal end.

Goldfried and d'Zurilla (1969) described a behavioral–analytic model for assessing the competence of the individual's responses to a problematic situation defined as novel or as presenting conflicting demands. Their model outlined four operations thought to be prerequisites for effective behavior. These operations include: (a) situational analysis—understanding of the problematic situation and its context; (b) response enumeration—sampling of possible alternative solutions; (c) response decision and evaluation—determining the degree of effectiveness of each of the potential solutions and deciding on an optimal solution; and (d) finally, the individual must skillfully carry out the selected response. Effective behavior, in any given situation, is viewed on a continuum. To be judged maximally effective, a response must be capable of reducing or eliminating the conflict, as well as minimizing other possible negative consequences that might ensue.

Simon (Newell & Simon, 1972) and Hayes (1981), on the other hand, have used the metaphor of the computer to analyze human information processing. Hayes described the following six sequences of actions that transpire when an individual solves a problem. First, the individual must identify the problem, that is, recognize that there is a problem to be solved. Next, he or she must represent, that is, understand the nature of the difficulty (i.e., "the gap") that the problem constitutes. Once the problem is mentally represented, the individual must engage in a search for the solution, choosing a method for crossing the gap. Once the individual has planned a solution to a problem, he or she must carry it out. Then, the solution has to evaluated by turning back to the problem statement and checking carefully if the solution satisfactory. Finally, the individual must engage in a process of "consolidation," that is, reflecting on the problem-solving experience, asking questions about it, and learning from the experience so that the problem will be easier to solve the next time it is confronted. In relatively easy problems, the individual may go through these actions in this order of actions and without any difficulties. In difficult, novel problems, the individual must perform a great deal of backtracking (i.e., reverting to previous steps). Successful problem solving depends on the effectiveness of carrying out each of these six actions.

McFall (1982) proposed a model in which social skills are differentiated from social competence. Competence is viewed as "a general evaluative term referring to the quality or adequacy of a person's overall performance in a particular task. Skills, however, are the specific abilities required to perform competently at a task" (pp. 12–13). McFall's model includes the following three major social skill processes: decoding skills, decision skills, and encoding skills. Each skill is considered to be a necessary, but not a sufficient, condition for competent responding, and all these information-processing steps are influenced by the individual's learning history and physical limitations.

The reviewed theories assume that the individual is confronted with a stimulus that may be conceptualized as a task, or as a problematic situation. The individual's behavior is assumed to be directed toward responding or solving the "problem." Each theory describes a specific set of cognitive operations or specific skills that are considered to be necessary for competent behavior or adequate solution.

Dodge (1986) formulated an integrative model of social competence that is based on the information-processing principles put forth by these theories. He offered a theoretical and empirical description of how social cognition processes, social behavior, and social adjustment may be related, particularly in the context of social problem solving. The model emphasizes the role of social–cognitive processes in mediating the relationship between environmental social stimuli and interpersonal behavior.

Description of the Model

According to the social information-processing model of children's social adjustment (Crick & Dodge, 1994; Dodge, 1986), children approach a particular situation or task with a biologically determined set of response capabilities and a database (i.e., their memory store of past experience, and a set of goals), and they receive input from the environment in the form of a set of social cues. Children's responses to those cues occur as a function of the way they process the social information.

The first step of social information processing for the child comprises encoding the social cues in the environment. Because of the tremendous amount of information presented in the social environment at a single moment, the child must learn skills of attending to appropriate cues, chunking information, and using rehearsal and mnemonic devices in order to store the information.

Once cues have been encoded, the next step requires the child to engage in a mental representation and interpretation process. The child must integrate the cues with past experiences and come to a meaningful understanding of the cues. This step is often indistinguishable from the first, in that it is difficult to assess a child's encoding of cues without simultaneously assessing his or her representation of those cues. In fact, the representation step may have a feedback loop to the encoding step, if the child determines that not enough information has been encoded to interpret the gestalt of the stimulus or if contradictory interpretations are made.

The third step in the reformulated model (i.e., Crick & Dodge, 1994) consists of clarifying goals. After interpreting the situation, it is proposed that the child selects a goal or desired outcome for the situation, or continues with a preexisting goal.

The next, fourth, step comprises accessing or constructing a response. It is hypothesized that the child engages in a process of searching for a possible behavioral response, or if the situation is novel, the child may construct a new behavioral response to the social cues.

The fifth step of processing involves a response decision. Ideally, the child learns to evaluate the potential consequences of each generated response and to estimate the probability of favorable outcomes while taking into account the environmental context and his or her own behavioral capabilities. The response decision process must have a direct feedback loop to the response search process. If the outcome evaluation leads to an unsatisfactory outcome estimate for every response generated, the competent response would consist of returning to an earlier stage of processing, in order to generate more possible responses.

When a response has been selected, the child proceeds to act it out at Step 6—the behavioral enactment step. This step also includes the processes of monitoring the effects of one's behavior on the environment and regulating that behavior accordingly. Verbal and motor skills are important at this stage. The child must possess linguistic and communicative skills and be able to enact a behavioral script, in order to respond competently.

Crick and Dodge's reformulated model of social information processing is a transactional one. That is, it is presumed that the process does not terminate at the point of enactment because it involves another person, who is also engaged in the six-step process already described. The model is one of a continual encoding of cues (input), operating on those cues, and enacting the outcome of the operations (output). Each output is also an input for the next operation. The steps exist in dynamic relation to each other. The encoding of cues influences how those cues are interpreted, but also the interpretation of cues influences how they are encoded. The response generation process sets the domain of response possibilities for the response decision process, but the decision process also has an impact on which responses get generated. Each step is a necessary part of competent responding. The steps, however, are not necessarily acted on in a conscious manner. Processing of social information can occur at an unconscious level. Conscious processing, however, is most likely to occur in highly problematic situations when a novel response is required, or when some clue brings the processing to the level of awareness.

The model describes competent processing of social information. The processing and interpretation of information at each of these steps will determine the nature of the response. If performance at some point in the progression is unskilled, either because of deficits in cognitive ability or due to biases in perception or interpretation of environmental stimuli, then the outcome will be maladaptive social behavior.

It is proposed in the reformulated model that processing occurs along simultaneous parallel paths, that is, individuals are engaged in multiple social information-processing activities at the same time, and not in a rigid sequential processing structure. The reformulated model also submits that, although processing is simultaneous for each of the steps, the path from a particular stimulus to a behavioral response follows a sequence of steps. Thus, the processing of that stimulus follows a time-related sequence, notwithstanding that processing in general occurs simultaneously at all steps.

The model was formulated specifically as a way of understanding individual differences in the social information processing of children who demonstrate aggression, but it also provides clear directions for researchers and clinicians interested in the assessment and treatment of social–behavioral deficits among students with LD.

Research Examining the Model

As seen in the earlier reviewed literature, many studies have demonstrated that children with LD differ from their NLD peers on various measures that assess the social-processing steps suggested in Dodge's (1986) social information-processing model. However, these studies have assessed only one or two processing steps at a time, yielding fragmented knowledge of these children's social information-processing skills. To date, only one comprehensive study has investigated the social information-processing skills of students with LD, in a single study, utilizing Dodge's model as a conceptual framework (Tur-Kaspa & Bryan, 1994). In this study, 30 students with LD from the third, fourth, seventh, and eighth grades, and two matched control groups who were not classified as having LD consisting of 29 low-achieving (LA) and 33 average-achieving (AA) students, were assessed on social information-processing skills, receptive and expressive vocabulary skills, and teacher ratings of social competence and school adjustment.

The results of this study indicated that AA students outperformed students with LD on all processing steps. That is, AA students scored significantly higher on the encoding process, on the representation process, on the response search process, on the response decision process, and on the enactment process.

Several researchers (Bursuck, 1983; Coleman, McHam, & Minnett, 1992; Sater & French, 1989) have suggested that academic deficiency rather than LD status mediates the social information processing differences found between students with LD and students without LD who attain low academic achievements. Tur-Kaspa and Bryan's (1994) data analyses indicated that the two groups differed significantly on two social information processing steps. Students with LD scored significantly lower than the LA students on the first step in the model, the encoding process. This finding corroborates much previous research indicating social perception deficits in children with LD when compared to NLD children (Bruno, 1981; Bryan, 1977; Dickstein & Warren, 1980; Maheady & Sainato, 1986; Stiliadis & Wiener, 1989; Wiig & Harris, 1974). Furthermore, this study also found students with LD to be deficient in the quality of self-generated solutions chosen when resolving social situations. Their preference for less competent solutions in comparison to their LA peers could not be attributed to a smaller pool of information on which to base their response decision, considering that the LD and LA groups did not differ on the number and type of solutions generated in the antecedent processing step. It is important to note that in these two processing steps, LA students did not significantly differ from AA students. The significant differences between the LD and LA groups on these two information processing steps further suggest that poor academic achievement alone does not appear to be an adequate explanation of the poor social skills of students with LD (La Greca & Stone, 1990a, 1990b; Vaughn, Hogan, Kouzekanani, & Shapiro, 1990).

Students with LD were found to be especially deficient in the encoding and the response decision processes, although they were comparable to LA and AA students in their social knowledge. The lack of significant differences between the three groups on the diversity of generated solutions and on the endorsement of different types of indicates that students with LD are knowledgeable and possess a repertoire of alternative solutions to handle social situations. They were as aware of the effectiveness of competent versus incompetent solutions as the LA and AA students. Nevertheless, when asked to select one of a given set of five different solutions, they preferred significantly more incompetent solutions than did AA students. These results lend additional support to previous studies (Bryan et al., 1981; Carlson, 1987; Stone & LaGreca, 1984), which found students with LD to demonstrate a basic social knowledge of what to say or what a desirable action might be in a given situation, yet they failed to implement this knowledge in their actions. According to Crick and Dodge's (1994) model, the child comes to the social task with a set of prior experiences that influence the child's social information-processing and social behavior. It might be that what looks like incompetent response decision process actually serves important, adaptive, and strategic social purposes for these children given their history of social difficulties and concomitant social environments (Donahue, Szymanski, & Flores, 1999).

The data analysis also revealed significant age differences across the three groups on several processing steps, although differences between the groups remained. Seventh–eighth graders outperformed third–fourth graders on the encoding process, number of solutions generated, and on their preference for competent solutions.

Bryan, Sullivan-Burstein, and Mathur (1998) examined the contribution of language and reading skills to the performance of students with LD on Dodge's (1986) five-step model, using only one out of five hypothetical social scenarios (i.e., peer entry) employed in Tur-Kaspa and Bryan's (1994) study. In addition, the more recent study examined the impact of four affect induction conditions on the social information processing skills of 45 students with LD and 50 students without LD in the seventh grade. The results of this study revealed main effects for language skills and affect induction.

Unlike the results of Tur-Kaspa and Bryan (1994), the later study did not find significant differences on social information-processing skills between students with and without LD. Use of the median-split method to form high and low language and reading groups, however, revealed that students scoring equal to and above the language median generated significantly more solutions and interpreted the scenario as significantly less hostile than did students below the language median. This finding supports the notion of a subgroup of students with LD who have language deficits that affect their academic and social skills.

With respect to the impact of mood induction on social information processing, Bryan et al. (1998) found that students in the self-induced positive affect condition (i.e., recall of happiest time in life) generated more solutions than did students in the neutral condition. Students in the externally created positive affect condition (i.e., listening to happy music) made more embellishments to the story solutions than did students in the neutral condition (i.e., counting numbers), and interpreted the social scenario as more positive than did students in the externally induced negative affect condition (i.e., listening to heavy metal music) or self-induced positive affect condition. The results of this study clearly emphasized the role that affect, and especially self-induced positive affect, plays in social cognition.

This finding, together with the results of the collective studies performed by Bryan and her colleagues (for a review see Bryan & Burstein, 2000), correspond with those of reported studies focusing on the contribution of mood states, emotionality (as a temperamental aspect), and emotion regulation skills to social competence. Ample literature has demonstrated how experimentally induced moods influence a wide variety of behaviors and cognitions (e.g., Isen, Daubman, & Nowicki, 1987; Schwarrz & Bless, 1991; Wright & Mischel, 1982). Recently, Lemerise, Harper, Caverly, and Hobgood (1998) found that induced moods influence children's goals for hypothetical provocation situations.

Eisenberg and her colleagues found that a combination of emotion regulation abilities and low emotionality predicted social competence concurrently and longitudinally (Eisenberg et al., 1997). Elementary school children with high emotionality combined with poor emotion regulation skills were found to be at risk for behavior problems, whereas those children with high emotionality and good emotion regulation skills were not at risk for behavior problems (Eisenberg et al., 1996).

Although Crick and Dodge (1994) explicitly asserted that emotion is an important component of social information processing, they also acknowledged that emotion's role is not well articulated in their model. Thus, Lemerise and Arsenio (2000) in their recent article proposed a revised integrated model of emotion processes and cognition in social information processing. They described the kinds of emotion processes that need to be integrated into Crick and Dodge's model, and argued that the inclusion of such processes would expand the model's explanatory power. On the basis of their revised model, Lemerise and Arsenio offered several specific hypotheses. At a general level they hypothesized that the intensity with which children experience emotions and their skill at regulating emotion can influence each step of social information processing. Specifically, children's high emotionality and poor emotions regulatory abilities may interfere with the encoding of social cues, assessing the situation from different cognitive and affective perspectives, and prevent a flexible approach to goal selection which takes into account contextual factors (Saarni, 1999). For example, they hypothesized that those children who are overwhelmed by their own or others' emotions may choose avoidant or hostile goals to reduce their own arousal. They also may be too overwhelmed and self-focused to generate a variety of responses and evaluate them from all parties' perspectives. On the other hand, good emotion regulators may be more likely to consider the situation from multiple perspectives, which should facilitate the selection of a more competent response. These hypotheses deserve examination in future research.

DISCUSSION AND SUGGESTIONS
FOR FURTHER RESEARCH

Research data have shown that children with LD exhibited a unique problem in the encoding of social information and exhibited a distinct response decision pattern in their tendency to select incompetent solutions to social situations. Nevertheless, they did seem to be knowledgeable about what an appropriate, desirable competent social solution should be.

The finding that students with LD could be differentiated from LA students on these social processing skills implies that the social skills deficits of students with LD are not likely to be a function of their low academic achievement status. This finding also suggests that future research on social skills and competence of students with LD should include comparisons with LA without learning disabilities as well as AA students.

Not all interpersonal problems indicate that a person lacks social knowledge or social skills. In addition to perceptual, cognitive, and behavioral skills, an individual must also possess certain attitudinal–motivational characteristics. In any given social situation, an individual must have the self-confidence and emotional resolve to act in an appropriate manner. Thus, it also may be that students with LD are not internally motivated for engaging in interpersonal relationships and for coping effectively with interpersonal problems. Students are generally not motivated to behave in ways that they believe will result in outcomes they believe will have little importance for their lives. Students who perceive little value in pursuing their interpersonal relationships may have little willingness to make the effort to initiate or maintain those relationships.

However, several studies have found that children with LD are equally eager to participate in social interactions as their NLD peers. In two studies that examined conformity to prosocial and antisocial situations in junior high school students, students with LD indicated that they would be as willing as their NLD classmates to participate with their peers in prosocial actions, and even more willing to participate with peers in antisocial actions (Bryan, Werner, & Pearl, 1982; Bryan, Pearl, & Fallon, 1989). It seems that students with LD have an interest in interacting with their peers, but they lack either the skills or the knowledge of how and when to use those rules appropriately for social interaction.

A large body of research indicates that the social climate experienced by many students with LD is likely to differ from that experienced by their NLD peers (i.e., low social status, social rejection, social withdrawn, negative peer interactions, and low self-esteem) (Pearl, 1992). Hence, the students with LD may not develop the same expectations of social situations, and may approach social tasks with a different set of goals or different motivations than do the AA students. This, in turn, may influence social task performance among students with LD.

According to Dodge (1986), a child comes to a social task with a set of prior experiences. These may consist of a particular way of perceiving the world, goals for social interactions, the child's self-concept, or transitory mood. Children's past experiences influence the way they process information. Recently, Lemerise and Arsenio (2000) emphasized the interrelation between cognition and affect. They suggested that individual differences in emotionality and emotion regulation can influence each step of social information processing. The nature of the emotional ties between a child and others involved in an encounter may also bias information processing. These hypotheses should be subjected to future research.

Research has indicated that students with LD do show improvement in their encoding of social stimuli and in their response decision process as they grow older. However, they still remain at high risk for social deficits in comparison to their NLD peers (Tur-Kaspa & Bryan, 1994). It should be noted, however, that cross-sectional studies can examine age differences, but only longitudinal research permits an inquiry into age effects (Gresham & MacMillan, 1997). Moreover, longitudinal studies are needed in order to better characterize the nature of these developmental trends.

Research has indicated that not all students with LD exhibit social skill problems. There is growing evidence that students with LD are not a homogeneous group with respect to their psychosocial characteristics (Hooper & Willis, 1989; Margalit & Al-Yagon, 1994). Research in neuropsychology, for example, is uncovering evidence that children with LD who have problems in arithmetic appear to have problems in social skills, spatial orientation, bimodal perceptual motor skills, problem solving, and social perception (Rourke, 1982; Semrud-Clikeman & Hynd, 1990). These researchers claimed that this profile is linked to problems in right hemisphere processing of information. Others, however, have argued that problems in the social domain are related to deficits in linguistic information processing (Donahue, 1986). The observed differences in social information-processing skills reported in the literature are likely to be specific to certain LD subtypes (Bryan et al., 1998). The subtyping issue has been further emphasized in recent studies examining the psychiatric comorbidity hypothesis (San Miguel, Forness, & Kavale, 1996). According to this hypothesis social skill deficits in individuals with LD may reflect the comorbidity of learning disabilities with psychiatric diagnoses (e.g., ADHD, depression, or dysthymia). In addition, given recent concern for social–behavioral characteristics of females versus males with LD, another direction for future research would be to investigate gender differences. In sum, further research is needed to identify those subgroups within the LD population who experience social problems. At the same time, it is also very important to identify those children with LD who fare well in their social lives. The identification of protective as well as risk factors for individuals with LD, and the relationships between these factors, will enable the facilitation of social–emotional adjustment among those experiencing such problems (Morrison & Cosden, 1997).

CONCLUDING REMARKS

How children who evidence LD manage to cope with the complexity of social stimuli surrounding them remains a challenging area for study. Research data have suggested that these children conceivably exhibit a unique social information-processing pattern, mainly in the encoding of social stimuli and in their response decision process.

Considerable accumulating empirical evidence pinpoints the importance of motivational and affective variables in social cognition. The first steps in pursuing this significant direction of research have been initiated by Bryan and her colleagues in recent studies that examined the impact of affect on cognition and behavior (Bryan & Burstein, 2000). Recent neurophysiological evidence suggests that emotion processes and cognitive processes influence one another, making it difficult to isolate cases of pure emotion or pure cognition (LeDoux, 1995). Future research must move forward to utilize multidimensional models that will capture the complexities of the reciprocal and interactive effects of cognitive, social, and affective variables. This kind of empirical research will offer an important contribution to our understanding of the social skills and social competence of students with LD.

REFERENCES

Axelrod, L. (1982). Social perception in learning disabled adolescents. *Journal of Learning Disabilities, 15,* 610–613.

Bachara, G. (1976). Empathy in learning disabled children. *Perceptual and Motor Skills, 43,* 541–542.

Baum, D. D., Duffelmeyer, F., & Geelan, M. (1988). Resource teacher perceptions of the prevalence of social dysfunction among students with learning disabilities. *Journal of Learning Disabilities, 21,* 380–381.

Bender, W. N. (1985). Differences between learning disabled and non-learning disabled children in temperament and behavior. *Learning Disability Quarterly, 8*, 11–18.

Bender, W. N. (1986). Teachability and behavior of learning disabled children. *Psychological Review, 59*, 471–476.

Bender, W. N., & Golden, L.B. (1988). Adaptive behavior of learning disabled and non-learning disabled children. *Learning Disabled Quarterly, 11*, 55–61.

Berg, F. L. (1982). *Psychological characteristics related to social problem solving in learning disabled children and their non-disabled peers.* Unpublished doctoral dissertation, University of Michigan, Ann Arbor.

Bruck, M., & Hebert, M. (1982). Correlates of learning disabled students' peer-interaction patterns. *Learning Disability Quarterly, 5*, 353–362.

Bruno, R. M. (1981). Interpretation of pictorially presented social situations by learning disabled and normal children. *Journal of Learning Disabilities, 14*, 350–352.

Bryan, J. H., Sonnefeld, J. L., & Greenberg, F. Z. (1981). Children's and parents' view of ingratiation tactics. *Learning Disability Quarterly, 4*, 170–179.

Bryan, T. (1974). Peer popularity of learning disabled children. *Journal of Learning Disabilities, 7*, 261–268.

Bryan, T. (1976). Peer popularity of learning disabled children: A replication. *Journal of Learning Disabilities, 9*, 307–311.

Bryan, T. (1977). Children's comprehension of nonverbal communication. *Journal of Learning Disabilities, 10*, 501–506.

Bryan, T. (1991). Assessment of social cognition: Review of research in learning disabilities. In L. H. Swanson (Ed.), *Handbook on the assessment of learning disabilities: Theory, research, and practice* (pp. 285–311). Austin, TX: Pro-Ed.

Bryan, T. (1997). Assessing the personal and social status of students with learning disabilities. *Learning Disabilities Research & Practice, 12*, 63–76.

Bryan, T., & Burstein, K. (2000). Don't worry, be happy: The effect of positive mood on learning. *Thalamus, 18*, 34–42.

Bryan, T., Pearl, R., & Fallon, P. (1989). Conformity to peer pressure by students with learning disabilities: A replication. *Journal of Learning Disabilities, 22*, 458–459.

Bryan, T., Sullivan-Burstein, K., & Mathur, S. (1998). The influence of affect on social-information processing. *Journal of Learning Disabilities, 31*, 418–426.

Bryan, T., Werner, M., & Pearl, R. (1982). Learning disabled students' conformity responses to prosocial and antisocial situations. *Learning Disability Quarterly, 5*, 344–352.

Bursuck, W. D. (1983). Sociometric status, behavior rating, and social knowledge of learning disabled and low-achieving children. *Learning Disability Quarterly, 6*, 329–338.

Bursuck, W. D. (1989). A comparison of students with learning disabilities to low achieving and higher achieving students on three dimensions of social competence. *Journal of Learning Disabilities, 22*, 188–194.

Carlson, C. I. (1987). Social interaction goals and strategies of children with learning disabilities. *Journal of Learning Disabilities, 20*, 306–311.

Center, D. B., & Wascom, A. M. (1986). Teacher perceptions of social behavior in learning disabled and socially normal children and youth. *Journal of Learning Disabilities, 19*, 420–425.

Chi, M. T. H., Feltovich, P., & Glazer, R. (1981). Categorization and representation of physics problems by experts and novices. *Cognitive Science, 5*, 121–152.

Coleman, J. M., McHam, L. A., & Minnett, A. M. (1992). Similarities in the social competencies of learning disabled and low achieving elementary school children. *Journal of Learning Disabilities, 25*, 671–677.

Crick, N. R., & Dodge, K. A. (1994). A review and reformulation of social information-processing mechanisms in children's social adjustment. *Psychological Bulletin, 115*, 74–101.

Dickstein, E. B., & Warren, D. R. (1980). Role-taking deficits in learning disabled children. *Journal of Learning Disabilities, 13,* 33–37.

Dodge, K. A. (1986). A social information processing model of social competence in children. In M. Perlmutter (Ed.), *Cognitive perspective on children's social and behavioral development: The Minnesota symposia on child psychology: Vol. 18* (pp. 77–125). Hillsdale, NJ: Lawrence Erlbaum Associates.

Donahue, M. (1986). Linguistic and communicative development of learning disabled children. In S. J. Ceci (Ed.), *Handbook of cognitive, social, and neuropsychological aspects of learning disabilities, Vol. 1* (pp. 263–289). Hillsdale, NJ: Lawrence Erlbaum Associates.

Donahue, M., Szymanski, C., & Flores, C. (1999). "When Emily Dickinson met Steven Spielberg": Assessing social information processing in literacy contexts. *Language, Speech, and Hearing Services in Schools, 30,* 274–284.

Eisenberg, N., Fabes, R. A., Guthrie, I. K., Murphy, B. C., Maszk, P., Holmgren, R., & Suh, K. (1996). The relations of regulation and emotionality to problem behavior in elementary school children. *Development and Psychopathology, 8,* 141–162.

Eisenberg, N., Fabes, R. A., Shepard, S. A., Murphy, B. C., Guthrie, I. K., Jones, S., Friedman, J., Poulin, R., & Maszk, P. (1997). Contemporaneous and longitudinal prediction of children's social functioning from regulation and emotionality. *Child Development, 68,* 642–664.

Emery, J. E. (1975). Social perception processes in normal and learning disabled children. *Dissertation Abstracts International, 36,* 1942A–1943B.

Epstein, M. H., Bursuck, W., & Cullinan, D. (1985). Patterns of behavior problems among the learning disabled: Boys aged 12–18, girls aged 6–11, and girls aged 12–18. *Learning Disability Quarterly, 8,* 123–129.

Flavell, J. H. (1974). The development of inferences about others. In T. Mischell (Ed.), *Understanding other persons* (pp. 66–116). Oxford, England: Blackwell.

Gerber, P. J., & Zinkgraf, S. A. (1982). A comparative study of social–perceptual ability in learning disabled and nonhandicapped students. *Learning Disability Quarterly, 5,* 374–378.

Goldfried, M. R., & d'Zurilla, T. J. (1969). A behavioral-analytic model for assessing competence. In C. D. Spielberger (Ed.), *Current topics in clinical and community psychology: Vol. 1* (pp. 151–196). New York: Academic Press.

Gresham, F. M. (1989). Social competence and motivational characteristics of learning disabled students. In M. Wang, M. Reynolds, & H. Walberg (Eds.), *The handbook of special education: Research and practice* (pp. 283–302). Oxford, England: Pergamon.

Gresham, F. M., & Elliott, S. N. (1989). Social skills deficits as a primary learning disability. *Journal of Learning Disabilities, 22,* 120–124.

Gresham, F. M., & MacMillan, D. L. (1997). Social competence and affective characteristics of students with mild disabilities. *Review of Educational Research, 67,* 377–415.

Gresham, F. M., & Reschly, D. L. (1986). Social skills deficits and low peer acceptance of mainstreamed learning disabled children. *Learning Disability Quarterly, 9,* 23–32.

Grolnick, W. S., & Ryan, R. M. (1990). Self-perceptions, motivations, and adjustment in children with learning disabilities: A multiple group comparison study. *Journal of Learning Disabilities, 23,* 177–184.

Hayes, J. R. (1981). *The complete problem solver.* Philadelphia: The Franklin Institute Press.

Holder, H. B., & Kirkpatrick, S. W. (1991). Interpretation of emotion from facial expression in children with and without learning disabilities. *Journal of Learning Disabilities, 24,* 170–177.

Hooper, S. R., & Willis, G. W. (1989). *Learning disability subtyping: Neuropsychological foundations, conceptual models, and issues in clinical differentiation.* New York: Springer-Verlag.

Horowitz, E. (1981). Popularity, decentering ability, and role-taking skills in learning disabled and normal children. *Learning Disability Quarterly, 4,* 23–30.

Isen, A. M., Daubman, K. A., & Nowicki, G. P. (1987). Positive affect facilitates creative problem solving. *Journal of Personality and Social Psychology, 52,* 1122–1131.

Jackson, S. C., Enright, R. D., & Murdock, J. Y. (1987). Social perception problems in learning disabled youth: Developmental lag versus perceptual deficit. *Journal of Learning Disabilities, 20,* 361–364.

Kavale, K. A., & Forness, S. R. (1996). Social skill deficits and learning disabilities: A meta-analysis. *Journal of Learning Disabilities, 29,* 226–237.

Kronick, D. (1981). *Social development of learning disabled persons.* San Francisco: Jossey Bass.

Kupersmidt, J. B., Coie, J. D., & Dodge, K. A. (1990). The role of poor peer relationships in the development of disorder. In S. R. Asher & J. D. Coie (Eds.), *Peer rejection in childhood* (pp. 274–305). New York: Cambridge University Press.

La Greca, A. M., & Stone, W. L. (1990a). Children with learning disabilities: The role of achievement in their social, personal, and behavioral functioning. In H. L. Swanson & B. Keogh (Eds.), *Disabilities: Theoretical and research issues* (pp. 333–352). Hillsdale, NJ: Lawrence Erlbaum Associates.

La Greca, A. M., & Stone, W. L. (1990b). LD status and achievement: Confounding variables in the study of children's social status, self-esteem, and behavioral functioning. *Journal of Learning Disabilities, 23,* 483–490.

Ladd, G. W., & Mize, J. (1983). A cognitive-social learning model of social skills training. *Psychological Review, 90,* 127–157.

LeDoux, J. E. (1995). Emotion: Clues from the brain. *Annual Review of Psychology, 46,* 209–235.

Lemerise, E. A., & Arsenio, W. F. (2000). An integrated model of emotion processes and cognition in social information processing. *Child Development, 71,* 107–118.

Lemerise, E. A., Harper, B. D., Caverly, S., & Hobgood, C. (1998). *Mood, social goals, and children's outcome expectations.* Poster presented at the biennial Conference on Human Development, Mobile, AL.

Maheady, L., & Sainato, D. M. (1986). Learning-disabled students' perceptions of social events. In S. J. Ceci (Ed.), *Handbook of cognitive, social, and neuropsychological aspects of learning disabilities: Vol. 1* (pp. 381–402). Hillsdale, NJ: Lawrence Erlbaum Associates.

Margalit, M., & Al-Yagon, M. (1994). Learning disability subtyping, loneliness and classroom adjustment. *Learning Disability Quarterly, 17,* 297–310.

McConaughy, S. H. (1986). Social competence and behavioral problems of learning disabled boys aged 6–11. *Journal of Learning Disabilities, 19,* 101–106.

McConaughy, S. H., & Ritter, D. R. (1986). Social competence and behavioral problems of learning disabled boys aged 6–11. *Journal of Learning Disabilities, 19,* 39–45.

McFall, R. M. (1982). A review and reformulation of the concept of social skills. *Behavioral Assessment, 4,* 1–33.

McKinney, J. D., & Feagans, L. (1983). Adaptive classroom behavior of learning disabled students. *Journal of Learning Disabilities, 16,* 360–367.

Morrison, G. M., & Cosden, M. A. (1997). Risk, resilience, and adjustment of individuals with learning disabilities. *Learning Disability Quarterly, 20,* 43–60.

Newell, A., & Simon, H. A. (1972). *Human problem solving.* Englewood Cliffs, NJ: Prentice-Hall.

Ochoa, S., & Olivarez, A. (1995). A meta-analysis of peer rating sociometric studies of pupils with learning disabilities. *The Journal of Special Education, 29,* 1–19.

Oliva, A. H., & Le Greca, A. M. (1988). Children with learning disabilities: Social goals and strategies. *Journal of Learning Disabilities, 21,* 301–306.

Owen, R. W., Adams, P. A., Forrest, T., Stolz, L. M., & Fisher, S. (1971). Learning disorders in children: Sibling studies. *Monographs of the Society for Research in Child Development, 36* (Serial No. 144).

Parker, J. G., & Asher, S. R. (1987). Peer relations and later personal relations: a meta-analytic review. *Psychological Bulletin, 117*, 306–347.

Pearl, R. (1987). Social cognitive factors in learning-disabled children's social problems. In S. J. Ceci (Ed.), *Handbook of cognitive, social, and neuropsychological aspects of learning disabilities: Vol. 2* (pp. 273–294). Hillsdale, NJ: Lawrence Erlbaum Associates.

Pearl, R. (1992). Psychological characteristics of learning disabled students. In N. N. Singh & I. L. Beale (Eds.), *Learning disabilities: Nature, theory, and treatment* (pp. 96–125). New York: Springer-Verlag.

Pearl, R., & Cosden, M. (1982). Sizing up a situation: LD children's understanding of social interactions. *Learning Disability Quarterly, 5*, 371–373.

Perlmutter, B. F., Crocker, J., Cordray, D., & Garstecki, D. (1983). Sociometric status and related personality characteristics of mainstreamed learning disabled adolescents. *Learning Disability Quarterly, 6*, 21–31.

Platt, J. J., & Spivack, G. (1975). *Manual for the Means-Ends Problem-Solving Procedure (MEMPS): A measure of interpersonal cognitive problem-solving skills.* Philadelphia: Hahnemann Community Health/Mental Retardation Center, Department of Health Services.

Polifka, J. A., Weissberg, R. P., Gesten, E. L., Flores de Apodaca, R., & Picolli, L. (1981). *The open middle interview (OMI) manual.* Unpublished manuscript, Rochester, NY: Center for Community Study, University of Rochester.

Pullis, M. (1985). LD students' temperament characteristics and impact on decisions by resource and mainstream teachers. *Learning Disability Quarterly, 8*, 109–122.

Ritter, D. R. (1989). Social competence and problem behavior of adolescent girls with learning disabilities. *Journal of Learning Disabilities, 22*, 460–461.

Rosenthal, R., Hall, J., Archer, D., DiMatteo, M. R., & Rogers, P. L. (1977). The PONS test: Measuring sensitivity to nonverbal cues. In P. McReynolds (Ed.), *Advances in psychological assessment: Vol. 4* (179–122). San Francisco: Jossey-Bass.

Rourke, B. P. (1982). Central processing deficiencies in children: Toward a developmental neuropsychological model. *Journal of Clinical Neuropsychology, 4*, 1–18.

Saarni, C. (1999). *The development of emotional competence.* New York: Guilford Press.

Saloner, M. R., & Gettinger, M. (1985). Social inference skills in learning disabled and nondisabled children. *Psychology in the Schools, 22*, 201–207.

San Miguel, S. K., Forness, S. R., & Kavale, K. A. (1996). Social skills deficits in learning disabilities: The psychiatric comorbidity hypothesis. *Learning Disability Quarterly, 19*, 252–261.

Sater, G. M., & French, D. C. (1989). A comparison of the social competencies of learning disabled and low achieving elementary-aged children. *The Journal of Special Education, 23*, 29–42.

Schneider, M., & Yoshida, R. K. (1988). Interpersonal problem-solving skills and classroom behavioral adjustment in learning-disabled adolescents and comparison peers. *Journal of School Psychology, 26*, 25–34.

Schwarrz, N., & Bless, H. (1991). Happy and mindless, but sad and smart? The impact of affective states on analytic reasoning. In J. Forgass (Ed.), *Emotion and social judgment* (pp. 55–71). Oxford, England: Pergamon Press.

Semrud-Clikemen, M., & Hynd, G. W. (1990). Right hemispheric dysfunction in non-verbal learning disabilities: Social, academic, and adaptive functioning in adults and children. *Psychological Bulletin, 107*, 196–209.

Shantz, C. H. (1983). Social cognition. In J. H. Flavell & E. M. Markman (Eds.), *Handbook of child development: Vol. 3. Cognitive development* (pp. 495–555). New York: Wiley.

Silver, D. S., & Young, R. D. (1985). Interpersonal problem-solving abilities, peer status and behavioral adjustment in learning disabled and non-learning disabled adolescents. *Advances in Learning and Behavioral Disabilities, 4*, 201–223.

Slate, J. R., & Saudargas, R. A. (1986). Differences in learning disabled and average students' classroom behaviors. *Learning Disability Quarterly, 9,* 61–67.

Spivack, G., Platt, J. J., & Shure, M. B. (1976). *The problem-solving approach to adjustment: A guide to research and intervention.* San Francisco: Jossey-Bass.

Stiliadis, K., & Wiener, J. (1989). Relationship between social perception and peer status in children with learning disabilities. *Journal of Learning Disabilities, 22,* 624–629.

Stone, W. L., & La Greca, A. M. (1984). Comprehension of non-verbal communication: A re-examination of the social competencies of learning-disabled children. *Journal of Abnormal Child Psychology, 12,* 505–518.

Swanson, L. H., & Malone, S. (1992). Social skills and learning disabilities: A meta-analysis of the literature. *School Psychology Review, 21,* 427–443.

Toro, P. A., Weissberg, R. P., Guare, J., & Liebenstein, N. L. (1990). A comparison of children with and without learning disabilities on social problem-solving skill, school behavior, and family background. *Journal of Learning Disabilities, 23,* 115–120.

Tur-Kaspa, H., & Bryan, T. (1993). Social attributions of students with learning disabilities. *Exceptionality, 4,* 229–243.

Tur-Kaspa, H., & Bryan, T. (1994). Social information-processing skills of students with learning disabilities. *Learning Disabilities Resaerch & Practice, 9,* 12–23.

Tur-Kaspa, H., & Bryan, T. (1995). Teachers' ratings of the social competence and school adjustment of students with LD in elementary and junior high school. *Journal of Learning Disabilities, 28,* 44–52.

Tur-Kaspa, H., Margalit, M., & Most, T. (1999). Reciprocal friendship, reciprocal rejection and socio-emotional adjustment: The social experiences of children with learning disorders over a one-year period. *European Journal of Special Needs Education, 14,* 37–48.

Vaughn, S., Hogan, A., Kouzekanani, K., & Shapiro, S. (1990). Peer acceptance, self-perceptions, and social skills of learning disabled students prior to identification. *Journal of Educational Psychology, 1,* 101–106.

Waterman, J. M., Sabesky, W. E., Silvern, L., Aoki, B., & McCaulay, M. (1981). Social perspective-taking and adjustment in emotionally disturbed, learning disabled and normal children. *Journal of Abnormal Child Psychology, 9,* 133–148.

Weiss, E. (1984). Learning disabled children's understanding of social interactions of peers. *Journal of Learning Disabilities, 17,* 612–614.

Wiig, E. H., & Harris, S. P. (1974). Perception and interpretation of non-verbally expressed emotions by adolescents with learning disabilities. *Perceptual and Motor Skills, 38,* 239–245.

Wong, B. Y. L., & Wong, R. (1980). Role-taking skills in normal achieving and learning disabled children. *Learning Disability Quarterly, 3,* 11–18.

Wright, J., & Mischel, W. (1982). Influence of affect on cognitive social learning person variables. *Journal of Personality and Social Psychology, 43,* 901–914.

Chapter 3

Development of Self-Understanding and Self-Esteem in Children and Adults With Learning Disabilities

Merith Cosden
Catherine Brown
Katherine Elliott
University of California, Santa Barbara

The development of a sense of self is a complex process for all children, and one that holds special challenges for children with learning disabilities (LD). The last decade of research on self-concept has changed our understanding of the structure of self-concept and its relationship to self-esteem (Harter, 1999). Children with LD vary in their self-esteem despite their negative academic experiences. Although studies have begun to identify factors related to self-esteem for children with LD, it is our premise that awareness, understanding, and acceptance of one's disability are critical elements to the development of positive self-regard. This chapter reviews the current literature on self-concept, self-esteem, and self-understanding in children with LD. Methods for developing positive self-understanding and self-esteem are discussed.

Why Study Self-Esteem?

Self-esteem is intuitively an important area of study. A review of the literature, however, reveals the ambiguity and complexity of this construct. High self-esteem has been considered from both positive and negative perspectives. On the positive side, a task force was established by the State of California in 1987 on self-esteem (Mecca, Smelser, & Vasconcellos, 1989), with the members of that group hypothesizing that the future of society would be tied to the perceived well-being of its citizens as measured by their self-esteem. On the other end of the continuum, a column by then President of the American Psychological Association, Martin Seligman, in the APA Monitor (Seligman, 1998) suggested that "baseless" self-esteem was one of society's major ills.

Most of the research on self-esteem has addressed it as a positive attribute, but there are some salient weaknesses with this work. For example, studies on self-esteem are largely correlational. Although some investigations view self-esteem as an outcome in itself, more typically self-esteem is viewed as a predictor of other outcomes ranging from academic performance, to eating disorders, to mental health (see Mruk, 1995 for a recent review). In most instances, the use of self-esteem as a predictor is based on theories that hold it as a precursor to other skills, rather than experimental designs or longitudinal studies. What we know about self-esteem is that it is associated with other self-perceptions and measures of functioning in school and in society. However, as noted by Seligman (1998), self-esteem can be artificially high when not developed in conjunction with positive skills or attributes, resulting in individual behavior problems as well as troubles for society.

In the 1960s, self-concept was viewed primarily as a unidimensional construct synonymous with self-esteem. This conceptualization of self-concept changed, however, with a variety of multidimensional models emerging (e.g., Bracken, 1996; Harter, 1990a; Marsh, 1993). Although the current major models of self-concept define domains differently, each includes separate measures of social competence and acceptance, academic skills, and physical appearance. Self-perceptions of academic and nonacademic competencies are also clearly separated. Studies utilizing these multidimensional measures have led to significant advancements in our understanding of the self-concept and the relationship of self-concept to self-esteem for children with and without LD.

Two additional methodological problems affect analysis of this large body of research. First, there is a lack of consensus regarding definitions of constructs such as self-concept, self-perceptions, self-understanding, and self-esteem. Although some investigators distinguish between these constructs (e.g., Harter, 1990a; Marsh, 1993) others do not (Bracken, 1996). These terms are defined as separate constructs in this chapter: *Self-concept* describes domain-specific self-perceptions; *self-esteem* pertains to one's overall sense of self-worth; and *self-understanding* refers to the accuracy with which individuals with LD understand the nature of their disability.

A second, and related, problem is that each of these constructs is assessed through self-report. By definition, self-esteem, self-concept, and self-understanding reflect the inner state of the individual as opposed to externally assessed skills or supports. Whereas this common methodology increases the likelihood of finding a relationship among the three variables, self-esteem, self-concept, and self-understanding do appear to be discernable, if interrelated, constructs.

Risk and Resilience

The constructs of risk and resilience gained salience subsequent to the publication of outcomes from the Kauai Longitudinal Study (Werner & Smith, 1992). This study monitored, and continues to monitor, the development of the 698 children born on that island in 1955. Many of the children in this sample were exposed to early risk, including perinatal trauma or poverty. The prospective nature of this study allowed investigators to examine the impact of risk factors on child development across the life span. The authors found that exposure to multiple risk factors increased the likelihood of the child having untoward outcomes later in life. However, the investigators also noted that these outcomes could be mitigated by the presence of "protective" factors, which included the child's verbal skills, an internal locus of control, and positive self-concept.

Using a risk and resilience framework to study LD allows one to account for individual differences with the population, while identifying factors related to both positive and negative outcomes (Morrison & Cosden, 1997). This research paradigm moves the literature from reliance on a deficit-oriented *between-group* model of study to a strength-based *within-group* method of analysis. Although this approach has gained acceptance (e.g., *Learning Disabilities Research & Practice: Special Issue*, Winter, 1993) there is still much to learn about factors that predict success and failure for children with LD (Werner, 1993).

In a recent study, Morrison and Cosden (1997) conceptualized the presence of LD as a risk factor that increased the likelihood of adverse outcomes but which, in and of itself, did not predict future behavior. The authors hypothesized that it was the combination of other aspects of the child's personal, familial, and social environment that determined whether the child would have successful or unsuccessful social, academic, and vocational outcomes. They also attempted to identify some of the *processes* by which different combinations of protective and risk factors operated. For example, having an agreeable temperament (one protective factor) is likely to increase the positive responses the child gets from others (a second protective factor) thus increasing the child's social support. Thus, it is not only important to understand the cumulative effects of risk and protective factors, but also the manner in which these factors enhance or inhibit each other.

In this chapter, self-understanding of one's LD is predicated to be a protective factor in relation to the development of positive self-perceptions and overall self-esteem. It is our premise that for students with LD self-esteem will be significantly affected by awareness and understanding of what it means to have a learning disability. To the extent that children (and adults) with LD understand the nature of their disability they will be better able to identify their strengths as well as weaknesses, and to utilize their skills and seek help when needed. In examining these relationships, we first consider how children, in general, develop self-awareness. Issues specific to developing an understanding of what it means to have LD are then examined.

DEVELOPMENT OF SELF-PERCEPTIONS

Theorists believe that children begin to form a sense of self at around age 5 (Eccles, Wigfield, Harold, & Blumenfeld, 1993). Early self-perceptions are formed on the basis of verbal and nonverbal cues from adults and peers. Further, children experience visceral feedback when they succeed or fail at tasks they attempt. At first, children incorporate this information in concrete ways. They accept that they are "good" at tasks when they master them without considering the difficulty of the activities or the ability of their peers to do similar work (Bear, Minke, Griffin, & Deemer, 1997). As a result of these cognitive limitations, children in elementary school typically have higher self-evaluations than do adolescents or adults. As children reach adolescence, their cognitive complexity increases. Self-perceptions change as adolescents begin to make social comparisons and recognize that they have a number of differentiated, and enduring traits.

Harter (1990b) described the changes that occur in the development of self-perceptions in terms of increasing levels of differentiation and changes in the domains by which children assess themselves. For the youngest group she has studied (4- to 7-year-olds) children appear to distinguish only four distinct areas of competence. These are: cognitive, physical, social, and behavioral. These domains become more differentiated for older elementary school students. For 8- to 12-year-olds, perceptions of self include scholastic competence, peer social acceptance, athletic skill, physical appearance, and behavioral conduct. Further, unlike younger children, elementary school children are also able to perceive themselves in a global way and provide ratings of global self-worth (Harter, 1990a). For adolescents, close friendship, romantic appeal, and job competence are additional domains in which self-judgments are made. These changes reflect the increased importance and differentiation of the social self.

As children mature, they make more social comparisons, self-perceptions become more "realistic," and self-esteem is likely to decline. For children with LD, this greater self-awareness also means acknowledging their differences from their peers.

SELF-PERCEPTIONS OF CHILDREN WITH LD

In studies where children with LD have been assessed using unidimensional scales of self-concept or self-esteem, they have scored lower than have children without LD (Chapman, 1988). This lower self-esteem was attributed to repeated school failures, awareness of being different than one's peers, problems in social acceptance, and incongruities in academic performance (Raviv & Stone, 1991).

Multidimensional measures of self-concept provided a new perspective on the self-perceptions of students with LD. The separation of academic and nonacademic competencies allowed investigators to see that although children with LD had lower academic self-perceptions than did their peers they did not necessarily have lower perceptions of their competencies in nonacademic domains (Ayres, Cooley, & Dunn, 1990; Chapman, 1988; Hagborg, 1999; Kistner, Haskett, White, & Robbins, 1987).

In addition, Harter (1990a) found that children with and without LD developed different structures to their self-perceptions. In particular, children who had LD were more likely than children without LD to differentiate their cognitive abilities from their specific academic skills. Children with LD were able to distinguish their perceptions of being smart or bright from their perceptions of having skills in particular academic areas (i.e., their ability to read, write, spell, or do math). Thus, Harter created two self-perception scales for elementary school children: one for children with LD, in which perceptions of intellectual ability and reading, writing, spelling, and math skills are assessed separately, and one for children without LD, which combines items on intellectual and scholastic ability into one subscale.

The finding that children with and without LD have different factor structures for viewing intellectual and academic abilities is important for two additional reasons. First, it indicates that children with LD are as capable as their nondisabled peers to differentiate and evaluate their competencies. Second, this difference suggests that the structure of self-concept is affected by the child's early experiences. Harter (1990a) suggested that the differentiation between cognitive ability and academic performance among children with LD reflects the special experiences of this population in the schools (p. 307).

Finally, studies have found large within-group variations in global self-esteem among children with LD. That is, although children with LD, as a group, tend to have lower self-esteem than do children without LD, there is considerable overlap across both groups. Using a risk and resilience framework, this overlap can be explained by identification of specific risk and protective factors for children with LD, as detailed next.

Nonacademic Strengths (Compensatory Hypothesis)

Development of nonacademic strengths appears to be a strong protective factor for children with LD. Studies find that self-perceptions of non-academic areas, including perceptions of one's physical attractiveness, social behavior, and athletic skills are associated with self-esteem (Cosden, Elliott, Noble, & Kelemen, 1999; Hagborg, 1996, 1999; Kloomok & Cosden, 1994; Renick & Harter, 1989). Hattie (1992) described this as an internal ipsative process, by which children compare their competence in one domain with competence in other domains, allowing their positive perceptions of stronger areas to compensate for their perceptions of their weaknesses. Given the apparent robustness of these findings, it is surprising how little attention has been given to the development of nonacademic aspects of the individual with LD.

Discounting the Importance of Academics

Harter (1990b) theorized that the congruence between perceptions of the importance of a domain and "doing well" in that area will contribute to one's perceptions of self-worth. She reported several findings to support this theory. First, she had children rate the importance of domains as well as their perceived competence in those same areas. By calculating a difference score, she was able to examine the impact of importance–perceived competence discrepancies on ratings of self-esteem. She reported significant correlations between discrepancy scores and ratings of self-worth, finding that lower discrepancies were associated with higher self-worth. Further, she noted that lower discrepancies were largely a result of children "discounting" the importance of those areas in which they did not perceive themselves as having higher skills.

Kloomok and Cosden (1994), however, reported different findings. They divided students with LD into three groups: those with high global–high academic self-concept, high global–low academic self-concept, and low global–low academic self-concept. They specifically examined the impact of *discounting* the importance of academic performance, as most students with LD would be expected to perceive their skills as relatively poor in this domain. They found that students in all three groups had discrepancy scores that reflected perceptions of academic performance as important. Although students with high global–high academic self-perceptions had smaller discrepancy scores, this was a function of higher ratings of their academic skills, rather than lower ratings of the importance of academics. Thus, the authors did not find evidence of discounting as a predictor of self-esteem. Others (e.g., Clever, Bear, & Juvonen, 1992) also have not found discounting to be a major protective factor. Thus, the role of discounting as a protective factor among students with LD is not clearly supported.

Support From Parents and Teachers

Social support is a strong protective factor for the development of global self-worth. Harter (1990b) built on the concept of the "looking-glass self" of Charles Horton Cooley to explain why self-esteem is affected by our belief in how others perceive us. She hypothesized that self-esteem is affected, at least in part, by others because "significant others are the social mirror into which one gazes to define the self" (p. 75). The data endorse her hypotheses. Across studies, children with LD who have higher self-esteem also express higher levels of peer and parent support (Harter, 1990b; Kloomok & Cosden, 1994; Rothman & Cosden, 1995).

It is important to note that the construct of social support can be assessed in two ways: by measures of perceived support, or through external indicators of assistance. This distinction is important, as problems in the first area (perceived support) reflect the individual's capacity to accurately appreciate his circumstances, while the latter area (external indicators of support) measures resource availability. When individuals with LD report low levels of social support, one or both of these problems may be evident. Relative to their nondisabled peers, students with LD may receive less support from teachers, parents, and peers as a result of their poor school performance or problematic social behavior. However, it is also possible that students with LD misperceive social cues and do not see support from others even when it is intended (Bender & Wall, 1994; Priel & Leshem, 1990). Examining parent and teacher perceptions of intended support, as well as the students' perception of support, can help locate the source of this problem.

Parental support, although most influential in early childhood, continues to affect one's self-worth throughout adulthood (Robinson, 1995). Students with LD who perceive greater support from their parents also report higher self-esteem (Kloomok & Cosden, 1994; Raviv & Stone, 1991; Rothman & Cosden, 1995). The manner in which parents convey support to their children with LD, however, is complex. Studies have found that parents of children with LD tend to have lower expectations for their children than do parents of children without LD (Tollison, Palmer, & Stowe, 1987). Furthermore, although parents and children rate the same skills as relatively high or low, parents tend to rate their children's achievements and self-esteem lower than do the children themselves (McLouglin, Clark, Mauck, & Petrosko, 1987; Raviv & Stone, 1991; Stone, 1997).

How do lower parental expectations affect identify development in children with LD? There is some indication that parents' ratings of their children's cognitive and academic skills, while lower than their child's, are moderately correlated with objective test scores (Stone, 1997). Further, parental knowledge about LD, and their openness, and acceptance of their child's disability, have been associated with the child's self-esteem (Raviv & Stone, 1991). This suggests that, in some instances, lower parental expectations may be adaptive, signifying awareness and acceptance of the child's disability (Tollison et al., 1987). On the other hand, parental expectations that are too low may inhibit the child from making efforts in areas in which they could succeed (Kistner et al., 1987). Thus, parental expectations that are too low will have a negative impact on children's self-perceptions, whereas overly high expectations will lead to frustration and family stress. Parental perceptions that accurately capture their child's strengths and weaknesses signal acceptance of the child and are experienced by the child as an indicator of support.

Furthermore, accurate parental understanding allows adults to advocate for their children. Wiener and Sunohara (1998) provided a concrete example of this in their study of parents who take an active role in facilitating their children's friendships. They interviewed parents who were trying to help their children with LD in their social development. These parents coached their children on how to approach friends, made sure that friends felt welcomed in their homes, and tried to fulfill the function of friend through engaging in fun, age-appropriate activities with their child. Understanding their children's strengths and weaknesses allowed these parents to offer them both emotional and practical support.

Given the high potential for experiencing both academic and social problems at school, it is not surprising that teacher feedback also has significant impact on students' self-esteem. Positive teacher feedback can mitigate the impact of academic problems, raising students' self esteem regardless of test scores (Bear & Minke, 1996). When students hear from their teachers that they are doing well, they see themselves as successful students, at least at the lower grade levels.

Teachers can also have a negative impact on students' self-perceptions. Teachers who are unaware that their students have LD, or who do not themselves understand what it means to have LD, may misattribute students' problems to laziness, lack of motivation, or having a bad attitude. Once a student has been identified with LD, teachers may see him or her in a stereotypical manner. Macintosh, Vaughn, Schumm, Haager, and Lee (1993) reported that middle-school teachers expected students with LD to have less motivation and lower academic self-concept. Although this is true for some children with LD, anticipating behavior problems may increase the likelihood of those problems occurring in others.

Peer Perceptions and Influence

As children approach adolescence, peer support has a more significant impact on their self-perceptions (Robinson, 1995), and can serve as either a risk or protective factor. Although a majority of students with LD maintain at least average social status, they are less likely to be popular and have a greater chance of being disliked by their peers (Conderman, 1995; Vaughn & Elbaum, 1999; Vaughn, Hogan, Kouzekanani, & Shapiro, 1990). Children who describe themselves as having less social acceptance and support also report lower self-esteem (Kloomok & Cosden, 1994).

As noted with regard to social support, *perceptions* of peer acceptance may not reflect *actual* peer acceptance. Perceptions may be influenced by a variety of factors, including prior expectations. For example, people who are depressed may not accurately see the overtures of others (Heath, 1995; Heath & Wiener, 1996). However, children with LD who experience social problems are likely to exhibit poor social skills associated with problems in processing social information (Bryan, 1997, 1998; Vaughn et al., 1990). Rourke and his colleagues (e.g., Harnadek & Rourke, 1994; Rourke, Young, & Leenaars, 1989) have identified a subgroup of children with a nonverbal learning disability who are characterized by poor social judgment and a lack of awareness of the impact of their behavior on others. Rourke hypothesized that the social isolation and depression experienced by this subgroup is directly associated with their problems in self-reflection and self-understanding.

Finally, social (peer) comparison may also be a risk factor for the development of self-esteem. Many studies have examined the impact of social comparisons, and one's social comparison group on the development of self-concept and self-esteem for children with LD. Students who spend the majority of their time in mainstream classes tend to use children without LD as a reference group, whereas children who spend the majority of their time in special education classes will compare their performance to that of other children with LD. In turn, it is hypothesized that students with LD who compare themselves to nondisabled students will report lower self-esteem, whereas those who use students with LD as a comparison group will report higher self-perceptions. This hypothesis has been supported by many, but not all, studies (e.g., Bear et al., 1997; Bryan, 1998; Renick & Harter, 1989). As noted by both Bear and Bryan, this process is likely to be context specific. That is, students will be differentially affected by academic environments that focus more or less on social comparison; and great variation can be expected on this dimension across mainstream and special education settings.

Self-Esteem Is Related to Self-Awareness

We have hypothesized (Cosden et al., 1999; Rothman & Cosden, 1995) that understanding what it means to have a learning disability is a significant protective factor in the development of positive self-esteem for students with LD. Several correlational studies support this (Cosden et al., 1999; Heyman, 1990; Kloomok & Cosden, 1994; Li & Moore, 1996; Rothman & Cosden, 1995).

The process of learning what it means to have a learning disability, however, appears to be a two-edged sword. On the one hand, understanding one's strengths and weaknesses is the first step in developing skills for successful educational, social, and vocational adaptation. On the other hand, self-understanding also means recognizing differences between oneself and others in ways that indicate that one is less capable than his or her peers.

For example, some studies find that children with LD who are accurate in their understanding of their social and academic problems are also more likely to report depression (Heath, 1995; Heath & Wiener, 1996). Unfortunately, the development of negative self-perceptions can influence belief in one's capacity to succeed across all domains, even those in which the student's disability does not interfere. For example, Ayres et al. (1990) found that students with LD who had lower self-esteem made global attributions for their failures to factors outside their control. Although these children had difficulties in some areas of academic functioning, their global attributions for failure contributed to a lack of persistence even for tasks at which they might have been successful. Conversely, some children with LD engage in "cognitive distortion" as a defense mechanism, overestimating their academic and social skills in order to protect their self-esteem (Alvarez & Adelman, 1986; Stone, 1997; Vaughn & Elbaum, 1999). Although this leads to higher self-esteem temporarily, it does not allow the individual to develop the skills needed to be successful in the future.

We hypothesize that many of the risk and protective factors associated with self-esteem are in some way related to self-understanding. For example, students who have a less pervasive view of their disability are more likely to be aware of their nonacademic areas of strength. As described earlier, accuracy in understanding also allows parents to take a more active, and effective, role in advocating for their children (Wiener & Sunohara 1998). Given the importance of developing accurate self-understanding, it is disturbing, if not surprising, that many children and adults, as well as many of their parents and teachers, do not have an accurate understanding of what it means to have LD.

DEVELOPING AN UNDERSTANDING OF WHAT IT MEANS TO HAVE LD

Children have difficulty developing an understanding of LD, in part, because there is no formal place in the Individualized Education Plan (IEP) process through which they are given this information. Thus, children obtain their knowledge about LD via informal means, through their parents or teachers or other school personnel—if they obtain information at all (Cosden et al., 1999). Inaccuracies in understanding what it means to have a learning disability, or no understanding, are the rule rather than the exception.

Limitations in our assessment tools also make it difficult to know what children "know." Until the 1990s, there were no formal scales for examining self-understanding among children or adults with LD. In response to this need, Heyman (1990) developed the Self-Perception of a Learning Disability (SPLD) scale. The SPLD is a self-report instrument with questions that covers three areas: whether students see their disability as delimited or global; whether they feel their disability is modifiable or permanent; and the degree to which they feel their disability is stigmatizing. Several studies (Heyman, 1990; Rothman & Cosden, 1995) have found a positive relationship between scores on the SPLD and global self-esteem. In addition, Rothman and Cosden found that children who had higher SPLD scores also had higher achievement scores and perceptions of greater behavioral and intellectual competence, social acceptance and support. Thus, students who saw their LD in a more positive manner also were aware of their academic and nonacademic strengths.

However, the SPLD mixes questions on knowledge about LD with questions on stigmatization. Thus, this scale is not a pure reflection of self-understanding. In a recent study, Cosden et al. (1999) administered the Self-Perception Profile for Learning Disabled Students (Renick & Harter, 1988), the Self Perception of a Learning Disability Scale (SPLD; Heyman, 1990), and a series of open-ended questions on what it meant to have a learning disability to elementary and junior high school students with LD. The investigators coded responses to open-ended questions about what it means to have LD for accuracy, and analyzed the relationship of these responses to SPLD and self-esteem scores. Several findings emerged from this analysis. A majority of elementary school students were not able to explain what it meant to have a learning disability; a majority of the students in the junior high sample had a response, but many of these responses were inaccurate, reflecting an overgeneralization of their academic problems. Students who described their learning disability as a "general" learning problem were more likely to have been told by a family member, whereas children who described LD as a circumscribed problem were more likely to have been told by a teacher.

Finally, open-ended descriptions of LD, coded for accuracy, were not associated with SPLD scores, indicating that these two measures yielded different information. Given the inability of most elementary school students to define LD, a secondary analysis was conducted solely with the junior high sample, comparing their coded responses to the "what is a learning disability" question with their scores on Harter's self-esteem scales. In this analysis, students who answered "I don't know" to "What is a learning disability?" had higher self-esteem scores than did students who gave a more definitive response. Thus, as suggested by earlier studies, self-esteem was lower for students beginning to understand their disability (Bear & Minke, 1996; Heath, 1995).

These studies indicate that for some students with LD the developmental of self-understanding is associated with lower self-esteem. However, this changes as children grow older, with self-understanding becoming a protective factor for adults with LD, associated with higher self-esteem and a decreased likelihood of depression. Studies indicate that successful adults with LD have greater self-awareness. Self-understanding allows them to utilize their strengths and advocate for their needs, seeking academic and vocational accommodations that build on their strengths and support their weaknesses (Adelman & Vogel, 1990; Spekman, Goldberg, & Herman, 1992; Vogel & Adelman, 1990; Vogel, Hruby, & Adelman, 1993).

The process by which children with LD gain a positive self-understanding is not clear. It appears that the emergence of self-understanding, and its impact on self-esteem, follows a developmental progression. At first, children with LD are unaware of their differences from other children. Even as those differences become apparent to others, children with LD may lack self-awareness due to difficulties in reading social cues or to cognitive distortions designed to protect their self-esteem. As their self-awareness increases, their self-esteem may decrease, at least temporarily.

A developmental shift occurs during adolescence, where self-understanding begins to lead to self-acceptance. We speculate that two types of changes may occur at this juncture. First, as the child's cognitive complexity increases, including their metacognitive abilities, they are more able to see themselves from multiple perspectives. That is, they are able to hold on to a self-perception that includes strengths and weaknesses without denying their disability, exaggerating their skills, or becoming overwhelmed by their academic problems. Second, with the passage of time, students become more knowledgeable about their disability, whether through their informal discussion with others or their own experiences attempting different tasks. We assume that by adulthood, most individuals with LD have gone through this process. For adults with LD the ability to identify strengths and weaknesses allows them to advocate for their needs and to seek opportunities that build on their skills, resulting in greater personal and vocational success.

Furthermore, we hypothesize that the developmental process through which children with LD gain self-understanding is guided by interactions with family, friends, and school personnel. These interactions can lead to accurate and positive understanding in some instances, and confusion or negative perceptions in others. The development of positive self-understanding is likely to be influenced by whether or not family members and teachers close to the child have an accurate understanding of LD, as well as the child's opportunities to discuss their disability with knowledgeable and caring others. The availability of significant others with whom to discuss their disability *over time* is particularly important, as the child's ability to understand the complexity of their disability and the questions they will have regarding the nature of their disability are likely to change over the course of their development. Conversely, children whose teachers and parents do not fully understand what it means to have LD, and children who do not have significant others with whom to discuss their disability, are not likely to develop accurate self-understanding. Instead, these children are likely to receive negative feedback for their school performance and social behavior, and to develop self-perceptions that either globalize their disability or are otherwise inaccurate (e.g., viewing themselves as slow or stupid). It is important for future research to consider how parent, teacher, and peer feedback may affect children with LD and their developing self-perceptions both negatively and positively.

IMPROVING SELF-UNDERSTANDING AND SELF-ESTEEM

To date, few programs have demonstrated positive changes in self-understanding or self-esteem for children with LD. In part, this is due to the paucity of research on counseling with this population. The invisibility of the LD diagnosis may foster the counselors' lack of awareness of its presence, and contribution, to their clients' problems. Poor compliance, intermittent attention, and difficulties in establishing a therapeutic relationship may be misinterpreted as resistance rather than viewed as a function of the LD by a therapist unaware of the client's condition.

Designing effective interventions to help children and adults with LD develop more accurate, and positive, self-perceptions will depend on several factors. Shirk and Harter (1996) noted that in order for interventions to be effective, they need to focus on the determinants of low self-esteem. This starts with an assessment of the nature and source of the child's problems.

Prout and Prout (1996) differentiated between primary and secondary problems in self-esteem. Primary self-esteem problems are those that precede the development of a disorder and play a central role in that disorder. For primary problems in self-esteem it is important to acknowledge that children with LD may experience low-self esteem, and other psychological difficulties as a result of circumstances that have little to do with their disability. The same types of adversity that affect all children, including poverty, parental discord, and environmental stressors, also impact children with LD. In these instances, interventions need to focus on problems that may not be directly related to the child's disability.

Secondary self-concept problems are a function of a disorder, disability, or condition. For children with LD secondary self-concept problems are likely to be common; that is, children with LD will experience lower self-esteem as a result of problems arising from their learning disability. For these instances, we propose developing interventions that can help children with LD identify and build on their strengths, especially their strengths in nonacademic areas. Although nonacademic strengths have been associated with self-esteem for students with LD (Kloomok & Cosden, 1994), few studies to date have attempted this. Hattie (1992) found this type of intervention to be effective for improving self-esteem within the general population. In a meta-analysis of 89 studies and more than 400 effect sizes Hattie found that one of the strongest effects was associated with intense outdoor programs that pose physical challenges to students, such as Outward Bound. It should also be noted that school-based programs, particularly those designed to enhance self-esteem by improving academic achievement, had the lowest effect sizes. Although Hattie does not report specific outcomes for children with LD, they are part of the larger samples. One can conjecture that other programs that help children with LD identify and build their strengths might also improve self-understanding and self-esteem by increasing student awareness of the specificity of their problems and by allowing them to experience success.

There is also a need for programs that will increase self-understanding. Particularly as students with LD transition into adulthood, ignorance about LD hampers their effective decision making (Ness & Price, 1990). Yuan (1994) developed one such program for college students with LD. Modules in the program addressed understanding LD, the causes of LD, characteristics of people with LD, identifying strengths, compensating for learning disabilities, and self-advocacy. Roffman, Herzog, and Wershba-Gershon (1994) described utilization of that program and note qualitative, positive findings in the development of both self-understanding and self-esteem. Although this study is small in scope, it does suggest a promising method for helping this population.

A pilot program, adapting this model for children and adolescents with LD, was implemented in one junior high school and one elementary school in Southern California (Kelemen, Elliott, Noble, & Cosden, 1998). Students were invited to participate in the program on the basis of their scores on SPLD and the Self-Perception Profile. Two groups were conducted at the junior high and two at the elementary level; each group had four or five students participating over a period of 8 weeks. Topics included defining LD, characteristics of people who have LD, identification of strengths and weaknesses, and development of compensatory strategies.

Posttest measures taken after the group ended yielded equivocal findings. That is, only 35% of the students showed improvements in their SPLD scores, while 50% noted higher self-esteem after participating in the group. A qualitative, post hoc examination of factors related to outcomes yielded two observations: Some of the students found the content hard to understand and integrate within the relatively short time frame; and the group process was difficult to maintain given individual variations in attention span, and learning styles.

Only a small number of interventions designed to increase self-understanding and self-esteem has been tested. Although the data are limited, they suggest directions for future consideration. Developmentally, younger children may not have the capacity to understand the complexity of their disability. Thus, programs need to be simple, focusing on the identification of internal strengths and weaknesses. As children approach adolescence their capacity to understand what it means to have LD will improve, such that they can benefit from interventions that are more sophisticated. Although the process of gaining self-understanding may initially lower self-esteem, it is expected that, over time, both self-understanding and self-esteem will improve. Knowing what it means to have a learning disability is an important outcome in itself, as it will allow students to help themselves, increasing their success in and out of school and, thereby, their feelings of self-worth.

Process of Intervention

In addition to developing content for student interventions, the counseling process for children and adults with LD needs to be examined. The challenges of counseling students with LD have been noted for a long time (e.g., Ledebur, 1977), although not well studied. Kelemen et al. (1998) described some of the problems faced in providing group counseling to children who have LD. They suggest repetition of ideas, small goals, and utilization of a multimedia format including nonverbal activities, such as collage and drawing. Special issues related to developing a therapeutic relationship have not been addressed in the literature, nor has how to help participants with LD provide or gain from group feedback.

Environmental Interventions

The aforementioned approaches are directed at the individual with LD. However, programs designed to enhance self-esteem may be even more effective when implemented at a systemic level. Bear et al. (1997) recommended interventions designed to help teachers help their students develop positive self-perceptions. Given the paucity of research in this area, Bear et al. suggest several ways in which teachers could structure their classrooms to reduce the social comparison process, a process that is likely to enhance self-esteem for children at the lower end of the academic spectrum. Suggestions include making grades private, avoiding use of ability groups, and individualizing tasks to assure some success for each student.

Similarly, interventions that focus on helping parents help their children could be fruitful. However, no published interventions were found that focused on helping parents help their children understand LD. The need for this type of program is suggested by the inaccuracy of information held by many parents and children, the impact of parental understanding on both instrumental and emotional support for their children, and the prolonged period of dependence which individuals with LD have on their family of origin (Spekman et al., 1992). Given the stress related to raising a child with LD (e.g., Dyson, 1996), programs should consider how to provide support as well as knowledge about LD in ways that will help parents learn to advocate for their children and to empower their children to advocate for themselves.

CONCLUSIONS

This chapter discusses self-understanding as a protective factor in the development of positive self-esteem for children who are at risk as a function of having LD. Understanding what it means to have LD helps the individual identify their strengths as well as their limitations, allowing them to explore opportunities in which they are likely to experience success, and to seek help where it is needed. Developmental issues related to understanding LD, and the interplay between self-understanding and self-esteem, require further exploration. Interventions are needed to address the development of self-understanding once a child is identified, as well as to help students with subsequent concerns about having LD across their life span.

ACKNOWLEDGMENT

The first author began her work on learning disabilities at the Chicago Institute for the Study of Learning Disabilities (CHILD) under the direction of Tanis Bryan. She thanks Tanis for her early support, and for opening this area of inquiry to her.

REFERENCES

Adelman, P. B., & Vogel, S. A. (1990). College graduates with learning disabilities—Employment attainment and career patterns. *Learning Disability Quarterly, 13,* 154–166.

Alvarez, V., & Adelman, H. S. (1986). Overstatements of self-evaluations by students with psychoeducational problems. *Journal of Learning Disabilities, 19,* 567–571.

Ayres, R., Cooley, E., & Dunn, C. (1990). Self-concept, attribution, and persistence in learning-disabled students. *Journal of School Psychology, 28,* 153–163.

Bear, G. G., & Minke, K. M. (1996). Positive bias in the maintenance of self-worth among children with LD. *Learning Disability Quarterly, 19,* 23–32.

Bear, G. G., Minke, K. M., Griffin, S. M., & Deemer, S. A. (1997). Self-concept. In G. G. Bear, K. M. Minke, & A. Thomas (Eds.), *Children's needs: Development, problems and alternatives* (pp. 257–269). Bethesda, MD: National Association of School Psychologists.

Bender, W. N., & Wall, M. E. (1994). Social-emotional development of students with learning disabilities. *Learning Disability Quarterly, 17,* 323–341.

Bracken, B. A. (1996). Clinical applications of a context-dependent, multidimensional model of self-concept. In B. A. Bracken (Ed.), *Handbook of self-concept: Developmental, social and clinical considerations* (pp. 463–504). New York: Wiley.

Bryan, T. (1997). Assessing the personal and social status of students with learning disabilities. *Learning Disabilities Research & Practice, 12,* 63–76.

Bryan, T. (1998). Social competence of students with learning disabilities. In B. Wong (Ed.), *Learning about learning disabilities* (2nd ed., pp. 237–271). San Diego: Academic Press.

Chapman, J. W. (1988). Learning disabled children's self-concepts. *Review of Educational Research, 58,* 347–371.

Clever, A., Bear, G. G., & Juvonen, J. (1992). Discrepancies between competence and importance in self-perceptions of children in integrated classes. *Journal of Special Education, 26,* 125–138.

Cosden, M., Elliott, K., Noble, S., & Kelemen, E. (1999). Self-understanding and self-esteem in children with learning disabilities. *Learning Disability Quarterly, 22,* 279–290.

Dyson, L. L. (1996). The experiences of families of children with learning disabilities: Parental stress, family functioning and sibling self-concept. *Journal of Learning Disabilities, 29,* 280–286.

Eccles, J. S., Wigfield, A., Harold, R. D., & Blumenfeld, P. (1993). Age and gender differences in children's self-and-task perceptions during elementary school. *Child Development, 64,* 830–847.

Hagborg, W. J. (1996). Self-concept and middle school students with learning disabilities: A comparison of scholastic competence subgroups. *Learning Disability Quarterly, 19,* 117–126.

Hagborg, W. J. (1999). Scholastic competence subgroups among high school students with learning disabilities. *Learning Disability Quarterly, 22,* 3–10.

Harnadek, M. C. & Rourke, B. P (1994). Principal identifying features of the syndrome of nonverbal learning disabilities in children. *Journal of Learning Disabilities, 27,* 144–154.

Harter, S. (1990a). Issues in the assessment of self-concept of children and adolescents. In A. M. La Greca (Ed.), *Childhood assessment: Through the eyes of a child* (pp. 292–325). New York: Wiley.

Harter, S. (1990b). Causes, correlates and the function role of global self-worth: A life-span perspective. In R. J. Sternberg & J. Kolligian (Eds.), *Competence considered* (pp. 67–97). New Haven, CT: Yale University Press.

Harter, S. (1999). *The construction of the self: A developmental perspective.* New York: Guilford Press.

Hattie, J. (1992). *Self-concept.* Hillsdale, NJ: Lawrence Erlbaum Associates.

Heath, N. L. (1995). Distortion and deficit: Self-perceived versus actual academic competence in depressed and nondepressed children with and without learning disabilities. *Learning Disabilities Research & Practice, 10,* 2–10.

Heath, N. L., & Wiener, J. (1996). Depression and nonacademic self-perceptions in children with and without learning disabilities. *Learning Disability Quarterly, 19,* 34–44.

Heyman, W. B. (1990). The self-perception of learning disability and its relationship to academic self-concept and self-esteem. *Journal of Learning Disabilities, 23,* 472–475.

Kelemen, E., Elliott, K., Noble, S., & Cosden, M. (1998). *Developing self-understanding in children with learning disabilities: A small-group counseling intervention.* California Association of School Psychologists, Santa Clara, CA.

Kistner, J., Haskett, M., White, K., & Robbins, F. (1987). Perceived competence and self-worth of LD and normally achieving students. *Learning Disability Quarterly, 10,* 37–44.

Kloomok, S., & Cosden, M. (1994). Self-concept in children with learning disabilities: The relationship between global self-concept, academic "discounting," nonacademic self-concept, and perceived social support. *Learning Disability Quarterly, 17,* 140–153.

Ledebur, G. W. (1977). The elementary learning disability process group and the school psychologist. *Psychology in the Schools, 14,* 62–66.

Li, L., & Moore, D. (1996). Acceptance of disability and its correlates. *The Journal of Social Psychology, 138,* 12–25.

Marsh, H. W. (1993). Relations between global and specific domains of self: The importance of individual importance, certainty and ideals. *Journal of Personality and Social Psychology, 65,* 975–992.

Macintosh, R., Vaughn, S., Schumm, J. S., Haager, D., & Lee, O. (1993). Observations of students with learning disabilities in general education classes. *Exceptional Children, 60,* 249–261.

McLoughlin, J. A., Clark, F. L., Mauch, A. R., & Petrosko, J. (1987). A comparison of parent–child perceptions of student learning disabilities. *Journal of Learning Disabilities, 20,* 357–360.

Mecca, A., Smelser, N. J., & Vasconcellos, J. (Eds.). (1989). *The social importance of self-esteem.* Berkeley, CA: University of California Press.

Morrison, G., & Cosden, M. (1997). Risk, resilience and adjustment of individuals with learning disabilities. *Learning Disability Quarterly, 20,* 43–60.

Mruk, C. J. (1995). *Self-esteem: research, theory, and practice.* New York: Springer.

Ness, J., & Price, L. A. (1990). Meeting the psychosocial needs of adolescents and adults with LD. *Intervention in School and Clinic, 26,* 16–21.

Priel, B., & Leshem, T. (1990). Self-perceptions of first and second grade children with learning disabilities. *Journal of Learning Disabilities, 23,* 642–673.

Prout, H. T., & Prout, S. M. (1996). Global self-concept and its relationship to stressful life conditions. In B. A. Bracken (Ed.), *Handbook of self-concept* (pp. 260–261). New York: Wiley.

Raviv, D., & Stone, C. A. (1991). Individual differences in the self-image of adolescents with learning disabilities: The roles of severity, time of diagnosis, and parental perceptions. *Journal of Learning Disabilities, 24,* 602–611, 629.

Renick, M. J., & Harter, S. (1988). *Manual for the self-perception profile for learning disabled students.* Colorado: University of Denver.

Renick, M. J., & Harter, S. (1989). Impact of social comparisons on the developing self-perceptions of learning disabled students. *Journal of Educational Psychology, 81,* 631–638.

Robinson, N. S. (1995). Evaluating the nature of perceived support and its relation to perceived self-worth in adolescents. *Journal of Research on Adolescents, 5,* 253–280.

Roffman, J. A., Herzog, J. E., & Wershba-Gershon, P. M. (1994). Helping young adults understand their learning disabilities. *Journal of Learning Disabilities, 27,* 413–419.

Rothman, H., & Cosden, M. (1995). The relationship between self-perception of a learning disability and achievement, self-concept, and social support. *Learning Disability Quarterly, 18,* 203–212.

Rourke, B. P., Young, G. C. & Leenaars, A. A. (1989). A childhood learning disability that predisposes those afflicted to adolescent and adult depression and suicide risk. *Journal of Learning Disabilities, 22,* 169–175.

Seligman, M. (1998). The American way of blame. *APA Monitor, 29,* (President's Column).

Shirk, S., & Harter, S. (1996). Treatment of low self-esteem. In F. M. Reinecke, F. Dattilio, & A. Freeman (Eds.), *Cognitive therapy with children and adolescents: A casebook for clinical practice* (pp. 175–198). New York: Guilford Press.

Spekman, N. J., Goldberg, R. J., & Herman, K. L. (1992). Learning disabled children grow up: A search for factors related to success in the young adult years. *Learning Disabilities Research and Practice, 7,* 161–170.

Stone, C. A. (1997). Correspondences among parent, teacher, and student perceptions of adolescents' learning disabilities. *Journal of Learning Disabilities, 30,* 660–669.

Tollison, P., Palmer, D. J., & Stowe, M. L. (1987). Mother's expectations, interactions, and achievement attributions for their learning disabled or normally achieving sons. *Journal of Special Education, 21,* 83–93.

Vaughn, S., & Elbaum, B. (1999). The self-concept and friendships of students with learning disabilities: A developmental perspective. In R. Gallimore, D. L. MacMillan, D. L. Speece, & S. Vaughn (Eds.), *Developmental perspectives on children with high-incidence disabilities* (pp. 81–107). Mahwah, NJ: Lawrence Erlbaum Associates.

Vaughn, S., Hogan, A., Kouzekanani, K., & Shapiro, S. (1990). Peer acceptance, self-perceptions, and social skills of learning disabled students prior to identification. *Journal of Educational Psychology, 82,* 101–106.

Vogel, S. A., & Adelman, P. B. (1990). Extrinsic and intrinsic factors in graduation and academic failure among LD college students. *Annals of Dyslexia, 40,* 119–137.

Vogel, S. A., Hruby, P. J. & Adelman, P. B. (1993). Educational and psychological factors in successful and unsuccessful college students with learning disabilities. *Learning Disability Research & Practice, 8,* 35–44.

Werner, E., & Smith, R. S. (1992). *Overcoming the odds: High risk children from birth to adulthood.* Ithaca, NY: Cornell University Press.

Wiener, J., & Sunohara, G. (1998). Parents' perceptions of the quality of friendships of their children with learning disabilities. *Learning Disabilities Research, 13,* 242–257.

Yuan, F. (1994). Moving toward self-acceptance: A course for students with learning disabilities. *Intervention in School and Clinic, 29,* 301–309.

Chapter 4

The Loneliness Experience of Children With Learning Disabilities

Malka Margalit
Michal Al-Yagon
Tel-Aviv University

Bryan's early studies (Bryan, 1974; Bryan & Bryan, 1978) initiated the comprehensive body of research that focused attention to the social difficulties of children with learning disabilities (LD). Meta-analysis studies (Kavale & Forness, 1996; Ochoa & Palmer, 1995) and research summaries (Bryan, 1997) demonstrated that students with learning disabilities often experience lower sociometric status and peer rejection more than their nondisabled peers. The objective of this chapter is to introduce the private experience of loneliness as reported by students with learning disabilities, to report research outcomes and future trends, pinpointing attention not only at the children's difficulties, but also at their resilience perspectives.

The loneliness experience is a global indicator of dissatisfaction from the quality or the quantity of individuals' social interrelations (Asher, Parkhurst, Hymel, & Williams, 1990). Peplau and Perlman (1982) defined loneliness as the unpleasant experience when individuals perceive a discrepancy between the desired and accomplished patterns of their social networks. It should be emphasized that loneliness is a different experience than solitude. In contrast to the negative affect experienced in loneliness, solitude is a developmental necessity, generally considered a positive experience and involves a deliberate choice to stay alone (Buchholz & Catton, 1999). Solitude may provide an opportunity for rest from stressful realities and anxiety-provoking people, or for enjoying the time alone for leisure activities, thinking, and creative work (Josselson, 1992; Marcoen & Goossens, 1990; Storr, 1988; Woodward, 1988).

The loneliness construct consists of two interrelated dimensions (Buchholz & Catton, 1999; Weiss, 1973): social loneliness and emotional loneliness. Social loneliness reflects the disruption of the social network and has been related to peer rejection. Emotional loneliness refers to a deficiency in intimate close relations (a good friend) and interpersonal bonding and has been related to attachment relations (Bowlby, 1969; Wood, Klebba, & Miller, 2000).

Attachment processes deal with the quality of the emotional ties between the mother and her infant (Josselson, 1992). The study on loneliness and attachment requires consideration of the complexity of interacting factors over time, and the developmental construct is characterized by the transformation of normative features and individual differences operating at the level of behavioral, emotional, and representational organization (Sroufe & Sampson, 2000).

Through developmental stages, children experience loneliness due to various groups of frustrations: The loneliness may represent for several children the unsatisfied need for close and intimate relationships with a small number of good and valued friends. Others may relate their loneliness to unfulfilled expectations for belonging to a larger and desired social group (Weiss, 1973). The loneliness experience may also represent the developmental difficulty of children with special needs to stay alone, and to keep involved in solitary activities (Margalit, 1991). The capacity to stay alone (Winnicott, 1965) is part of a healthy maturational process, and the developmental difficulty of several children to remain alone may contribute to their increased need for interpersonal contacts.

The study of children with learning disabilities (Margalit, 1994; Pavri & Monda-Amaya, 2000; Sabornie, 1994) revealed that their personal characteristics may not only predispose them to the loneliness experience, but also may render it more difficult for them to cope with these aversive feelings. Loneliness indicates a subjective stress experience, yet the study of individuals with learning disabilities revealed that their loneliness experience is often a reflection of realistic social difficulties, resulting in their poor social network, low social status and peer rejection (Valas, 1999).

Three main factors were often identified as predicting social difficulties and loneliness experiences among children with learning disabilities: (a) the knowledge deficit—the children have not acquired the age-appropriate knowledge needed for developing satisfactory social relations, pinpointing attention at their deficient social cognition (Pearl, 1992); (b) the performance deficit—the children have not secured the skills to translate age-appropriate social knowledge into effective interpersonal behaviors. These children may learn what is the expected behavior at various situations, but have difficulties in translating their knowledge base into age-adequate performance (Vaughn & La Greca, 1992); (c) these children have adopted the behavioral style of rejected and lonely children, accepting the reputation of isolated individuals and beliefs as to how lonely youngsters often behave (Margalit, 1994). Their interpersonal approach and nonverbal communication reveal their alienated self-concept, and their beliefs in their inability to develop satisfying social relations. In line with the social model that examines relationships as the function of interactions between individuals, ecological conditions, and cultural codes and values (Vaughn, McIntosh, & Hogan, 1990), this chapter discusses the loneliness experience reported by students with learning disabilities as related to different age groups, and ecological conditions within a systemic model. This model assumes that gender and environments, family climate, and peer relations are related to different aspects of self-perceptions and can be viewed as parts of dynamic, interactive processes in which the child is both influenced by and influences the social processes.

LONELINESS AMONG DIFFERENT AGE GROUPS

Loneliness levels of children with learning disabilities were compared to nondisabled children in different age groups from preschool to adolescents. At the preschool stage, before the academic failure was established, the study of loneliness among children at risk for developing learning disabilities has a unique significance for understanding the syndrome. In order to examine the consistency of the loneliness experience, the loneliness measure (Asher et al., 1990) was compared at the beginning and end of the academic year for 379 preschool children (238 children at risk for developing learning disabilities and 141 typical developing children). The results of the study (Margalit & Al-Yagon, 2000) revealed that at the end of the year, both groups of children felt less lonely (see Fig. 4.1). However, the loneliness level of the children at risk remained significantly higher, and the correlation between the beginning and end of the year was moderate and significant.

Different types of inclusion for these children reflect the attempts to provide support for children at risk in the least restricted and stigmatizing environment. In a study that examined the relation between different types of inclusion and the loneliness experience of children at risk for developing learning disabilities (Margalit, 1998), 187 preschool children (ages ranged from 4;9 to 6;3 years, $M = 5.5$, $SD = 0.37$) were assessed. The sample consisted of students from 23 preschool systems divided into three major groups. The first two groups were students in full inclusion systems, with team teaching of regular and special education's teachers in each preschool: Group A—60 children (47 boys and 13 girls) who were considered at risk for developing learning disabilities; Group

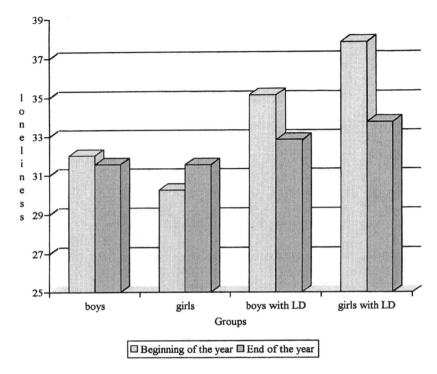

FIG. 4.1.   Loneliness at preschools through the year ($N = 379$ students).

B—76 normally developing peers from the same preschool (56 boys and 20 girls); Group C—51 children (38 boys and 13 girls), regular students in 17 preschools, who were considered at risk for developing learning disabilities, yet got their remedial support in a municipality-supported afternoon center, and not in their preschool settings during school time. The goals of this study were to examine the loneliness experience among these groups of students in two ecological conditions: those in regular systems to those in full-inclusion systems (each preschool in the full-inclusion systems consisted of 10 students at risk for developing learning disabilities, and about 20 normative developed students and two teachers; Margalit, 1998).

The comparisons of both groups of students—those at risk for developing learning disabilities and their normative developing peers—revealed significant differences. Children at risk reported higher levels of loneliness than their peers. However, no significant differences were found between the two groups of children at risk for developing learning disabilities, regardless of their different educational environments and type of inclusion and support. Thus the increased loneliness experience may be considered an intrinsic factor to the disability conceptualization and to the deficit experience. In addition, it should be emphasized that not all children at risk reported increased levels of loneliness. In each of the earlier mentioned studies, a group of children with developmental delays did not feel lonelier than their peers.

In an attempt to identify the different sources of loneliness, attachment conceptualization was examined. Because learning disabilities cannot be identified at the infancy age stage, in order to examine the attachment experience, we used the mothers' narratives about early mother–infant relations. Mothers approach their newborn babies with certain assumptions and beliefs about the infants' needs and abilities and their competencies and priorities as mothers. Their assumptions and expectations are reinforced by signals from the babies, indicating to the mothers their importance to the infants. If the mother's perceptions of the infant's needs and abilities are limited, due to her emotional stress or her perception of the child's slow development, and if the child's increased needs for attention are not met by the mother, this child may receive a restricted input, too little attention, and a limited range of shared parent–child activities.

The recognition of the bidirectional nature of the influence, with mothers of temperamentally difficult preschool children reporting more psychosocial difficulties revealed that mothers were more prone to anxiety and their competence as parents. These mothers reported they felt less emotionally close to their children, and found their parenting role restricted their lives to a greater extent. In a recent study, Al-Yagon and Margalit (2000) explored the multiple perspectives of risk factors in predicting adaptive functioning among preschool children. This study examined 145 mother–child dyads divided into two groups: Group 1—70 mothers and their children with developmental delays (51 boys, 19 girls); Group 2—75 mothers and their normally developing children (46 boys, 29 girls). The children with developmental delays at risk for developing learning disabilities and their peers were students in inclusive kindergartens (age range 5 to 6;5 years). Risk factors comprised of three groups of measures: the child characteristics; the maternal and familial ecological variables; and the child's attachment style as described by mothers. Different sources of information were used: children's self-reports, mothers' narratives, and teachers' ratings. Path analysis (Amos analysis) was used to compare the multidimensional risk model for the two groups.

The results indicated different patterns of relations between the model's components for the two groups, demonstrating different sources for the experience of loneliness. Feeling of loneliness was explained by the attachment style among the group of children at risk for developing learning disabilities. In this group of children, "secure" attachment, as viewed by mothers, contributed significantly to lower levels of loneliness. In the group of the normally developing children, the role of the attachment style, as a factor that predicted adaptation was not substantiated. For the first group, children's difficult temperament contributed directly to an insecure pattern of mother–children attachment, lower maternal sense of coherence, and a lower level of family cohesion. In addition, the difficult temperament of children contributed indirectly to their reports of loneliness (through the attachment style as a mediator) and to teacher-evaluated child adjustment (through the family cohesion mediator).

In summary, the studies on preschool children focused attention on the loneliness experience even before the learning difficulties were established, and within different inclusion models. The relation of attachment relations and family climate to children's loneliness was established, pointing attention to the complex interrelating factors even at this early age.

ELEMENTARY SCHOOL

At the elementary school-age stage, the learning disabled children are identified and assessed, following their academic failure. Research documented their cognitive difficulties and learning deficiencies. However, there is growing attention to the social difficulties among children with learning disabilities, and their higher levels of loneliness than their peers (Margalit & Al-Yagon, 2000; Margalit & Efrati, 1996). It should be noted that various studies documented that girls with learning disabilities reported higher levels of loneliness than boys (see Fig. 4.2). The consistency of these results (correlation of .55, $p < .01$; $N = 2400$ students) and the gender impact calls attention to girls with learning disabilities. It is commonly accepted that fewer girls than boys are identified as having learning disabilities. However, additional focused research is needed to clarify the gender-related adjustment.

Research often relates loneliness to peer ratings, examined peer nomination as a measure of children's popularity, and reciprocal nomination as an indicator of friendship relations. Research documented that popularity and friendship measures are moderately related to loneliness reports for children with and without learning disabilities. In an attempt to further examine the loneliness experience among children with learning disabilities, the role of reciprocal negative nominations among peers (having children in your class whom you don't like, and they don't like you—"identified enemies") has been explored (Margalit, Tur-Kaspa, & Most, 1999). This study revealed the unique contribution of having identified enemies in class. Results confirmed that within the group of students with learning disabilities, those children who had at least one identified enemy in class, felt lonelier and less coherent than children with learning disabilities who

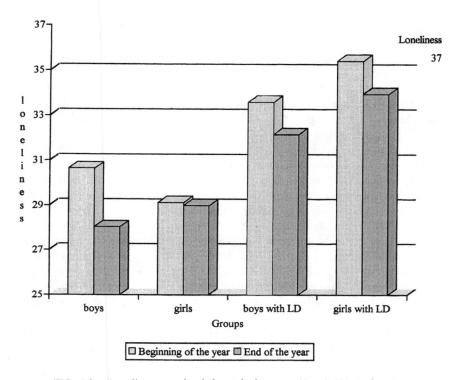

FIG. 4.2.   Loneliness at school through the year (*N* = 2,400 students).

had no "class enemies." Such significant within-group differences were not found in the comparison groups, revealing the social–emotional vulnerability of the children with learning disabilities to social distress. They attributed increased importance to peer attitudes, due to their limited social network, especially the negative ones. Hierarchical multiple regression analysis revealed that the loneliness experience was significantly predicted by the personal measure of resilience, the interpersonal measure of peer reciprocal rejection, and cognitive conception of friendship qualities. Children with learning disabilities who had at least one identified "enemy" in class, experienced higher levels of loneliness and viewed themselves as less coherent than did their nondisabled peers (Margalit, Tur-Kaspa, & Most, 1999).

In order to study the unique contribution of the academic difficulties to the subjective experience of students with learning disabilities, Valas (1999) examined the psychological adjustment among two groups of children with academic difficulties: students with learning disabilities and low-achieving students and compared them to their average achieving peers. The sample consisted of 1,434 students drawn from regular school classes.

Results confirmed the theoretical model (using LISREL as a path analysis) and demonstrated that students with learning disabilities were less accepted by peers, had lower self-esteem, and felt lonelier than their nondisabled peers. The comparisons of students with learning disabilities with the low achievement students (when controlling for academic achievement and intelligence) revealed that the students with learning disabilities were less accepted by peers and felt lonelier. On the other hand, they were less depressed. It is possible that the students with learning disabilities felt less pressure for achievements and accept their disability, while the students with low achievement were more depressed as an outcome of their academic failure. The results suggested that in addition to the academic difficulties, students with learning disabilities experienced higher levels of loneliness, particularly in primary school.

It is commonly accepted that teachers' impressions and beliefs have a clear impact on children's personal experiences. However, it was not clear if teachers' perceptions might reflect the personal experience of children's loneliness. The examinations of teachers' ratings between two groups of students at the beginning and end of the year, revealed that teachers are aware of students' alienation (Margalit, Mioduser, Al-Yagon, & Neuberger, 1997). The students' loneliness predicted teachers' assessment of students' social difficulties in addition to the teachers' evaluations of learning and behavioral difficulties at the beginning of the year. The comparisons of teachers' perception and students' loneliness revealed a significant consistency and consistent differences between children with learning disabilities and nondisabled peers.

The entrance of technology into our life questioned our established concepts of interpersonal relations, challenged our established conceptualization of connectedness and alienation realizing, and pointed attention to the new opportunities related to distance communications and interrelations. In order to clarify the model of loneliness, and the students perceptions of themselves in their world, 756 students (second to fourth grades) participated in the study: 368 students with learning disabilities (196 boys and 172 girls) and 388 students with average achievements (214 boys and 174 girls; Weissberg, 2000). The construct "sense of coherence" has been used in this study together with the loneliness reports (Antonovsky, 1979, 1987). The sense of coherence construct is a generalized worldview, reflecting the extent to which an individual has dynamic confidence that his or her internal and external environments are structured and predictable, and that there is a high probability that life situations will work out as well as can be expected (Antonovsky, 1979, 1987). An inclination to perceive the world as ordered and explicable, enables the individual to develop a cognitive assessment of the difficulties stemming from stressors, and facilitates the active search for appropriate coping strategies.

Similar to earlier research in this study (Weissberg, 2000), group comparisons revealed that students with learning disabilities were less accepted by peers; they reported lower levels of sense of coherence than their peers, and higher levels of loneliness. Developmental trends were also identified and older students felt more coherent and less lonely. In order to examine simultaneously all variables, a Structural Equation Modeling analysis (SEM) was used (EQS method) and a common loneliness model was identified for both groups.

In addition to the demographic variables: age, gender, and group belonging (LD/NonLD), three factors predicted the loneliness experience: personal—the sense of coherence; interpersonal—expressed by peer nominations; and instrumental—the attitudes toward computers mediated the aversive loneliness experience. Separate analysis of the model for each group revealed that for the group of average achievement students, all five predictors were significant: age, gender, personal including attitudes, and interpersonal variables. For the group of students with learning disabilities, only two measures remained significant: the personal perceptions in terms of the sense of coherence and the attitudes toward computers. The results of this study pointed to the significant role of computers in predicting lower levels of loneliness for students with learning disabilities.

The instrumental mediation for loneliness experience—the computers—needs additional examination to clarify if the role of technology in the children's life starts to challenge the traditional loneliness and companionship conceptualizations. The examinations of how e-friends and web-peers may mediate the loneliness can clarify the types of possible direct impacts (in terms of expending social networks) and indirect impacts (in terms of self-perceptions and social place in the class). We have also to examine the impact of computers' involvement as an out-of-school activity for securing a different status in class for the student with learning disabilities.

ADOLESCENCE

Research on loneliness at the adolescent stage emphasized the importance of the experience (Hamid & Lok, 2000). Lonely youth possessed limited social networks, had fewer close friends of both sexes, and received less support from their classmates. Generally, their interpersonal relationships were less satisfying, and within their family, their relationships with their father were less satisfying. They were less trusting of authority figures and less optimistic about the trustworthiness of others. The loneliness experience of students with learning disabilities at the adolescence age group was also investigated in various studies, reporting similar results. For example, Sabornie (1994) compared 38 students with learning disabilities and their matched nondisabled peers from sixth- and seventh-grade middle-school students. Similar to earlier research, the students with learning disabilities reported higher levels of loneliness as compare to their matched peers.

Different social environments and unique ecological conditions can be expected to predict the development of different interrelations, and loneliness experience. Margalit and Ben-Dov (1995) compared adolescents with LD to nondisabled students within two different environmental conditions: the Israeli kibbutz and the city social system. The kibbutz community is a special socialist group that provides social, economic, educational, and medical resources according to individual need. In this unique community the value of social relations is emphasized, and children stay together in children's homes most of their waking hours. They go to their parents' homes only late in the afternoon. In several communities at the time of the research, they even slept in these communal children's homes. The study investigated social skills and identified loneliness patterns among 122 adolescents with LD and 120 non-LD students from these two social systems: the kibbutz and the city. The research teams consisted of individuals from the kibbutz movement and from the city. Two opposite hypotheses were raised. The kibbutz's researchers expected the children to experience less loneliness in the society that was saturated by social relations. The city researchers expected the kibbutz children with learning disabilities to experience higher levels of loneliness, assuming that in this environment children with learning disabilities are expected to developed social relations even when they are not mature enough for these ongoing relations. Confronting this social pressure, they may feel higher levels of loneliness. The overall analysis did not support the opposing hypothesis, and revealed that both groups of students with learning disabilities (the city as well as the kibbutz youngsters) experienced higher levels of loneliness than their nondisabled peers. They were rated by teachers as less adjusted socially, and by peers as less accepted than the nondisabled group, regardless of their different social environments. Yet, when compared to students with learning disabilities in the city, the kibbutz students were evaluated by peers as having more friends and by teachers as demonstrating more self-control. However, they did not differ in their loneliness levels or in their peer ratings.

Sabornie and Thomas (1989) compared social affective traits among three groups of students: a group of children with learning disabilities, a group of students with behavior disorders, and a nondisabled group. In this study, the students with learning disabilities and behavior-disordered students did not differ on their loneliness levels and social and adjustment variables.

These studies demonstrated that throughout different samples and different age groups (from preschool to adolescents), and from different ecological conditions, students with learning disabilities reported higher levels of loneliness (Margalit, 1994), but not all students revealed these differences when compared to their peers. The loneliness experience was predicted by their personal experience of coherence, and by out-of-school activities such as the preference for computers. In addition, the role of social status and peer ratings was emphasized in explaining loneliness especially for the nondisabled group. These results focused interest at the personal roots of loneliness without ignoring the interpersonal perspectives.

WHO IS NOT LONELY?

Research also pointed out that not all children with learning disabilities experience more loneliness than their nondisabled peers. In most studies (Margalit, 1994), a small group of youngsters was identified. They did not view themselves as lonely individuals more than their peers. The search for resilience and adjustment focuses interest on this unique group of children among the students with learning disabilities, who demonstrated age-adequate social skills, and average scores on their sense of coherence reports, regardless of their continuous academic difficulties.

Most diagnostic and intervention efforts for students with learning disabilities are based on a clinical model, which identifies and diagnoses the children's cognitive difficulties. Such an approach relies on conceptualizations of disability and pathology as a basic rationale for understanding children with learning disabilities. Garmezy (1983), in his comprehensive survey of childhood stressors, focused attention on the importance of individual and environmental factors that can influence resilience and stress-resistance in children. The rise in experimental interventions, using concepts such as stress-resistance, ego-resilience, and invulnerability, in contrast with terms such as deficits, special difficulties, and pathology, hold unique significance for children with learning disabilities. As already mentioned, the sense of coherence construct is a generalized belief that the individual feels when coping with demands placed upon him or her by stress factors (Antonovsky, 1979, 1987). A tendency to perceive the world as structured and predictable enables the individual to understand difficulties and facilitate the active search for appropriate strategies.

In line with the sense of coherence conceptualization, in order to promote the chances of successful coping with stressors, children must be able to understand the problem they are facing, have at their disposal the necessary resources, view the problem as important, be motivated and have hope to solve it. Life stressors are many and varied. A strong sense of coherence is closely related to a wide and varied repertoire of coping strategies, and to flexibility in selecting the particular coping strategy that seems most appropriate for the situation at hand (Antonovsky, 1987).

Antonovsky and Sourani (1988) considered the sense of coherence construct not as a specific coping style, but rather as a characteristic of flexibility in selecting appropriate coping behaviors. An individual who demonstrates a high level of coherence would succeed in transforming his or her potential resources into reality, and thus will more adequately be able to cope with life stressors.

Children with learning disabilities often viewed themselves as less coherent individuals. However, many studies identified among them a unique group of students who do not experience social distress and loneliness more than their nondisabled peers (Vaughn & La Greca, 1992). This focused interest on the resilient group of students with learning disabilities who are not lonely, revealed that they demonstrated age-adequate social skills. The salutogenic model (Antonovsky, 1979, 1987), which suggests a complementary approach to the pathological model and explains successful coping with stressors, highlights the strengths and capacity of these individuals for successful adjustment, without ignoring their academic difficulties. Antonovsky (1987) differentiated between the pathologenic approach, which seeks to explain why people get sick, and the salutogenic approach (focusing on the origins of health and coping), which seeks to explain why people do not become ill, staying healthy and active. The pathogenic orientation uses the commonly accepted cause–effect model; once the disease is defined, a constant search is made for the true causes of maladjustment or a specific illness, with the belief that identifying these causes will lead to the identification of the most appropriate remediation of the maladjustment. In contrast, the salutogenic orientation focuses interest on probability models, trying to identify factors that will predict resistance to difficulties, buffering pressures and disappointments, and promotes effective coping with stressful situations.

Age-appropriate social interrelations can be reached when children feel themselves coherent and competent, and are willing to initiate and experiment with interrelations outside of their personal boundaries. Thus, separations and connections were found to be conceptually interrelated, affecting each other in a reciprocal manner and involving internal and external processes (Winnicott, 1965). Self-reported sense of coherence, social skills, and peers' social acceptance predicted significantly (and negatively) the youngsters' loneliness experience (Margalit, 1991).

Environmental conditions may further promote or limit children's abilities to develop satisfactory peer relations. Children's deficiencies may predispose them to developing unsatisfactory or frustrating interpersonal relations. This predisposition can be understood only through detailed investigations of the reciprocal interactions between the children and significant adults within different environmental climates and over time.

SIGNIFICANT ADULTS' PERSPECTIVES:
MOTHERS' AND TEACHERS' PERCEPTIONS

The developmental aspects of sense of self, personal identity, and social relations, all seem to be related to familial aspects, and to the understanding of the loneliness experience. Loneliness and social isolation within the family environment has been expressed not only by children but also by parents. Confronted with the pain, stress, increased demands, and unwanted life changes introduced by their children's disabilities, parents often reported that they feel lonely (Antonovsky, 1993). Rooted in the psychoanalytic tradition (Josselson, 1992; Winnicott, 1965), it has been conceptualized that difficulties in early infant–parent relations may predict increased loneliness at a later developmental stage.

Family reactions to the disabling children have been widely studied, with a focus on parents' decreased coherence, unique patterns of family climates, coping, and affective level (Turnbull et al., 1993). The expressions of the children's loneliness seem to perpetuate parental distress and loneliness. All of these aspects interact with the child's disabilities and more difficult temperament, leading to higher levels of loneliness both in parents and children. In these families, decreased cohesion and closeness among their members were reported, more conflictual relations, and the independence and personal growth of the individual family members were reduced and challenged (Margalit, 1990).

Comparisons between perceptions of loneliness (Unger, 1992; Zehavi, 1992) further clarified the perspectives of significant adults when confronted with the children's distress. The perceptions of teachers and mothers were studied within this ecological paradigm. Teachers of students with learning disabilities rated their students as more lonely than did the mothers and the students' self-reports, and this difference was not significant for the nondisabled group. Teachers viewed the loneliness experience of the youngsters as more severe than did the mothers and the youngsters themselves. Teachers are often the only adults who observe the child in comparison to their peers and within ongoing social interactions and tasks. It is not clear if the different ratings represented the teachers' realistic assessments of the children, or reflected their own sense of helplessness, distress, and beliefs that they lack the knowledge and skills needed to deal with children's loneliness. Discussions with teachers revealed that many of them felt unprepared to deal with children's frustrations in the social domain. Mothers seemed to be more in tune with their children's loneliness experience than were the teachers. These outcomes challenge the paradigm for teachers' preparation. In times of inclusion, teachers should be sensitized to the emotional distress and alienation experience of students with and without special needs.

COMPANIONSHIP AND LONELINESS

The research focus on companionship has revealed the full complexity of the interpersonal processes, concentrating on qualitative and quantitative advantages of having a good friend. If within the peer world, a good friend is expected to attend to one's major relational needs (Parker & Asher, 1993), then it can be expected that the poorer quality of friendship, as reported by individuals with learning disabilities, may be closely related to their loneliness feelings.

Parker and Asher (1993) listed unique provisions that good friendship relations may contribute. Good friends may communicate care and concern to their mates. They can provide help in times of need, sometimes share their intimate feelings or thoughts ("telling secrets"), and often spend enjoyable time together. Another important aspect of friendship relates to conflicts and disagreements. The amount of conflicts among children provided an important index, but the conflict resolution style also added a crucial perspective to the understanding of interrelations. Unresolved conflicts may increase the experience of social isolation. Children with learning disabilities (Margalit, 1994) were less accepted by peers, had fewer friends, and their companionship provisions patterns were different from those of their nondisabled peers. They felt that their friends cared less for them, spent less time together in enjoyable activities ("hanging around"), and also had more unresolved conflicts in their relations.

SUBTYPING OF LONELINESS AND BEHAVIOR ADJUSTMENT

An additional important step in understanding the difficulties of the students with learning disabilities and planning effective interventions is the move from a generalized approach for studying loneliness to the identification of different subgroups of children. In a study that combined the conceptualization of internalizing versus externalizing psychopathology (Achenbach, 1982; Hymel, Rubin, Rowden, & LeMare, 1990), with the evaluation of loneliness (Asher et al., 1990), four subgroups have been identified: two subgroups of lonely children and two subgroups of nonlonely children (Margalit & Al-Yagon, 1994).

The first group was characterized as withdrawn, nonaggressive, introverted, shy, extremely lonely, and isolated. It was rated by teachers as evidencing internalizing maladjustment, and consisting of children who were anxious, apprehensive, timid, and low in social assertiveness; whereas the second lonely group was characterized as aggressive, sometimes hyperactive, and often noted for deficient problem solving, poor social skills, and retaliations of anger and hostility related to attributional bias. As for the two nonlonely groups, both evidenced good social skills. One nonlonely group demonstrated typical externalizing maladjustment, consisting of aggressive children with age-appropriate social skill abilities and a controversial social status. Teachers viewed them as demonstrating low self-control skills. The other nonlonely group was relatively adjusted, with introverted tendencies and its remaining difficulties were within the academic scope.

The attempt to further explore the unique relations between loneliness and maladjustment behaviors called for the comparisons of students with learning disabilities and students with behavior disorders. In line with the inconsistent differences reported between these two groups (Epstein, Bursuck, & Cullinan, 1985; Fessler, Rosenberg, & Rosenberg, 1991), the subtyping approach has been adopted, using social and behavioral maladjustment variables as the criteria for subtyping (Hooper & Willis, 1989, Margalit, 1995). The subtyping approach emphasized the distinction between the group of students with learning disabilities and the group of students with behavior disorders. The learning disabled group revealed lower social skills scores and were less represented in the aggressive and not lonely subgroup. The behavior disordered group disclosed more extreme levels of externalizing and internalizing maladjustment. A differential impact of social skills training was found for the different subgroups of children (Margalit, 1995). Indeed, the pre–post comparisons of the assessed measures revealed that following intervention, the students felt less lonely, were more accepted by their peers, had higher levels of self-control, and displayed less internalizing and externalizing maladjustment. However, the examination of the intervention effects within the subtyping model highlighted its differential strength.

The subgroup of lonely students with strong internalizing tendencies reported at the beginning of the intervention the highest levels of loneliness. Following the intervention, they felt less lonely. However, they remained passive in their expectation for the desired change in their social status. Their teachers commended them for their high self-control, yet remarked on their extremely low social initiation. Students with learning disabilities in this subgroup presented a clear decrease in their internalizing tendencies. This finding was not significant for the students with behavior disorders.

The subgroup of students with externalizing and lonely students that was noted by their behavior difficulties, were rated by their teachers before intervention, as demonstrating externalizing difficulties and the lowest self-control when compared to the other subgroups. Their peers did not accept them, and they were aware of their social difficulties. They wished to gain friendship, yet failed to control their frustration and anger, and got easily into trouble. Following intervention, they felt less lonely, showed better self-control, and less externalizing maladjustment. The students with learning disabilities increased their self-control skill and revealed less externalizing maladjustment. The students with behavior disorders did not reveal significant changes in their externalizing maladjustment.

The subgroup of students who demonstrated externalizing maladjustment, yet felt socially competent, initiated social interactions, and seldom experienced loneliness. They were relatively accepted by peers, and felt that they had many friends. Following intervention, they were even more accepted by peers.

The results of this study (Margalit, 1995), pointed attention to the advantages of a subtyping model not only for diagnosis, but also for directing intervention plans. It clearly indicated that although the aggressive and social isolation behavior of students with learning disabilities and students with behavior disorders may look similar, they need differential processes to reach significant changes. The results suggested that students with learning disabilities need a focused emphasis on social skill acquisition and active coping with loneliness, whereas students with behavior disorders benefited better from an emphasis on self-control skills. Only individualized interventions and detailed observations of social processing and outcomes may clarify in future research the differential patterns and roles of the disruptive behavior for the two subgroups. In line with Vaughn and La Greca's (1992) notion of fitting intervention to population needs, a comprehensive assessment of behavior profile is needed, and adapted intervention procedures to help the children in their abilities to cope with loneliness.

COPING WITH LONELINESS

Individuals not only experienced social distress in a unique and subjective manner, but also reacted differently to the painful experience of loneliness. Some children felt helpless and sorry for themselves, feeling ineffective in their coping style. Others reported that they do not feel very lonely, demonstrating their resilience and effective coping. The study of different coping strategies among these children (Margalit, 1994) not only further establishes the existence of their unique and distinct approaches to stressful situations, but also helps in developing individualized interventions.

In several studies, similar to Cassidy and Asher's (1992) procedure, students were interviewed in order to clarify their understanding of the loneliness meaning, and to find out their coping strategies: What they do when they feel lonely. The survey pointed out the distinction between more active and approach coping strategies and strategies that rely essentially on avoidance of the problem. External trends, toward promoting social skills and generating intimate social interrelations and toward increasing networking with peer groups at school age, and internal trends, toward cultivating satisfying solitary interests and activities, and enhancing abilities to stay alone without feeling loneliness, were both present within the different strategies. Different categories of activities have been identified (Woodward & Kalyan-Masih, 1990), reflecting individual differences in the children's ability to initiate effective and appropriate coping activities.

Different children cope with their loneliness using varying levels of approach and avoidance coping. Without ignoring the complex and dynamic patterns of coping strategies, higher levels of passive and avoidance coping with loneliness were evident among the groups of disabled students. In addition, the outcomes of coping efforts may be evaluated according to the proportion of solitary versus social activities exhibited in the children's performance repertoire. The study of students with learning disabilities (Margalit, 1994) revealed more solitary solutions and the children stayed engaged in enjoyable activities that can be performed alone. Students rated self-initiated strategies as most helpful in coping with loneliness (Pavri & Monda-Amaya, 2000).

INTERVENTION MODELS

The choice of a model for interventions targeting loneliness among children with learning disabilities must be closely related to loneliness theory. The ecological conceptualization of loneliness as a multivariate construct related to individual differences and environmental characteristics, holds implications for the construction of effective interventions. Interventions should be designed to be concurrently related to sources of loneliness in the individual's current functioning and developmental history, reflecting continuous interactions between environmental and individual goals, and between expectations and attitudes toward solitary activities. Intervention goals may be directed toward changing the child or changing the environment in terms of family and school, integrating both the systemic and the skill deficit models to promote personal empowerment, satisfying social interactions and decreasing the loneliness experience.

Empowerment has often been viewed as the process that facilitates the individual's identification and recognition of needs and the ability to use existing personal competencies in order to obtain resources to meet these needs. Within a salutogenic perspective (Antonovsky, 1987), that attempts to identify factors promoting activities located at the healthy end of the continuum (fostering socialization and decreasing loneliness), the empowerment approach has been using enabling experiences to promote children's competence and sense of control. The systemic climate creates opportunities for competencies to be experienced.

This systemic approach devotes interventional efforts not only for the children who demonstrate interpersonal dissatisfaction, but also at their peers and significant adults. Parents and teachers can structure environments in order to promote companionship and satisfactory peer interrelations. Developing a knowledge base about the social life of their children, and becoming aware of different developmental aspects of interpersonal relations such as aggressiveness and shyness, may enable these adults in affecting their children's interpersonal relations. Parents and teachers can be effective in helping children cope with loneliness by creating opportunities and promoting social behaviors and skills, initiating satisfactory solitary and social play activities, and helping children deal with their emotions (Ladd, 1988). In order to help them develop effective interventions, two related aspects should be examined in depth: skill selection and procedure selection.

Identification of the deficient skills must be based on individualized assessments and developed within age-related objectives. Laboratory studies highlighted various aspects of the children's social skill deficits, including negative views of the self and others, unresponsiveness to others in social interactions, and inappropriate patterns of self-disclosure. Skill selection should be geared to individual needs, with an emphasis on developmental and systemic considerations, and detailed observations.

Different procedures were found to be effective in social skill training programs, such as modeling, peer tutoring, role playing, and problem-solving sequences. Adult-mediated and peer-mediated approaches were applied, in order to initiate change not only within the child who feels lonely and needs training in friendship-making skills, but also in the environment in order to encourage and promote companionship opportunities (Rizzo, 1988).

Personal and social change following successful interventions rely extensively on different methods of empowerment (Bandura, 1988) such as providing individuals with knowledge, skills, and resilient self-beliefs of efficacy to alter aspects of their lives over which they have control. Personal beliefs and perceived self-efficacy about one's capabilities to organize and implement the actions necessary for attaining designated levels of performance in different areas have been found important in mediating behavioral change. Judgments of personal efficacy affect the individual's choice of activities and selection of environments (Ozer & Bandura, 1990).

Finally, the empowering model has focused intervention efforts toward promoting change in the processes and outcomes that are directed at the children's experiences of themselves, their peers, and adults. In this interventional approach, the value of social skill training has not been ignored.

These empowering approaches attempt to activate the individual's search for individualistic answers to social needs and may foster his or her sense of coherence, and the ability to develop both meaningful connections and areas of interest for enjoyable solitary activities. It should be recognized that throughout life, individuals consistently attempt to control and regulate their social life by moving from periods of social interrelations—in which we prefer to spend time with other people, to solitude periods, when they want to be left alone. Empowerment approaches acknowledge the different routes to helping children in coping with loneliness, and the importance of multiple interventional methods in promoting competency and social growth.

SUMMARY

This chapter examined loneliness among children with learning disabilities from developmental and ecological perspectives. Studies have shown consistent increased levels of loneliness among children with learning disabilities from different age groups and ecological conditions. In addition, the study of children with learning disabilities demonstrated that their personal characteristics may not only predispose them to the loneliness experience, but may also contribute to their ability to cope with these unpleasant feelings. The study on preschool children emphasized the loneliness experience of these students, even before the learning difficulties were established, and within different inclusion models. The contribution of the attachment style and family climate to children's loneliness and adjustment was established for the group of children at risk, pointing attention to the complex interrelating factors of the child and the family characteristics.

Reviewing studies of elementary and high school students with learning disabilities revealed the gender impact in addition to the unique contribution of personal conceptions and the buffering power of peer relations. The follow-up from the beginning to the end of the academic year revealed that as a group, children felt less lonely at the end of the academic year, yet students with learning disabilities remained lonelier than their nondisabled peers. It can be concluded that most lonely children remained lonelier than their peers, and the correlation between the beginning and end of the academic year were moderate and significant.

Within the ecological conceptualization, this chapter examined the perceptions of teachers and mothers. Results indicated that teachers and mothers were distressed by the children's expressions of loneliness, and often felt unprepared to deal with children's social needs. Moreover, the results demonstrated the importance of subgroups' identification in promoting the understanding of loneliness, and special attention should be directed at the characteristics of those children with learning disabilities who did not feel lonelier than their peers. In line with resilient models, the chapter emphasized the need for additional exploration of this unique group of children with learning disabilities, who demonstrated age-adequate social skills.

Future research and intervention experimentation will contribute to the multifactor approach in planning social skills learning strategy programs. Empowering models of intervention focused efforts toward promoting significant changes by directing attention at the children's experiences (joint impact of affective and cognitive processing) of themselves, their peers, and adults. These empowering approaches attempt to activate the individual's search of individualistic answers for social needs and may foster his or her sense of coherence, and the ability to develop both meaningful connections and areas of interest for enjoyable social and solitary activities. Future research should clarify means and outcomes of focused attempts toward changing the child experience of loneliness and changing the environment in terms of family and school, integrating both the systemic and the skill deficit models to promote personal empowerment, satisfying social interactions and to decrease the loneliness experience. However, a word of caution should be expressed. Everyone experiences loneliness at some time, and the goals of the loneliness research are not to prevent the aversive yet basic human experience, but to increase the understanding of the alienation affect and to promote coping strategies through skill training and identifying moderating ecological factors.

REFERENCES

Achenbach, T. M. (1982). *Developmental psychopathology* (2nd ed.). New York: Wiley.

Al-Yagon, M., & Margalit, M. (July, 2000). *Multiple perspectives on children at-risk for developing learning disorders*. Paper presented at the International Special Education Congress, Manchester, UK.

Antonovsky, A. (1979). *Health, stress and coping*. San Francisco: Jossey-Bass.

Antonovsky, A. (1987). *Unraveling the mystery of health*. San Francisco: Jossey-Bass.

Antonovsky, A. (1993). The implications of the Salutogenesis: An outsider's view. In A. P. Turnbull, J. M. Patterson, S. K. Behr, D. L. Murphy, J. G. Marquis, & M. J. Blue-Banning (Eds.), *Cognitive coping, families and disability* (pp. 111–122). Baltimore: Paul Brookes.

Antonovsky, A., & Sourani, T. (1988). Family sense of coherence and family adaptation. *Journal of Marriage and the Family, 50*(2), 79–92.

Asher, S. R., Parkhurst, J. T., Hymel, S., & Williams, G. A. (1990). Peer rejection and loneliness in childhood. In S. R. Asher & J. D. Coie (Eds.), *Peer rejection in childhood* (pp. 253–273). Cambridge, England: Cambridge University Press.

Bandura, A. (1988). Self-efficacy conception of anxiety. *Anxiety Research, 1*, 77–98.

Bowlby, J. (1969). *Attachment and loss: Vol. 1. Attachment*. New York: Basic Books.

Bryan, T. H. (1974). Peer popularity of learning disabled children. *Journal of Learning Disabilities, 7,* 621–625.

Bryan, T. (1997). Assessing the personal and social status of students with learning disabilities. *Learning Disabilities, Research & Practice, 12*(1), 63–76.

Bryan, T. H., & Bryan, J. H. (1978). Social interactions of learning disabled children. *Learning Disabilities Quarterly, 1,* 33–38.

Buchholz, E. S., & Catton, R. (1999). Adolescents' perceptions of aloneness and loneliness. *Adolescence, 34,* 203–213.

Cassidy, J., & Asher, S. R. (1992). Loneliness and peer relations in young children. *Child Development, 63,* 350–365.

Epstein, M. H., Bursuck, W., & Cullinan, D. (1985). Patterns of behavior problems among the learning disabled: Boys aged 12–18, girls aged 6–11 and girls aged 12–18. *Learning Disability Quarterly, 8*(2), 123–129.

Fessler, M. A., Rosenberg, M. S., & Rosenberg, L. A. (1991). Concomitant learning disabilities and learning problems among students with behavioral/emotional disorders. *Behavioral Disorders, 16,* 97–106.

Garmezy, N. (1983). Stressors of childhood. In N. Garmezy & M. Rutter (Eds.), *Stress, coping and development in children* (pp. 43–84). New York: McGraw-Hill.

Hamid, P. N., & Lok, D. P. P. (2000). Loneliness in Chinese adolescents: A comparison of social support and interpersonal trust in 13 to 19 year olds. *International Journal of Adolescence and Youth, 8*(1), 45–63.

Hooper, S. R., & Willis, W. G. (1989). *Learning disability subtyping.* New York: Springer-Verlag.

Hymel, S., Rubin, K. H., Rowden, L., & LeMare, L. (1990). Children's peer relationships: Longitudinal prediction of internalizing and externalizing problems from middle to late childhood. *Child Development, 61,* 2004–2021.

Josselson, R. (1992). *The space between us.* San Francisco: Jossey-Bass.

Kavale, K. A., & Forness, S. R. (1996). Social skill deficits and learning disabilities: A meta-analysis. *Journal of Learning Disabilities, 29*(3), 226–237.

Ladd, G. W. (1988). Friendship patterns and peer status during early and middle childhood. *Developmental and Behavioral Pediatrics, 9,* 229–238.

Marcoen, A., & Goossens, L. (1990, April). *Loneliness and aloneness in adolescence: Introducing a multidimensional measure and some developmental perspectives.* Paper presented at the annual American Educational Research Association conference, Boston.

Margalit, M. (1990). *Effective technology integration for disabled children: The family perspective.* New York: Springer-Verlag.

Margalit, M. (1991). Understanding loneliness among students with learning disabilities. *Behavior Change, 8,* 167–173.

Margalit, M. (1994). *Loneliness among children with special needs: Theory, research, coping and intervention.* New York: Springer-Verlag.

Margalit, M. (1995). Social skill learning for students with learning disabilities and students with behavior disorders. *Educational Psychology, 15*(4), 445–457.

Margalit, M. (1998). Sense of Coherence and loneliness experience among preschool children with learning disabilities. *Journal of Learning Disabilities, 31*(2), 173–180.

Margalit, M., & Al-Yagon, M. (1994). Learning disability subtyping, loneliness and classroom adjustment. *Learning Disability Quarterly, 17*(4), 297–310.

Margalit, M., & Al-Yagon, M. (2000, December). *Loneliness and adjustment among students with learning disabilities.* Paper presented at the Annual Meeting of the Israeli International Dyslexia Association, Tel-Aviv.

Margalit, M., & Ben-Dov, I. (1995). Learning disabilities and social environments: Kibbutz versus city comparisons of social competence and loneliness. *International Journal of Behavioral Development, 18*(3), 519–536.

Margalit, M., & Efrati, M. (1996). Loneliness, coherence and companionship among children with learning disorders. *Educational Psychology, 16*(1), 69–79.

Margalit, M., Mioduser, D., Al-Yagon, M., & Neuberger, S. (1997). Teachers' and peers' perceptions of children with learning disorders: consistency and change. *European Journal of Special Needs Education, 12*(3), 225–238.

Margalit, M., Tur-Kaspa, H., & Most, T. (1999). Reciprocal nominations, reciprocal rejections and loneliness among students with learning disorders. *Educational Psychology, 19*, 79–90.

Ochoa, S. H., & Palmer, D. J. (1995). A meta-analysis of peer rating sociometric studies with learning disabled pupils. *Journal of Special Education, 29*, 1–19.

Ozer, E. M., & Bandura, A. (1990). Mechanisms governing empowerment effects: A self-efficacy analysis. *Journal of Personality and Social Psychology, 58*, 472–486.

Parker, J. G., & Asher, S. R. (1993). Friendship and friendship quality in middle childhood. *Developmental Psychology, 29*(4), 611–621.

Pavri, S., & Monda-Amaya, M. (2000). Loneliness and students with learning disabilities in inclusive classrooms: Self-perceptions, coping strategies and preferred interventions. *Learning Disabilities Research and Practice, 15*(1), 22–33.

Pearl, R. (1992). Psychosocial characteristics of learning disabled students. In N. N. Singh & I. L. Beale (Eds.), *Learning disabilities: Nature, theory and treatment* (pp. 96–125). New York: Springer-Verlag.

Peplau, L. A., & Perlman, D. (1982). Perspectives on loneliness. In L. A. Peplau & D. Perlman (Eds.), *Loneliness: A sourcebook of current theory, research and therapy* (pp. 1–18). New York: Wiley.

Rizzo, T. A. (1988). The relationship between friendship and sociometric judgements of peer acceptance and rejection. *Child Study Journal, 18*, 161–191.

Sabornie, E. J. (1994). Social-affective characteristics in early adolescents identified as learning disabled and nondisabled. *Learning Disability Quarterly, 17*(4), 268–279.

Sabornie, E. J., & Thomas, V. (1989). *Social/affective adjustment of mildly handicapped and nonhandicapped early adolescents*. Paper presented at the annual AERA meeting, San Francisco.

Sroufe, L. A., & Sampson, M. C. (2000). Attachment theory and systems concept. *Human Development, 43*, 321–326.

Storr, A. (1988). *Solitude*. New York: Ballantine.

Turnbull, A. P., Patterson, J. M., Behr, S. K., Murphy, D. L., Marquis, J. G., & Blue-Banning, M. J. (1993). *Cognitive coping, families and disabilities*. Baltimore: Paul Brooks.

Unger, Y. (1992). *Social competence and feelings of loneliness among adolescents with LD: Self-reports and mothers' and teachers' ratings*. Unpublished MA thesis, Tel Aviv University.

Valas, H. (1999). Students with learning disabilities and low-achieving students: Peer acceptance, loneliness, self-esteem, and depression. *Social Psychology of Education, 3*(3), 173–192.

Vaughn, S., & La Greca, A. M. (1992). Beyond greetings and making friends: Social skills from a broader perspective. In Y. L. Wong (Ed.), *Contemporary intervention research in learning disabilities: An international perspectives* (pp. 96–114). New York: Springer-Verlag.

Vaughn, S., McIntosh, R., & Hogan, A. (1990). Why social skills training doesn't work: An alternative model. In T. E. Scruggs & B. Y. L. Wong (Eds.), *Intervention research on learning disabilities* (pp. 279–303). New York: Springer-Verlag.

Weiss, R. S. (1973). *Loneliness: The experience of emotional and social isolation*. Cambridge, MA: MIT Press.

Weissberg, L. (2000). *The non-academic world in school*. Unpublished masters thesis, Tel Aviv University.

Winnicott, D. W. (1965). The capacity to be alone. In D. W. Winnicott (Ed.), *The maturation processes and the facilitating environment* (pp. 29–36). New York: International Universities Press.

Wood, B. L., Klebba, K. B., & Miller, B. D. (2000). Evolving the biobehavioral family model: The fit of attachment. *Family Process, 39*(3), 319–344.

Woodward, H. (1988). *The solitude of loneliness.* Lexington, MA: Lexington Books.

Woodward, J. C., & Kalyan-Masih, V. (1990). Loneliness, coping strategies and cognitive styles of the gifted rural adolescent. *Adolescence, 25,* 977–988.

Zehavi, I. (1992). *Comparison between students with LD and nondisabled students on social competence and feelings of loneliness.* Unpublished masters thesis, Tel Aviv University.

Chapter 5

Students With Learning Disabilities and Their Classroom Companions

Ruth Pearl
University of Illinois at Chicago

A book published several years ago received a lot of attention in both the professional literature and the popular press. In it the author made a claim that parents have little influence on their children's personality development, aside from passing on their genes. What counts, according to this author, is the children's peer group (Harris, 1998).

This claim is undoubtedly overstated, but it is clear that the relationships children have with their peers are important. For one thing, it is now clear that it is critical to take into account classroom social relations if we want children to meet the academic objectives we have set for them. Several researchers have pointed out that there are many goals students may try to achieve in school and among them, for most children, are socially oriented goals. In fact, for many students, social goals in school may be valued more highly than learning goals (Dweck, 1996; Wentzel, 1996).

But beyond being a critical consideration for accomplishing our academic aspirations for children, it is also clear that if we are concerned about children's general well-being, their social relationships deserve attention. A currently prominent theory asserts that individuals have three basic psychological needs. Two of these needs are for feelings of competence and feelings of autonomy. But the third need, critical for healthy psychological adjustment, is for feelings of relatedness (Deci & Flaste, 1995; Deci & Ryan, 1985). For students, this need manifests itself in the desire to develop connections and associations with others in their classroom (Deci, Vallerand, Pelletier, & Ryan, 1991).

Since Tanis Bryan's groundbreaking research on the social relation-ships of children with learning disabilities (LD) almost 30 years ago, it has become evident that many of these children have relationships with peers that warrant concern. In Bryan's (1974) study, students in the third, fourth, and fifth grades were asked to nominate classmates who were and were not desired as friends, classroom neighbors, and guests at a party. The children were also asked questions like, "Who is handsome or pretty?" and "Who finds it hard to sit still in class?" The students with learning disabilities received both fewer positive nominations and more negative nominations than did the nondisabled students. Notably, a fol-low-up study conducted the next year when the children were in new classes and, for the most part, with different classmates, found that the stu-dents with learning disabilities continued to receive fewer positive and more negative nominations (Bryan, 1976).

Sociometric research conducted since these early studies has continued to find that, compared to children without learning disabilities, a dispro-portionate number of children with LD are less well accepted, more re-jected, or more neglected than their nondisabled classmates, in kinder-garten prior to identification through high school (Bruinicks, 1978a, 1978b; Coben & Zigmond, 1986; Conderman, 1995; Cook & Semmel, 1999; Donahue & Prescott, 1988; Garrett & Crump, 1980; Gottlieb, Gott-lieb, Berkell, & Levy, 1986; Horowitz, 1981; Hoyle & Serafica, 1988; Kistner & Gatlin, 1989; Levy & Gottlieb, 1984; Madge, Affleck, & Lowen-braun, 1990; Margalit & Freilich, 1999; Ochoa & Palmer, 1995; Perl-mutter, Crocker, Cordray, & Garstecki, 1983; Scranton & Ryckman, 1979; Sheare, 1978; Siperstein, Bopp, & Bak, 1978; Siperstein & Goding, 1983; Tur-Kaspa, in press; Vaughn, Hogan, Kouzekanani, & Shapiro, 1990; Wiener, Harris, & Shirer, 1990). For example, in one study, more than half the students with learning disabilities had low social status (Stone & La Greca, 1990). Approximately half of these low-status students received ratings from peers indicating that they were rejected, while half received ratings indicating neglect. Several meta-analyses of sociometric studies have found that, in general, only somewhere between 16% and 22% of stu-dents with LD are as well liked as their nondisabled peers (Kavale & Forness, 1996; Ochoa & Olivarez, 1995; Swanson & Malone, 1992).

Although it is evident that not all students with learning disabilities have problems obtaining peer acceptance (e.g., Conderman, 1995; Dud-ley-Marling & Edmiaston, 1985; Perlmutter et al., 1983; Prilliman, 1981; Sabornie & Kauffman, 1986; Sainato, Zigmond, & Strain, 1983; Sater & French, 1989) or in developing reciprocated friendships (Bear, Juvonen, & McInerney, 1993; Vaughn, McIntosh, Schumm, Haager, & Callwood, 1993), peer relationships are a problem for many, and this raises an addi-tional concern. The sociometric studies tell us something about how well children are liked, but they don't tell us about which classmates the children are actually associating with. Even children who are generally not well liked may have some companions with whom they "hang out." And for children with learning disabilities, the peers they spend time with may be particularly important. This conclusion emerges from a series of studies, conducted in collaboration with Tanis Bryan and others, that suggests that students with learning disabilities may be particularly vulnerable to the influence of their peers. These studies, described in following section, were especially concerned with whether students with learning disabilities might be vulnerable in a way that could get them involved in misconduct.

SUSCEPTIBILITY TO PEER INFLUENCE FOR MISCONDUCT IN STUDENTS WITH LEARNING DISABILITIES

At least two components are involved in peer influence (Kandel, 1978). The first is the process of differential selection of individuals into particular types of peer groups. This is likely to be a bidirectional process: Children desire to associate with some peer groups more than others, and are encouraged or discouraged by the members of different groups to join them. This is often on the basis of some shared characteristic, for example, gender, race, or aggressive behavior (cf. Farmer, Pearl, & Van Acker, 1996). Then, once associated with a peer group, children become subject to the second component of peer influence: Members of the group influence each other through the process of mutual socialization.

A number of factors led us to suspect that children and adolescents with LD might be more likely than other children to be selected into groups with high levels of problem behaviors and at more risk for socialization into misconduct. One reason is the difficulty many students with LD have in being accepted by their classmates. These students, therefore, might be particularly receptive to seemingly friendly overtures from peers. Some support for this hypothesis comes from a recent study by Settle and Milich (1999) who found that after an unfriendly interaction, children with LD evaluated themselves and the other child more negatively than did nondisabled students. In contrast, after a friendly interaction, they evaluated themselves and the other child more positively. This suggests that interactions with amicable peers may be especially welcomed by children with learning disabilities, possibly regardless of characteristics of those peers.

There are also data to suggest that problem behaviors may actually give students an entrée into some social groups. For instance, in first-grade classrooms characterized by high levels of aggression, aggressive behavior was positively related to boys' (although not girls') peer acceptance

(Stormshak et al., 1999). Similarly, data on older students led other researchers to suggest that "Adolescents with a history of troubled friendships or marginal peer relations, would therefore rely more extensively on deviance to establish new friendships" (Poulin, Dishion, & Hass, 1999, p. 57). Hence, it may be that problematic behaviors of students with learning disabilities who have had problems obtaining peer acceptance can actually be an asset (at least for boys) for gaining peer associates.

Once in a social group, it seems possible also that children with LD may be disproportionately susceptible to joining in misconduct if it is engaged in by their peer associates. The low social status of many students with learning disabilities may make them especially concerned about fitting in, and therefore more willing than other students to conform, regardless of the nature of their peers' activity. Furthermore, the social cognitive deficits that appear to be typical of many students with learning disabilities may increase their vulnerability to peer influence. Students with LD sometimes have difficulty in roletaking the perspective of others (Bruck & Hebert, 1982; Dickstein & Warren, 1980; Horowitz, 1981; Wong & Wong, 1980) and in comprehending the meaning of subtle or ambiguous social cues (Axelrod, 1982; Bruno, 1981; Bryan, 1977; Dimitrovsky, Spector, Levy-Schiff, & Vakil, 1998; Gerber & Zinkgraf, 1982; Holder & Kirkpatrick, 1991; Jackson, Enright, & Murdock, 1987; Pearl & Cosden, 1982; Saloner & Gettinger, 1985; Wiig & Harris, 1974). This research suggests that students with learning disabilities who have such problems may be less discerning than other students of the nature of a proposed activity, and may not recognize instances in which they are being deliberately misled. In addition, if students with LD have had social experiences different from those typical of their classmates, they may not have acquired the same type of knowledge about situations in which they could get in trouble. The lack of this type of knowledge could put them at greater risk.

Finally, linguistic and pragmatic limitations (Donahue, in press) may make it more difficult for some students with LD to effectively handle difficult situations. Difficulties in language comprehension could lead them to misconstrue what is being proposed. Problems in language production could make it difficult for them to fend off undesirable invitations, even if they recognize the potential of a situation for getting them in trouble.

Expectations About Situations Involving Misconduct

One study in this series (Pearl, Bryan, & Herzog, 1990) examined high school students' expectations for different situations in which one teenager invited another to engage in misconduct (e.g., shoplifting or stealing a car). We wanted to see if the students with learning disabilities were as knowledgeable as other students about how a situation like this would be likely to play out. If they were less aware, it would suggest that they might not be as prepared as other students if the situation actually happened to them.

The students were interviewed to determine their expectations for what someone who wanted them to join in misconduct would say, what would happen if the request were accepted or refused, and what would motivate the decision to accept or refuse. The students came from a number of public high schools with different types of populations—urban high schools with predominantly African-American or Hispanic students, and suburban schools with a majority of Caucasian students.

To summarize the findings, the expectations of students with learning disabilities differed in several respects from those of nondisabled students. One difference was in their response to the question of how a request would be stated. Students with LD were more likely than nondisabled students to predict requests that were direct and to the point (e.g., "Let's take this car"), whereas the nondisabled students more frequently anticipated requests that were couched in terms indicating a payoff to the listener (e.g., "We'll have fun") or minimizing the negatives involved in the act (e.g., "We'll bring the car right back"). In other words, the students with learning disabilities were more likely than nondisabled students to expect exhortations to be straightforward and forthright, while the nondisabled students expected the speaker to use persuasive ploys. In addition, students with LD were less likely to mention the possibility of getting caught in response to the question of what might happen if bids to engage in misconduct were accepted, and were more likely than non-LD to think if the requests were refused, the person refusing the request would feel bad. Finally, the students with LD showed less insight about these situations in that they suggested fewer reasons for why someone would accept these requests, and spontaneously suggested fewer alternative scenarios for what might ensue if the requests were accepted or refused.

One question we had about the findings of this study was whether the fact that it required the students to actually orally produce statements may have been a factor in the finding that the students with LD seemed to expect more direct requests than the other students. That is, we had asked them to tell us what a person making the request would say, and it is possible that that the students with LD came up with the direct, simple requests more than other students because they were easier to express. So a follow-up study (Pearl & Bryan, 1992) was conducted with a questionnaire that did not require the students to orally produce a statement, but simply to choose which of two statements they thought was more likely. This study confirmed that students with learning disabilities were more likely than those without to expect succinct, straightforward requests. These studies

suggest that the expectations of students with LD may leave them less prepared than other students to deal with the wiles of mischievous peers.

Detection of Deception

The next study evaluated students' ability to detect deception, a skill that
could help protect them from others' attempts to take advantage of them
(Pearl, Bryan, Fallon, & Herzog, 1991). Recognizing deception can be a
complex task. The first step in the detection of deception, recognizing
that a statement is inconsistent with the facts, is itself likely to be a challenge for individuals of limited social cognitive skill. Further, to recognize
that the statement was not only mistaken but in fact a deliberate lie, the
deceptive intent of the speaker must also be noted. The results of several
referential communication studies, which found that students with LD assumed that speakers were as forthcoming as possible (Donahue, 1984;
Donahue, Pearl, & Bryan, 1980), suggested that students with LD were
more likely to assume a speaker's veracity than are other students. We hypothesized, therefore, that students with LD would tend to assume a
speaker was being truthful, and therefore might not detect deception as
readily as their classmates without disabilities.

In this study, junior high school students listened to a series of tape-
recorded stories, each of which described an interaction between two characters and concluded with a statement made by one of the characters. In
some of the stories, information provided in the story indicated that the
concluding statement was intentionally deceptive. By examining the pattern of responses to questions asked after each story, it was possible to determine whether there were group differences in correctly identifying
these deceptive statements. The results indicated, as hypothesized, that
the students with LD were less able than their non-LD classmates to detect
the deception. Interestingly, further analyses indicated that the students
with LD recognized that the statements were not true; however, they were
more likely to think that although the speaker was wrong, he or she was
sincere and not deliberately deceptive.

Acquiescence to Peer Pressure to Engage in Misconduct

Finally, junior high school students' self-reported willingness to conform
to the activities of peers was examined (Bryan, Werner, & Pearl, 1982). A
questionnaire described a variety of hypothetical situations in which their
friends pressured them to join in activities in which they really did not
wish to participate. The students were asked to indicate what they would
do in these situations. We hypothesized that because many students with
LD find less peer acceptance than their classmates, they may be more will-

ing to go along with the wishes of friends out of a desire not to appear different and to win peer approval.

The findings were that there were no differences between groups when asked about the prosocial situations; both groups reported that they would agree to participate in many of these activities. However, when asked about situations involving misconduct, non-LD students were more likely than students with LD to indicate they would refuse to participate. In addition, students with LD reported feeling less concern than nondisabled students when they did engage in misconduct. A second study with a different sample of junior high school students (Bryan, Pearl, & Fallon, 1989) again found that students with LD expressed greater willingness than other students to go along with the wishes of their friends to participate in misconduct.

The results of these and other studies support the hypothesis that students with LD may be particularly vulnerable to peer influence. One part of this vulnerability appears to be that these students are less discriminating than nondisabled students about the type of activities they're willing to participate in at the urging of peers. The students with LD reported a greater willingness to acquiesce to friends' requests to engage in misconduct, less concern after participating in such activities, and more anticipated negative affect for refusing requests to join in these activities.

However, it also appears that many of these students seem to lack knowledge and skills that could alert them to the possibility that they might be led astray by what seem to be friendly peers. The students with LD were more likely than nondisabled peers to expect direct, straightforward requests, and less likely to expect persuasive appeals. This finding may mean that these students are less wary than other students when requests are not so directly stated. The non-LD students were savvy to the fact that peers trying to involve them in undesirable activities might attempt to cajole them. If, in contrast, the students with LD are not as aware that persuasive attempts are likely, it is possible they may be more susceptible to the persuasive attempts that are made. In addition, compared to the non-LD students, the students with LD had less awareness of the possible consequences of misconduct, and appeared to be less skillful in recognizing lies.

CLASSROOM ASSOCIATES OF STUDENTS WITH LEARNING DISABILITIES

If students with LD are vulnerable to the influence of their peers, as these studies suggest, it becomes important to identify the classmates with whom these children are likely to associate. This is particularly true if, as has been suggested, "the identity of the child's friends is a significant consideration in predicting developmental outcome" (Hartup, 1996, p. 7). Although one way to get this information might be through classroom observations to see who interacts with whom, a more efficient method is to use a procedure called "social cognitive mapping." This method asks the children, "Are there any students in your class who hang around together a lot? Who are they?" The children then make lists of the different groups of children who associate together. By using this information, one can get a good picture of who in the classroom associates with whom. There is substantial agreement among children in their reports of these groups, and validity studies show that children do in fact interact more with children reported to be in their group (Cairns, Gariépy, Kinderman, & Leung, 1997; Cairns, Leung, Buchanan, & Cairns, 1995).

This method was used in a study, conducted in collaboration with Thomas Farmer, Richard Van Acker, Philip Rodkin, and others, of 59 fourth, fifth, and sixth-grade classrooms (Pearl et al., 1998). The classrooms were in public schools in Chicago, Chicago suburbs, and rural and small urban areas of North Carolina. Each classroom had at least two students with mild disabilities who attended the general education classroom for at least 50% of the school day. Forty-nine percent of the sample was Caucasian; 44% was African-American; and 7% was Hispanic. Approximately 13% of the sample was identified as having mild disabilities; children with learning disabilities made up the majority of this group.

Initial analyses provided a general picture of classroom social groups. An average of 4.63 groups were named per classroom, with an average of 5.19 students per group. Forty-five percent of the groups were composed of only girls, 42% were composed of boys, and 13% were of mixed gender.

Group Membership Versus Isolation

The first issue addressed was whether children with mild disabilities were named to a social group at all. We found that although most children with mild disabilities were named to a social group, a higher proportion of them were not. Although 7% of children in general education were isolated, this was true of 19% of children with mild disabilities.

Which children with mild disabilities were in classroom social groups? In addition to having asked the children about who hung out with whom, we also had asked them to nominate classmates who fit different characteristics, for instance, being a leader or being shy. So for this question, these peer nominations were examined. Preliminary analyses indicated that the same children tended to be nominated for the categories indicating misconduct—that is, the categories of "disruptive," "starts fights," and "gets in trouble"—so these items were combined. Similarly, the same children tended to be identified for the categories indicating desirable classroom behavior—"studious" and "cooperative"—so these items were combined into a composite we called prosocial.

We found that girls with mild disabilities in groups were more likely than the isolated girls with mild disabilities to be perceived of as a leader and prosocial. Boys with mild disabilities in groups were more likely than isolated boys with mild disabilities to be perceived of as a leader, athletic, and—in a troubling finding—high in misconduct. To restate this latter finding, the boys with mild disabilities who were in groups were more likely than those who were not to be considered by peers to be high in misconduct. This difference was not found for boys without disabilities. So, although nondisabled boys in groups were no more likely to be perceived as high in misconduct than were nondisabled boys who were not in groups, it may be that for boys with mild disabilities, being high in misconduct either resulted from membership in their social group, or was a means of entrée into it.

Membership in High Misconduct or High Prosocial Groups

What kind of groups were the children with mild disabilities in? Were they distributed in the same way as nondisabled students among social groups where members were high in positive characteristics or high in misconduct, or were they disproportionately in one type of a group? To study this, we again looked at the nominations the children made for the different categories of behavior. We identified social groups where the mean score of the nondisabled students in the group was at or above the 80th percentile in peer-assessed prosocial behavior, or at or above the 80th percentile in peer-assessed misconduct.

We found that most students with mild disabilities were not in groups high in misconduct, and most students in groups high in misconduct did not have mild disabilities. Specifically, 49% of the students with mild disabilities were in groups that were about average in prosocial and problem behavior, 11% were in prosocial groups, and 21% were in groups high in problem behavior. At least 80% of every group high in problem behavior was comprised of nondisabled students. Nonetheless, students with mild disabilities were overrepresented in groups high in misconduct and underrepresented in the prosocial groups. Furthermore, an analysis that looked at the proportion of group members with mild disabilities found that the highest proportions were in the groups with the highest level of problem behaviors (Farmer, Van Acker, Pearl, & Rodkin, 1999). To summarize, a disproportionate number of students with mild disabilities found companions who were high in problematic behavior.

The next analyses sought to identify which students with mild disabilities were in which type of group. Children were considered to be high in prosocial behavior or high in problem behavior if their scores on these factors were at or above the 80th percentile for all children with mild disabilities. Results indicated that the characteristics of the students were strongly related to those of their peer group. Thirty-two percent of the high prosocial students with mild disabilities were members of high prosocial groups, while these groups contained only 3% of the students with mild disabilities who were high in problem behavior, and 8% of the students with mild disabilities who average in prosocial and problem behavior. Similarly, high problem behavior groups contained 34% of the students with mild disabilities who were high in problem behavior, but only 7% of the prosocial students with mild disabilities, and 20% of the students who were average in prosocial and problem behavior. There were no significant differences in the percentage of high prosocial, high problem behavior, or average students with mild disabilities who affiliated in groups that were average in prosocial and problem behavior, or who were isolated.

Role Played in Problem Groups

And what role did the students with mild disabilities who were members of high problem behavior groups play in their group? Were they important, central members of the group, or were they more marginal members? We identified this by looking at how often children were named as belonging to a particular social group. If they were named as members of a group less often than other children were named, the assumption is made that their membership was not as salient or central to the group.

We found that general education students in problem behavior peer groups tended to have higher centrality scores within their groups than did students with mild disabilities. This was at the .07 probability level, so it was very close to being significant. When the analysis was restricted to the groups that were most prominent in the classrooms, the groups that almost all the children mentioned, the difference was highly significant ($p = .004$). Thus, the children with mild disabilities appeared less likely to have prominent roles in their groups than did the non-LD students (Farmer et al., 1999).

A number of issues about the classroom peer associations of children with mild disabilities are evident in this research. First, what was said before bears repeating: Most of the children with mild disabilities were in a social group, and most were in groups that were not high in misconduct. Nevertheless, there are some reasons for concern. A disproportionate number of children with mild disabilities were not named to any social group, and of the children who were named to a group, a disproportionate number were in groups high in problematic characteristics. The fact that children with mild disabilities tended to occupy a marginal status in their group, coupled with the findings described earlier that they may be especially susceptible to peer influence, suggests that these associations may not necessarily be positive. If these children are vulnerable to peer influence, it is certainly not good news that a disproportionate number of them are hanging out with classmates who are high in misconduct. This may have been why the boys with mild disabilities who were in groups were more likely than those who were isolated to be high in misconduct themselves. Or, alternatively, perhaps these students' problem behaviors served to increase their peer acceptance and interaction.

An additional concern has to do with the nature of the relationships within a group. Classroom groups are not necessarily characterized by supportive friendships among their members; indeed, members may not even particularly like each other. Studies demonstrate that the children's friendships vary in such features as closeness, security, and conflict (e.g., Bukowski, Hoza, & Boivin, 1994; Parker & Asher, 1993). These studies indicate that in addition to concerns about whether children are included in a group and, if they are, the type of group in which they are included, one must also pay attention to the quality of the relationships children within groups have with each other. Thus, although most students with LD have some classroom companions, whether their classroom associates provide the degree of "relatedness" considered important for healthy psychological adjustment (Deci & Flaste, 1995; Deci & Ryan, 1985) is unknown.

To untangle more precisely the dynamics of how the children's characteristics influence and are influenced by their membership in classroom social groups requires following children's social relationships over time, and examining in more detail the nature of children's relationships within classroom groups. Nevertheless, the results of this research suggest that programs designed to assist students with disabilities in developing positive behaviors probably need to focus on classroom social structures—the groups of children's classroom associates—as well as on the skills and behaviors of individual students.

To summarize, children with LD show variability in their peer relations, just as they do in so many other domains. Some children with LD are well accepted by their peers; yet many others are not. And, while the majority of students with learning disabilities at least appear to have classroom associates, there is reason to be concerned that these may not always promote the positive outcomes we would hope. Nearly three decades after Tanis Bryan's pioneering research, the peer relationships of children with learning disabilities continue to warrant concern.

ACKNOWLEDGMENTS

The research cited in this chapter was supported by grants H023A50033, H023C70103, and PR158GH500 from the U.S. Department of Education, Office of Special Education and Rehabilitative Services.

REFERENCES

Axelrod, L. (1982). Social perception in learning disabled adolescents. *Journal of Learning Disabilities, 15*, 610–613.

Bear, G. G., Juvonen, J., & McInerney, F. (1993). Self-perceptions and peer relations of boys with and boys without learning disabilities in an integrated setting: a longitudinal study. Learning Disability Quarterly, 16, 127–136.

Bruck, M., & Hebert, M. (1982). Correlates of learning disabled students' peer interaction patterns. *Learning Disability Quarterly, 5*, 353–362.

Bruininks, V. L. (1978a). Actual and perceived peer status of learning disabled students in mainstream programs. *Journal of Special Education, 12*, 51–58.

Bruininks, V. L. (1978b). Peer status and personality of learning disabled and nondisabled students. *Journal of Learning Disabilities, 11*, 29–34.

Bruno, R. M. (1981). Interpretation of pictorially presented social situations by learning disabled and normal children. *Journal of Learning Disabilities, 14*, 350–352.

Bryan, T. H. (1974). Peer popularity of learning disabled children. *Journal of Learning Disabilities, 7*, 621–625.

Bryan, T. H. (1976). Peer popularity of learning disabled children: A replication. *Journal of Learning Disabilities, 9*, 307–311.

Bryan, T. H. (1977). Children's comprehension of non-verbal communication. *Journal of Learning Disabilities, 10*, 501–506.

Bryan, T., Pearl, R., & Fallon, P. (1989). Conformity to peer pressure by students with learning disabilities: A replication. *Journal of Learning Disabilities, 22*, 458–459.

Bryan, T., Werner, M., & Pearl, R. (1982). Learning disabled students' conformity responses to prosocial and antisocial situations. *Learning Disability Quarterly, 5*, 344–352.

Bukowski, W. M., Hoza, B., & Boivin, M. (1994). Measuring friendship quality during pre- and early adolescence: The development and psychometric properties of the Friendship Qualities Scale. *Journal of Social and Personal Relationships, 11*, 471–484.

Cairns, R. B., Gariépy, J. -L., Kinderman, T., & Leung, M. -C. (1997). *Identifying social clusters in natural settings*. Unpublished manuscript. Chapel Hill: University of North Carolina, Center for Developmental Science.

Cairns, R. B., Leung, M. -C., Buchanan, L., & Cairns, B. D. (1995). Friendships and social networks in childhood and adolescence: Fluidity, reliability, and interrelations. *Child Development, 66*, 1330–1345.

Coben, S. S., & Zigmond, N. (1986). The social integration of learning disabled students from self-contained to mainstream elementary school settings. *Journal of Learning Disabilities, 19*, 614–618.

Conderman, G. (1995). Social status of sixth- and seventh-grade students with learning disabilities. *Learning Disability Quarterly, 18*, 13–24.

Cook, B. G., & Semmel, M. I. (1999). Peer acceptance of included students with disabilities as a function of severity of disability and classroom composition. *Journal of Special Education, 33*, 50–61.

Deci, E. L., & Flaste, R. (1995). *Why we do what we do: The dynamics of personal autonomy.* New York: Putnam.

Deci, E. L., & Ryan, R. M. (1985). *Intrinsic motivation and self-determination in human behavior.* New York: Plenum.

Deci, E. L., Vallerand, R. J., Pelletier, L. G., & Ryan, R. M. (1991). Motivation and education: The self-determination perspective. *Educational Psychologist, 26,* 325–346.

Dickstein, E. B., & Warren, D. R. (1980). Role taking deficits in learning disabled children. *Journal of Learning Disabilities, 13,* 378–382.

Dimitrovsky, L., Spector, H., Levy-Schiff, R., & Vakil, E. (1998). Interpretation of facial expressions of affect in children with learning disabilities with verbal or nonverbal deficits. *Journal of Learning Disabilities, 31,* 286–292, 312.

Donahue, M. L. (1984). Learning disabled children's conversational competence: an attempt to activate the inactive listener. *Applied Psycholinguistics, 5,* 21–35.

Donahue, M. (in press). "Hanging with friends": Making sense of research on peer discourse in children with language and learning disabilities. In E. Silliman & K. Butler (Eds.), *The language-learning disabilities continuum: New partners in research, technology, and education.* Mahwah, NJ: Lawrence Erlbaum Associates.

Donahue, M., Pearl, R., & Bryan, T. (1980). Learning disabled children's conversational competence: Responses to inadequate messages. *Applied Psycholinguistics, 1,* 387–403.

Donahue, M., & Prescott, B. (1988). Reading disabled children's conversational participation in dispute episodes with peers. *First Language, 8,* 247–258.

Dudley-Marling, C. C., & Edmiaston, R. (1985). Social status of learning disabled children and adolescents: A review. *Learning Disability Quarterly, 8,* 189–204.

Dweck, C. S. (1996). Social motivation: Goals and social cognitive-processes. A comment. In J. Juvonen & K. R. Wentzel (Eds.), *Social motivation: Understanding children's school adjustment* (pp. 181–195). New York: Cambridge University Press.

Farmer, T. W., Pearl, R., & Van Acker, R. (1996). Expanding the social skills framework: A developmental synthesis perspective, classroom social networks, and implications for the social growth of students with disabilities. *Journal of Special Education, 30,* 232–256.

Farmer, T. W., Van Acker, R. M., Pearl, R., & Rodkin, P. C. (1999). Social networks and peer-assessed problem behavior in elementary classrooms. *Remedial and Special Education, 20,* 244–256.

Garrett, M. K., & Crump, W. D. (1980). Peer acceptance, teacher references, and self-appraisal of social status among learning disabled students. *Learning Disability Quarterly, 3,* 42–48.

Gerber, P. J., & Zinkgraf, S. A. (1982). A comparative study of social-perceptual ability in learning disabled and nonhandicapped students. *Learning Disability Quarterly, 3,* 42–48.

Gottlieb, B. W., Gottlieb, J., Berkell, D., & Levy, L. (1986). Sociometric status and solitary play of LD boys and girls. *Journal of Learning Disabilities, 19,* 619–622.

Harris, J. R. (1998). *The nurture assumption: Why children turn out the way they do.* New York: Free Press.

Hartup, W. W. (1996). The company they keep: Friendships and their developmental significance. *Child Development, 67,* 1–13.

Holder. H. B., & Kirkpatrick, S. W. (1991). Interpretations of emotion from facial expressions in children with and without learning disabilities. *Journal of Learning Disabilities, 24,* 170–177.

Horowitz, E. C. (1981). Popularity, decentering ability, and roletaking skills in learning disabled and normal children. *Learning Disability Quarterly, 4,* 23–30.

Hoyle, S. G., & Serafica, F. (1988). Peer status of children with and without learning disabilities—A multimethod study. *Learning Disability Quarterly, 11,* 322–332.

Jackson, S C., Enright, R. D., & Murdock, J. Y. (1987). Social perception problems in learning disabled youth: Developmental lag versus perceptual deficit. *Journal of Learning Disabilities, 20,* 361–364.

Kandel, D. B. (1978). Homophily, selection and socialization in adolescent friendships. *American Journal of Sociology, 84,* 427–436.

Kavale, K. A., & Forness, S. R. (1996). Social skill deficits and learning disabilities: A meta-analyisis. *Journal of Learning Disabilities, 29,* 226–237.

Kistner, J. A., & Gatlin, D. F. (1989). Sociometric differences between learning-disabled and nonhandicapped students: Effects of sex and race. *Journal of Educational Psychology, 81,* 118–120.

Levy, L., & Gottlieb, J. (1984). Learning disabled and non-LD children at play. *Remedial and Special Education, 5,* 43–50.

Madge, S., Affleck, J., & Lowenbraun, S. (1990). Social effects of integrated classrooms and resource room/regular class placements on elementary students with learning disabilities. *Journal of Learning Disabilities, 23,* 439–445.

Margalit, M., & Freilich, R. (1999). Examining changes in loneliness experience, sense of coherence and social status, in Israeli inclusive education. *Thalamus, 17,* 62–65.

Ochoa, S. H., & Olivarez, A. (1995). A meta-analysis of peer rating sociometric studies of pupils with learning disabilities. *Journal of Special Education, 29,* 1–19.

Ochoa, S. H., & Palmer, D. J. (1995). Comparison of the peer status of Mexican-American students with learning disabilities and non-disabled low-achieving students. *Learning Disability Quarterly, 18,* 57–63.

Parker, J. G., & Asher, S. R. (1993). Friendship and friendship quality in middle childhood: Links with peer group acceptance and feelings of loneliness and social dissatisfaction. *Developmental Psychology, 29,* 611–621.

Pearl, R., & Bryan, T. (1992). Students' expectations about peer pressure to engage in misconduct. *Journal of Learning Disabilities, 25,* 582–585, 597.

Pearl, R., Bryan, T., Fallon, P., & Herzog, A. (1991). Learning disabled students' detection of deception. *Learning Disabilities Research and Practice, 6,* 12–16.

Pearl, R., Bryan, T., & Herzog, A. (1990). Resisting or acquiescing to peer pressure to engage in misconduct: Adolescents' expectations of probable consequences. *Journal of Youth and Adolescence, 19,* 43–55.

Pearl, R., & Cosden, M. (1982). Sizing up a situation: Learning disabled children's understanding of social interactions. *Learning Disability Quarterly, 3,* 3–9.

Pearl, R., Farmer, T. W., Van Acker, R., Rodkin, P. C., Bost, K. K., Coe, M., & Henley, W. (1998). The social integration of students with mild disabilities in general education classrooms: Peer group membership and peer-assessed social behavior. *Elementary School Journal, 99,* 167–185.

Perlmutter, B. F., Crocker, J., Cordray, D., & Garstecki, D. (1983). Sociometric status and related personality characteristics of mainstreamed learning disabled adolescents. *Learning Disability Quarterly, 6,* 21–31.

Poulin, F., Dishion, T. J., & Hass, E. (1999). The peer influence paradox: Friendship quality and deviancy training within male adolescent friendships. *Merrill-Palmer Quarterly, 45,* 42–61.

Prilliman, D. (1981). Acceptance of learning disabled students in the mainstream environment: A failure to replicate. *Journal of Learning Disabilities, 14,* 344–346.

Sabornie, E. J., & Kauffman, J. M. (1986). Social acceptance of learning disabled adolescents. *Learning Disability Quarterly, 9,* 55–60.

Sainato, D. M., Zigmond, N., & Strain, P. (1983). Social status and initiations of interaction by learning disabled students in a regular education setting. *Analysis and Intervention in Developmental Disabilities, 3,* 71–87.

Saloner, M. R., & Gettinger, M. (1985). Social inference skills in learning disabled and nondisabled children. *Psychology in the Schools, 22,* 201–207.

Sater, G. M., & French, D. C. (1989). A comparison of the social competencies of learning disabled and low achieving elementary-aged children. *Journal of Special Education, 23,* 17–27.

Scranton, T., & Ryckman, D. (1979). Sociometric status of learning disabled children in an integrative program. *Journal of Learning Disabilities, 12,* 402–407.

Settle, S. A., & Milich, R. (1999). Social persistence following failure in boys and girls with LD. *Journal of Learning Disabilities, 32,* 201–212.

Sheare, J. B. (1978). The impact of resource programs upon the self-concept and peer acceptance of learning disabled children. *Psychology in the Schools, 15,* 406–412.

Siperstein, G. N., Bopp, M. J., & Bak, J. J. (1978). Social status of learning disabled children. *Journal of Learning Disabilities, 11,* 98–102.

Siperstein, G. N., & Goding, M. J. (1983). *Social integration of learning disabled children in regular classrooms.* Greenwich, CT: JAI Press.

Stone, W. L., & La Greca, A. M. (1990). The social status of children with learning disabilities: a reexamination. *Journal of Learning Disabilities, 23,* 32–37.

Stormshak, E. A., Bierman, K. L., Bruschi, C., Dodge, K. A., Coie, J. D., & the Conduct Problems Prevention Group (1999). The relation between behavior problems and peer preference in different classroom contexts. *Child Development, 70,* 169–182.

Swanson, H. L., & Malone, S. (1992). Social skills and learning disabilities: A meta-analysis of the literature. *School Psychology Review, 21,* 427–443.

Tur-Kaspa, H. (in press). The socio-emotional adjustment of adolescents with learning disabilities during high school transition periods. *Journal of Learning Disabilities.*

Vaughn, S., Hogan, A., Kouzekanani, K., & Shapiro, S. (1990). Peer acceptance, self-perceptions, and social skills of learning disabled students prior to identification. *Journal of Educational Psychology, 82,* 101–106.

Vaughn, S., McIntosh, R., Schumm, J. S., Haager, D., & Callwood, D. (1993). Social status, peer acceptance, and reciprocal friendships revisited. *Learning Disabilities Research and Practice, 8,* 82–88.

Wentzel, K. R. (1996). Social goals and social relationships as motivators of school adjustment. In J. Juvonen & K. R. Wentzel (Eds.), *Social motivation: Understanding children's school adjustment* (pp. 226–247). New York: Cambridge University Press.

Wiener, J., Harris, P. J., & Shirer, C. (1990). Achievement and social-behavioral correlates of peer status in LD children. *Learning Disability Quarterly, 13,* 114–127.

Wiig, E. H., & Harris, S. P. (1974). Perception and interpretation of nonverbally expressed emotions by adolescents with learning disabilities. *Perceptual and Motor Skills, 38,* 239–245.

Wong, B. Y., & Wong, R. (1980). Role-taking skills in normal achieving and learning disabled children. *Learning Disability Quarterly, 3,* 11–18.

Chapter 6

Friendship and Social Adjustment of Children With Learning Disabilities

Judith Wiener
Ontario Institute for Studies in Education
of the University of Toronto

Children with learning disabilities (LD) have been shown in many research studies to have difficulties with social relationships and social interaction, to have a low academic self-concept, and to have a variety of emotional difficulties (see Greenham, 1999; Morrison & Cosden, 1997 for recent reviews of this literature). The presence of these difficulties has been well-documented, and is generally acknowledged as an issue of concern that needs to be addressed by researchers, teachers, and other practitioners. The problem is that there is less agreement about the factors that contribute to these social and emotional difficulties.

In this chapter I describe a study that compares children with and without learning disabilities in terms of their friendship patterns, peer acceptance, social skills, feelings of loneliness, self-concept, and depressive symptoms. The details of the methodology and the results of this study are described in several other publications (Hoosen & Wiener, 1996; Kuhne, 1999; Larie & Wiener, 2001; Pires & Wiener, 2001; Power, 1999; Richards & Wiener, 1996; Tardif, & Wiener, 2001; Wiener, 1998a; Wiener, Kuhne, & Schneider, 1996; Wiener & Schneider, 1999; Wiener & Schneider, 2002). The results generally confirm that of previous studies with regard to specific differences between children with and without LD. In this chapter I endeavor to integrate the findings from the previous publications in order to formulate a conceptual framework that will guide future research and practice. The major focus of this chapter is the contextual and internal factors that predict the social and emotional adjustment of children with LD.

OBJECTIVES OF THE STUDY

The study had four broad objectives.

1. to explore the friendship patterns of children with LD;
2. to make explicit the relationships between friendship and self-concept, loneliness, and depression in children with and without LD;
3. to discover whether children experiencing both LD and attention deficit–hyperactivity disorder (ADHD) display patterns of social and emotional functioning similar to those of other LD youngsters; and
4. to establish how the type of special education placement experienced by children with LD impacts on their social and emotional functioning.

We focus on friendship because there is considerable evidence that children who have close friends are psychologically better adjusted than children who do not (Bagwell, Newcomb, & Bukowski, 1998; Newcomb & Bagwell, 1996; Schneider, Wiener, & Murphy, 1994; Vandell & Hembree, 1994). Furthermore, this area has received scant treatment by researchers on the social and emotional functioning of children with LD and the few studies that exist have mainly compared the number of friends children with and without LD claim they have. These studies have yielded confusing results. Some investigators found no differences between children with and without LD in the number of friends they have (Juvonen & Bear, 1992; Vaughn, McIntosh, Schumm, Haager, & Callwood, 1993; Vaughn & Haager, 1994). These investigators also did not find that children with LD had a higher proportion of friends with LD than did other children. In all of these studies the children were placed in elementary school full-inclusion settings. Tur-Kaspa, Margalit, and Most (1999) and Vaughn and Elbaum (1999), however, did find that children with LD had fewer friends than children without LD.

We decided to broaden the conceptualization of friendship exemplified by the existing studies on friendship of children with LD to examine the characteristics of their friends, the stability of their relationships, and the quality of their relationships. As some children with LD are transported to schools outside of their home school in order to receive special education placement, we wondered whether they might have more out-of-school friends than children without LD. Given the problems children with LD have with social interaction skills (Swanson & Malone, 1992), it also seemed likely that they might choose children who are younger than them or children with learning problems as friends, and that their friendships may be less stable than those of children without LD.

We could not find any previous studies on the stability of friendship of children with LD. We anticipated that the friendships of children with LD might be less stable than the friendships of children without LD because of evidence that, over the course of a school year, the peer status of children with LD is less stable relative to their counterparts without LD (Kuhne & Wiener, 2000; Vaughn, Elbaum, & Schumm, 1996).

Two previous studies have investigated the quality of friendships of children with LD. Wenz-Gross and Siperstein (1997) found that children with LD and children with mild cognitive delays reported less contact with their friends. They also reported lower levels of intimacy, validation, and loyalty in their relationships than did children without LD. Vaughn and Elbaum (1999), on the other hand, found no differences in the degree of companionship children and adolescents with and without LD reported they had in their friendships, but that children with LD reported less support for self-esteem and less intimacy in their relationships. In both of these studies the investigators sought the opinions of the children with LD about the quality of their relationships, but did not seek the opinions of their mutual friends.

The essence of the first objective was to describe the friendship patterns of children with LD and compare them to children without LD. The next three objectives, on the other hand, were developed in order to elucidate some of the internal and contextual factors in children with LD which may play a role in determining their friendship patterns. Objective 2 explored the association between the number of close friends children have, the quality of their relationships with their best friend, and self-concept, loneliness, and depression. We hypothesized that children with LD who had more reciprocated friendships, or higher quality friendships would have a healthier social self-concept and overall self-esteem, and would be less lonely. Although there have been no studies explicitly including children with LD which explored the association between friendships and how children with LD feel about themselves, developmental studies have shown that children with higher quality friendships are less likely to be lonely and to have a more positive self-concept (Berndt, 1996; Parker & Asher, 1993).

Objective 3 examined aspects of the comorbidity hypothesis with regard to comorbidity of LD and ADHD. San Miguel, Forness, and Kavale (1996) suggested that the social problems of children with LD are "largely due to extreme scores within LD samples" (p. 258) of children with psychiatric disorders such as ADHD and depression. As discussed by Wiener (1998b), this is an intriguing hypothesis with scant evidence to support or refute it. Although the comorbidity of LD and ADHD is high (Barkely,

1998; Biederman, Newcorn, & Sprich, 1991), there have been few studies that have systematically compared the social and emotional functioning of children with LD who do not have ADHD with children with LD who have comorbid ADHD. The results of those studies that have been conducted indicate that children with both LD and ADHD are more likely to be rejected by peers and to have both internalizing and externalizing behavior problems as rated by teachers than children who are only identified as having LD or ADHD (Flicek, 1992; Wiener, Harris, & Duval, 1993). Children with LD and no comorbid ADHD in these studies, however, were still deficient in comparison with their normally functioning peers.

Objective 4 compared the friendship patterns and social and emotional functioning of children with LD in four types of special education settings—Resource Room, In-Class Support, Self-Contained Class, and Full-Inclusion. This aspect of the study has immense practical importance. The controversy regarding the relative effectiveness of more and less inclusive placements in facilitating the social and emotional adjustment of children with learning disabilities has clearly not been resolved. Studies conducted prior to 1980 have typically focused on comparing children in resource room settings with children in self-contained special education classes. The overall finding has been that children placed in contained special classes fare worse on most academic and social measures than children in integrated settings such as resource rooms. Carlberg and Kavale (1980), in their meta-analytic review, however, found that the studies suggest that the overall finding of the superiority of integration did not necessarily apply to children with LD. Recent studies have not been effective in resolving the controversy. The studies have been of two types. One type of study has compared various aspects of social and emotional functioning of children with and without LD in specific inclusion settings, but has not compared the functioning of children with LD across settings (Juvonen & Bear, 1992; Vaughn et al., 1993). The second type of study has examined teacher characteristics which facilitate the inclusion of children with LD academically and socially (e.g., Schumm, Vaughn, Gordon, & Rothlein, 1994; Stanovich & Jordan, 1998). In the present study, however, we compare children with LD whose placement was determined by the same criteria but the type of setting is more or less inclusive depending on the philosophy of the school.

METHODOLOGY

The participants in the study were 232 children, 117 (67 boys, 50 girls) of whom had LD and 115 (68 boys, 47 girls) did not have LD. The children were in Grades 4 to 8 in nine schools (55 classrooms) from two suburban school districts near Toronto, Canada. The children with LD were identified as having a learning disability by the Identification, Placement, Review Committee of the school districts, and were receiving some form of special education services. All of the children in the sample had a Verbal, Performance, or Full Scale IQ of 80 or greater. The children with LD were functioning below the 25th percentile in reading, spelling, or mathematics on a standardized individual achievement test. Although all of the children had been living in Canada for at least 6 years, English was a second language for 16% of the parents of the children with LD and 17% of the parents of the children without LD. The children represented a range of SES.

As our major focus was to obtain a solid description of the friendship patterns of the children, we assessed four aspects of friendship. First, we determined the number of friends children had by asking them in the context of a structured interview to list their friends, by giving the children's parents and teachers a questionnaire in which they listed the children's friends, and by asking the friends whom the children nominated who their friends were. Thus, we were able to determine not only who the children thought were their friends (which we term Nominated Friends), but also whether the friendships were reciprocated by the friend, or (in the case of out of school friendships or nominated friends whose parents did not consent to participation in the study) whether the children's parents and teachers agreed that the friendships were mutual. Friendships that were corroborated by parents or teachers, or reciprocated by peers are referred to as Corroborated or Reciprocated (CR) friendships. Second, we asked the children, parents and teachers specific questions about the friendships in order to determine the characteristics of the friends including the gender and age of the friends, whether the friends had learning problems, and the context in which the children interacted. Third, we assessed the stability of the friendships by repeating the children's friendship interview 3 months after the initial interview. Friendships were considered stable if the children nominated the same friend a second time. Fourth, we used the Friendship Quality Questionnaire–Revised (FQQ-R; Parker & Asher, 1993) to assess the quality of the children's friendships.

Peer acceptance was measured using a rating scale technique. We gave the participants in the study and at least 15 of their classmates a class list comprised of all children in the class whose parents provided consent to participate in the study. The children rated how much they liked the students on the list on a 4-point scale.

The participants in the study were also given several standardized measures of social and emotional functioning, which have been used in many studies with children with LD. Self-concept was assessed by the Self- Perception Profile for Learning Disabled Children (SPPLD; Renick & Harter,

1988), loneliness was assessed by the Loneliness and Social Dissatisfaction Scale (Asher, Hymel, & Renshaw, 1984), social skills and problems behaviors were assessed using the teacher version of the Social Skills Rating System (SSRS; Gresham & Elliot, 1990), and depressive symptoms were assessed using the Children's Depression Inventory (CDI; Kovacs, 1992).

Most of the analyses exploring the first two objectives (to describe the friendship patterns of children with LD and the association between friendship and self-concept, loneliness, and depression) involved some form of comparison between the 117 children with LD and the 115 children without LD. Gender and grade (Grades 4–6; 7–8) effects were also investigated. To explore comorbidity with ADHD (Objective 3), the children with LD were divided into two groups—those with significant symptoms of ADHD according to parent and teacher ratings on the ADHD Rating Scale (DuPaul, 1990) and those without significant symptoms of ADHD. The cut-off was scores of 2 or 3 (on a 0–4 point scale) on 10/14 items for boys or on 8/14 items for girls on either the teacher or parent scale and a minimum score of 10 on the lower scale. The resultant sample was comprised of 36 children with LD who met our criteria for ADHD, and 71 children with LD who did not.

Only the children with LD were included in the analyses regarding special education placement. The children came from four types of placements. The 26 children in the In-Class Support placement (15 boys, 11 girls) attended three different schools. They were placed in the general education classroom for the entire school day and received assistance from the special education teacher, who came into the general education class to work with a small group of children, for 30 to 60 minutes per school day, with the modal amount of time being 40 minutes. The 45 (20 boys, 16 girls) children in the Resource Room placement attended five different schools. They were placed in the general education classroom for most of the school day and withdrawn to a separate room for special education assistance for between 30 to 90 minutes per school day, with the modal amount of time being 40 minutes. The children in both the In-Class Support and Resource Room placements were identified by the Identification, Placement, Review Committee of the school districts as having mild to moderate learning disabilities. The 23 (16 boys, 7 girls) children in the Self-Contained Special Education Class placement were in three different classes comprised of 8 to 10 children. They spent at least half of the school day in the special education classroom and were typically integrated for subjects such as physical education, music, and art. The 21 (14 boys, 7 girls) children in the Inclusion setting were also from three different classrooms which were comprised of between 28 and 32 children, 8 to 10 of whom were identified with LD. They spent the entire school day in the general education classroom. The classes each had two teachers, one of whom had special education qualifications. The teachers team-taught, and usually used mixed-ability grouping when they divided the children into groups. The children in both the Self-Contained Special Education Class and the Inclusion placements were identified by the Identification, Placement, Review Committee of the school districts as having severe learning disabilities.

RESULTS

Objective 1: Friendship Patterns of Children With LD

Consistent with the findings of previous studies (i.e., Juvonen & Bear, 1992; Vaughn & Haager, 1994), we found that children with and without LD did not differ in Nominated Friends—the number of friends the children thought they had. Boys with LD, however, had fewer mutual friends (as measured by Reciprocated Friendships and by CR Friends) than the other children. Girls with LD did not differ from children without LD in terms of the number of mutual friends they had. This may be explained by the fact that boys with LD nominated a higher proportion (just over 30%) of friends who did not attend their school. Girls with LD and children without LD, on the other hand, had fewer than 25% of friends who did not attend their school. (These out-of-school friends frequently lived near the participants but attended a different school such as a local Catholic school or a school with a French immersion program. In some cases, the friend attended the local public school but the participant with LD was bused to a different school for special education. Some of the out-of-school friends were children of the parents' friends.) Out-of-school friends were not given the opportunity to reciprocate the nomination, and it would be unlikely that teachers would corroborate the friendship.

Not surprisingly, children with LD also had more friends whom their teachers viewed as having learning problems than children without LD (45% for children with LD compared to 24% for children without LD). Almost all of the friendships of the children in the sample were same-age peers to the extent that among the children without LD only 0.6% of Nominated Friends and no CR Friends were two or more years younger than them. Although children with LD also tended to nominate peers as friends, the fact that 6% of their Nominated Friends and 3.5% of their CR Friends were two or more years younger than them may suggest some difficulties.

Overall, approximately 70% of the Nominated Friends and 82% of the CR Friends of the children in the sample were stable over a 3-month period. We found developmental differences, however, in the degree to which the friendships of children with LD were stable. The friendships of children with LD in Grades 4 to 6 were less stable than those of children without LD, whereas there were no between-group differences in stability of friendships for children in Grades 7 to 8. The developmental literature indicates that stability of friendships tends to increase from Grades 1 to 4, but does not change in Grades 4 to 8, the age range of the present study. This pattern was found for the comparison group of children without LD. One possible explanation for the relative instability of the friendships of children with LD in Grades 4 to 6 is that children with LD are less mature in their friendship patterns than children without LD.

We analyzed the friendship quality data from the FQQ–R in three ways. First, we examined the self-reported quality of friendship of children with and without LD with their single very best friend. Second, as friendship is a dyadic phenomenon (Schneider et al., 1994), we felt it was important to assess the views of the best friends of the children in the sample. Therefore, we compared the mean value of the friendship quality ratings of dyads where neither member had a learning disability, with dyads where one or more children had a learning disability. We were able to do this for 77 same-sex dyads (39 boy dyads, 38 girl dyads) of which 37 dyads were comprised of two children without LD, 3 dyads of two children with LD, 15 dyads of one child with and one child without LD, and 22 dyads of one child with LD and a friend whose LD status was not ascertained. Third, for the 15 dyads comprised of one child with, and one child without LD, we compared the views of these two children on the quality of the relationship.

Parker and Asher (1993) found that the FQQ–R had six factors. Our factor analysis of the FQQ–R revealed nine factors because, in our analysis, three of Parker and Asher's original factors (Companionship and Recreation, Validation and Caring, and Conflict Resolution) were divided into two factors. Two of our nine factors referred to aspects of companionship (School Companionship, and Out of School Companionship), three factors referred to the aspects of the relationship that typically is seen as reflective of emotional closeness (Help and Sharing, Trust and Caring, Disclosure, and Validation), and three factors referred to the amount of conflict in the friendship and the ways that conflicts were resolved (Conflict, Conflict Resolution through Talking, and Relationship Repair).

With regard to self-reported quality of friendship, children with LD reported that they felt less validated by their friends than did children without LD. Validation was measured by items such as "My friend tells me I'm good at things"; "My friend tells me I'm pretty smart." Children with LD also reported more conflict in their relationships claiming that they and their best friend get mad at each other a lot, argue a lot, fight, and bug each other. Furthermore, children with LD claimed that they had more trouble with Relationship Repair (do not make up easily with their best friend when they have a fight) than did children without LD.

A different pattern emerged when the friendship quality of dyads were analyzed. Dyads containing a member with LD were more likely to report that their single best school friend was less likely to provide companionship at school than did dyads without a member with LD. School companionship was measured by items such as "My friend and I always sit together at lunch," "pick each other as partners," "play together at recess," and "help each other with school work." Dyads with a member with LD, however, were more likely to report that their relationships involved more disclosure than did dyads without a member with LD. Disclosure was assessed by items such as "My friend and I are always telling each other about our problems," and "I can think of lots of secrets my friend and I have told each other."

The analysis of the discrepancy between the reports of the members of the 15 dyads comprised of one member with and one member without LD provided some explanation for the higher levels of disclosure reported in dyads containing at least one member with LD. In these dyads, the member with LD tended to report higher levels of Disclosure, Help and Sharing, and Trust and Caring than did the member without LD. Help and Sharing was assessed by items which involve mutuality such as "My friend and I help each other with chores or other things a lot," "do special favors for each other" but also by items that could involve a one-way relationship such as "When I'm having trouble figuring out something, I usually ask my friend for help and advice," and "My friend often helps me with things so I can get done quicker." Trust and Caring includes items such as "My friend would still like me even if all the other kids didn't like me," and "My friend cares about my feelings." It is interesting to speculate on why children with LD report that their friendships are higher in quality with respect to the emotional closeness domain than their mutual friends without LD. It is possible that the children with LD were engaging in wishful thinking and as a result positively distorted the quality of the relationship. According to Heath (1995), children with LD often positively distort their self-ratings of academic skills. It is also possible that the mutual friendships of children with and without LD are somewhat unidirectional. Perhaps the children with LD seek help, confide in, and trust their friends more than do the dyad members without LD.

Objective 2: Social Relationships and Social and Emotional Adjustment

Our initial analyses involved comparison of children with and without LD on the measures we used in the study. Our findings confirmed those of several previous studies (see Greenham, 1999, for a review of this literature) in that children with LD were found to be deficient in relation to children without LD on most of the measures. Specifically, children with LD were less accepted by peers, had poorer social skills and higher levels of problem behaviors as rated by teachers, experienced more loneliness and social dissatisfaction, had lower academic self-concepts, and had higher levels of depressive symptoms than children without LD. Children with and without LD did not differ in self-esteem (Global Self-Worth on the SPPLD) and the nonacademic self-concept scales on the SPPLD.

The major question we posed was the degree to which various aspects of social and emotional adjustment measured in this study were predicted by the peer relationship measures including peer acceptance, number of Nominated, Reciprocated, and CR friends, and quality of friendship. Peer acceptance, as measured by ratings by same-sex peers, correlated positively with overall self-esteem and self-perception of social acceptance, and negatively with loneliness and depressive symptoms in both children with and without LD.

Number of Nominated Friends, number of Reciprocated Friends, and number of CR Friends were all associated with a lower level of loneliness and better self-perception of social acceptance in both children with and children without LD. In other words, if children believe they have friends, even if the friendship does not appear to be reciprocated, they are likely to feel less lonely and believe they are accepted by peers. There were differences between children with and without LD in the pattern of correlations between the friendship variables and overall self-esteem and depressive symptoms. In children with LD, number of Reciprocated school friendships was associated with higher self-esteem, and number of Reciprocated and CR friendships were both associated with less depressive symptoms. None of the correlations between Reciprocated and CR friendships with overall self-esteem and depressive symptoms were significant for children without LD. With regard to quality of friendship, having a friend who is a good companion at school is associated with less loneliness for both children with and children without LD. On the other hand, having a friend who is a good companion outside of school was associated with higher overall self-esteem and less loneliness only in children with LD.

Objective 3: Comorbidity With ADHD

For the most part, having ADHD added to the social difficulties of children with LD in predictable ways. As might be anticipated, the children with both LD and ADHD (LD+ADHD) had more teacher-rated externalizing and hyperactive problem behaviors and were seen by teachers as being less socially skilled than children with LD who did not have ADHD (LD–ADHD). Children with LD+ADHD had a smaller proportion of their nominated friendships reciprocated by peers, had more friends with teacher-rated learning problems, and reported more conflict in their relationships than children with LD–ADHD. On all of the foregoing variables, both groups of children with LD were deficient in comparison with children without LD.

Children with LD+ADHD also reported higher levels of depressive symptoms than children with LD–ADHD and comparison children without LD, but children with LD–ADHD did not differ from children without LD in terms of number of depressive symptoms. Although both children with LD+ADHD and LD–ADHD were less accepted by peers and reported higher levels of loneliness and a lower academic self-concept than children without LD, the two groups of children with LD did not differ from each other with respect to these issues. The extent to which these findings support the San Miguel et al. (1996) comorbidity hypothesis is discussed later.

Objective 4: The Impact of Special Education Placement

As described earlier, we compared children with LD in four types of special education placements on the friendship measures and most of the measures of social and emotional functioning. One of the striking results was that there were no differences between children in the In-Class Support and Resource Room placements on any of the measures. The children in these two placements had similar number of friends, similar quality of relationships, and similar levels of peer acceptance. They also had similar scores on the measures of social skills, problem behaviors, self-concept, loneliness, and depression. Essentially, our data revealed that pulling children out of the general education class for short periods each day (30 to 90 minutes) to receive special education assistance neither enhanced their social and emotional adjustment nor led to increased problems with social and emotional adjustment.

In spite of the fact that many of the students in Inclusion programs were identified by the school as having more severe learning disabilities than children in In-Class Support and Resource Room placements, we also did not find differences between these three groups on any of the measures. There were, however, several important differences in social and emotional functioning of children in Self-Contained Special Education Classes and in Inclusion Programs. (The children in both of these placements were identified using the same criteria as having severe LD.) Children in Self-Contained Special Education Classes reported a reduced level of companionship with their best school friends at school, and a higher level of conflict in their relationships than children in Inclusion Programs. The children in Self-Contained Special Education classes also were rated by teachers as being more deficient in social skills and having more problem behaviors than the children in Inclusion Programs. Finally, the children in Self-Contained classes experienced higher levels of loneliness and social dissatisfaction, and higher levels of depression than children in Inclusion Programs.

DISCUSSION

Risk and Resilience Theory

The theoretical base for interpretation of the findings from the present study is risk and resilience theory. According to Keogh and Weisner (1993), a risk is a "negative or potentially negative condition that impedes or threatens normal development" (p. 4). Resilience, on the other hand, is a process or capacity for an individual who is vulnerable due to adverse circumstances to achieve a positive adaptation (Rutter, 1983). Protective factors may facilitate the successful adaptation of a child who is at risk. Protective factors may include constitutional characteristics such as an easy temperament or above average intellectual ability, and environmental factors such as a supportive family and school environment (Garmezy, 1983). Keogh and Weisner (1993) articulated four assumptions, which formed the basis of a risk and resilience analysis presented by Morrison and Cosden (1996).

> (a) a learning disability, if accurately determined, reflects internal problems in processing information that typically affect school performance; (b) a learning disability puts the individual at risk for subsequent nonacademic problems , at school, at home, and in the community, but the scope and severity of these problems vary; (c) protective and risk factors act in combination to affect outcomes for individuals with learning disabilities; and (d) specific protective and risk factors vary as a function of the person's age, stage of development, and the ecocultural context in which he or she is functioning. (p. 45)

As Morrison and Cosden point out, considerable literature has been devoted to risk factors associated with learning disabilities. The results of the present study, and that of many other studies on specific aspects of the social and emotional functioning of children with learning disabilities (Greenham, 1999) have clearly established the validity of the first two assumptions articulated by Morrison and Cosden (i.e., that children with LD are at risk for both academic and nonacademic problems at home, at school, and in the community.) In the present study, compared to children without LD, children with LD had problems with social skills, problem behaviors, and peer relationships, had lower academic self-concepts, and experienced more loneliness and depression. The key issue is figuring out, among children with LD, which factors might lead to greater severity of these nonacademic problems, and what protective factors lead to successful adaptation.

One of the difficult questions in this analysis is to define risk and resilience among children with LD. On the one hand, it is possible to examine the factors that predict risk of problematic peer relations including low peer acceptance, having few friends, or low quality friendships. On the other hand, one might examine the question of whether having positive peer relationships is a protective factor in terms of mitigating against loneliness, depression, or low self-esteem. The problem is that the data in the present study are correlational; longitudinal data would be needed to fully answer the question. Nevertheless, in the absence of longitudinal data, examining the implications of the results of this study may still be useful.

Risk Factors for Problematic Peer Relations

The findings of the present study identified two factors that put children with LD at risk for problems with peer relations: self-contained special education class placement, and comorbidity with ADHD.

Special Education Placement. Although a great deal has been written about the impact of special education placement on the functioning of children with special needs (e.g., Carlberg & Kavale, 1980; Fuchs & Fuchs, 1994; Gartner & Lipsky, 1987; Wang, Reynolds, & Walberg, 1990), and there are many studies examining the social competence of children with LD in specific inclusion settings (e.g., Juvonen & Bear, 1992; Vaughn et al., 1993), there are few recent studies comparing children with LD in various types of placements in terms of a variety of measures of social and emotional functioning. This makes our findings especially important. Contrary to the claims of the earlier advocates of full inclusion, withdrawing children with LD to a resource room for between 30 and 90 minutes per school day, as opposed to providing equivalent levels of special education support within the general education classroom, seemed to have no impact on the children's peer relationships, social skills, self-concept, and feelings of loneliness.

On the other hand, placement in a Self-Contained Special Education class for at least half of the school day did have some negative effects compared to Inclusion placements, even when the children in the self-contained class were compared with others who were identified as also having severe LD and needing intensive support. The children in the Self-Contained Special Education classes reported increased loneliness, and a lower quality of friendship with their single best friend in that their friend was less likely to be a good companion at school, and the relationships involved more conflict compared to children with similar severity of LD in Inclusion programs. The children in the special education classes played together on the school yard, and frequently identified each other as friends. Their self-reported high level of conflict in their relationships, however, were consistent with our observations, and those of their teachers, that these children seemed to constantly bicker with their friends. Perhaps the positive peer models in the Inclusion programs serve to decrease the amount of conflicts among the children with LD. Although some of the children with LD in the Inclusion program in our study were not attending their home school in order to receive the high intensity support of a general education classroom with two teachers, one of whom having special education qualifications, they were not clearly labeled as LD. This might have occurred because their general and special education teachers team-taught, and with the exception of specific skill instruction in language and mathematics, mixed-ability grouping was used. This may explain why the pattern of functioning of the children with LD in the Inclusion program was similar to the children with more mild LD in the In-Class Support and Resource Room programs and differed from their counterparts in the Self-Contained Special Education classes.

Other studies have revealed that children with LD in self-contained special education classes were more likely to have neglected peer status (i.e., to be socially isolated but not necessarily overtly rejected by regular class peers) than children with LD in more integrated settings (Coben & Zigmond, 1986; Wiener, Harris, & Duval, 1993). The findings from the present study also confirm those of a qualitative study on children's perceptions and attitudes about their placement (Demchuk, 2000). All of the eight 9- to 12-year-old children in a self-contained class poignantly recounted their feelings of being excluded and victimized, and attributed these feelings to their full-time placement in a special education class.

The findings about the risk of self-contained special education class placement with regard to problematic peer relations is illustrated by the experience of Sarah, a 13-year-old girl who is currently in Grade 8 in a large middle school. Both this middle school and her previous elementary school are comprised of children from middle-class backgrounds and children from a subsidized housing project. Sarah, who was adopted, is from a stable, supportive middle-class family. Sarah has learning disabilities in both reading and mathematics which necessitated placement in a half-time learning disabilities class when she was in Grade 4. Her mathematics disabilities are especially severe. Although she is athletic, has fairly good verbal and social skills, and has a number of friends outside of school, she has been the object of chronic victimization at school. She is especially hurt by taunting about her adoption and her learning disabilities. When she is victimized, she becomes anxious and depressed, and conveys to her mother that she does not want to go to school. She is afraid to tell teachers and school administrators about what is happening because she fears reprisals from the bullies.

The victimization seems to occur in clusters, with periods of relatively good peer acceptance in between. Victimization intensified in Grade 4 concomitant with her placement in the half-time learning disabilities class in which she was the only girl. She had no friends in the special education class, and was rejected by several girls in her general education class who persuaded other students not to play with her. In Grade 7, when she moved to middle school, she obtained assistance in the resource room for mathematics and language arts. As all of the students in the school rotated to different classes for different subjects, and she was in a regular home room class, her placement in special education was not evident to many of the students. Furthermore, four of the students in the learning disabilities class were girls, one of whom became her best friend. She also acquired a few friends in her home-room class. She was no longer persistently bullied, and seemed to develop a more positive self-concept.

Our data regarding the risk factor of self-contained class placement explain why Sarah had intermittent, but serious, peer relationship difficulties. When she simply received special education support in the resource room for a short period each day, her classmates viewed her as someone who just needed a bit of help. As she did not have significant social skill deficits or severe problem behaviors, she was generally accepted. Placement in the self-contained class, on the other hand, was stigmatizing. Children who had been her playmates in Grades 1 to 3 now viewed her as someone with behavior and social problems, like some of her peers in the special education class. She became the target of a few bullies, which led to further rejection by former friends. Complicating her problems was the fact that she was the only girl in the special education class, making it difficult for her to make friends there. The bullying and peer rejection had a negative impact on her social self-concept, and she became lonely and depressed.

Comorbidity With ADHD. On first glance, the results of the present study appear to support San Miguel et al.'s (1996) conclusion that the differences between children with and without LD in social skills are largely due to the presence of children with comorbid psychiatric disorders such as ADHD in the sample of children with LD. The results confirmed those of previous studies that children with LD+ADHD are less accepted by peers and have higher levels of teacher-rated problem behaviors and less developed social skills than children with LD–ADHD (Flicek, 1992; Wiener et al., 1993). Our data also indicate that children with LD+ADHD have a lower proportion of reciprocated friendships, more friends with learning problems, and experience more conflicts in their relationship with their best friend than children with LD–ADHD. Children with LD+ADHD also reported higher levels of depressive symptoms than children with LD–ADHD.

It appears that the hyperactive–impulsive behaviors of children with ADHD permeate their social relationships, leading to more conflict and social rejection, and fewer mutual friendships. There is some evidence that children with LD+ADHD are not very aware of these problems. Their self-concept was generally similar to children without LD, and they did not appear to experience higher levels of loneliness than other children. Nevertheless, these findings indicate that ADHD is a risk factor in terms of the peer relations, emotional and social adjustment of children with LD.

Although our findings show that comorbidity with ADHD is a risk factor for children with LD, they do not completely support the comorbidity hypothesis as articulated by San Miguel et al. (1996). These investigators essentially suggested that children with LD who do not have other disorders would not differ from comparison children without LD in terms of social skills and other aspects of social and emotional functioning. There were, however, significant differences between children with LD–ADHD and children without LD on almost all of the variables discussed earlier, with the functioning of children with LD–ADHD being more deficient than the comparison children. (The exceptions were nonacademic self-concepts, depressive symptoms, and problem behaviors on the SSRS.) These findings indicate that although comorbidity with ADHD increases the risk of social and emotional difficulties in children with LD, children with LD who do not have ADHD still have social and emotional difficulties when compared to children without LD.

The findings regarding comorbidity with ADHD as a risk factor are illustrated by the case study of Andrew, who was diagnosed with ADHD–Combined Type at the age of 6 by a pediatrician. Due to the severity of his hyperactivity, impulsivity, and inattention, he received 70 mg of Ritalin daily to control his symptoms. He was enrolled in a private special education school and he received remedial assistance after school 3 days per week. Due to his parents' concern about his meager academic progress, he was referred for a psychological assessment when he was in Grade 6. At that time he was found to be reading at a late Grade 2 level, and to have severe phonological processing difficulties. His mathematics skills were at a beginning Grade 4 level.

When on Ritalin, Andrew could concentrate on academic tasks for periods of up to 2 hours and typically reflected before responding. Nevertheless, he had low affect, and did not make eye contact. When he was not on Ritalin, Andrew could only attend to task for 2 to 3 minutes. He responded impulsively, and frequently became agitated and aggressive. At school, outbursts were common at the end of the morning and afternoon when his Ritalin was no longer having an effect.

Andrew was poorly accepted by the other students in the class. He had one friend whom he telephoned regularly, but had only visited this child once. Andrew had never invited a child to his house. Andrew's parents were very concerned about his academic achievement, but were not concerned about his problems with social relationships. His teachers and caregivers were all concerned about his behavioral outbursts, and about his impoverished social contacts.

Protective Factors

Identifying protective factors (i.e., factors that seem to provide children with LD, who are defined as the risk group, with a buffer from a problem, but do not protect children without LD) required considerable investigation. It is important to note that protective factors are not the opposite of risk factors (Garmezy, 1983). As poor peer acceptance was associated with loneliness and depressive symptoms, and reduced overall self-esteem and self-perception of social acceptance in both children with and without LD, low peer acceptance is clearly a risk factor for impaired social and emotional adjustment. This finding regarding the overall risk of low peer acceptance is consistent with the literature that peer rejection is such a powerful phenomenon that children who are rejected are at risk for a variety of social and emotional problems both in childhood (e.g., French & Waas, 1985) and later in life (e.g., Roff, Sells, & Golden, 1972). Peer acceptance, however, is technically not a protective factor because it does not differentially protect the children with LD—the risk group.

There was some indication that the number of mutual friends that children with LD have and some aspects of the quality of their friendships are protective factors (i.e., having more mutual friends and higher quality relationships are protective of self-esteem and buffer them from loneliness and depression.) Number of Reciprocated Friendships was associated with higher overall self-esteem and reduced levels of depressive symptoms only in children with LD. Number of CR friendships was associated with reduced depressive symptoms in children with LD but not children without LD. These data imply that having mutual friends was an important contributor to the well being of children with LD but may not be an important contributor to the well being of children without LD.

The correlations between the self-reported quality of friendship variables and self-esteem, social self-concept, and loneliness were generally quite low with the highest correlations being approximately .24, making the conclusions somewhat tentative. Although having a best friend who was a good companion at school was associated with lower levels of loneliness for both children with and without LD, having a friend who was a companion outside of school (My friend and I "live really close to each other," "do fun things together a lot," "go to each other's house after school and on weekends") was only associated with lower levels of loneliness and with higher self-esteem for children with LD. It is possible, then, that for children with LD who experience so much difficulty in school, having a close out-of-school friend is a protective factor. Several of the parents of children with LD in Wiener and Sunohara's (1998) qualitative study on parents' beliefs about the friendships of children with LD spoke about the value of such a friend, essentially corroborating the conclusion that this may be a protective factor. Having a close out-of-school friend may be less important for children without LD who are more likely to have close friends at school.

The results presented here suggest that if risk factors are minimized and certain protective factors are in place, children with LD are unlikely to have difficulties with social adaptation and emotional adjustment. Therefore, the third and final case study concerns a child with LD who has very good social and emotional adjustment. Michael was diagnosed as having a learning disability at the age of 10, when he was beginning fifth grade. Psychoeducational testing revealed well above average verbal and nonverbal abilities. Michael also had very highly developed mathematics abilities. He lives in an upper middle-class residential area of a large Canadian city, and attends a public school that mainly serves the upper middle-class community in which he lives. At the beginning of fifth grade, his decoding skills were at a beginning Grade 3 level, and his reading comprehension at a beginning Grade 4 level. His reading disabilities were traced to difficulties with phonological processing and short-term memory, especially for sequential, nonmeaningful, information. Michael's father, who was an engineer, claimed that he and Michael had similar difficulties. Michael began receiving remedial assistance in the resource room for 40 minutes per day in Grade 5.

Michael has excellent social skills, and has consistently been well-liked by adults and other children. Both at school and at camp he is typically regarded as a leader by his peers. He has several close friends and a very supportive family. Although he became acutely aware of his academic difficulties in Grade 4, when he had a teacher who did not make any accommodations for his reading difficulties and seldom praised any of the students in her class, he was generally self-assured and had high self-esteem. Placement in the resource room did not seem to have any impact on Michael's self-esteem or peer relationships.

Studies have revealed that approximately one third to one half of children with LD, like Michael, do not have significant social interaction difficulties (Greenham, 1999; Wiener, 1987). As discussed by Morrison and Cosden (1997), students like Michael whose learning disabilities are very specific, who do not have nonverbal learning disabilities with the associated social skill deficits, and who have strong social supports from family and friends are more likely to be socially and emotionally adjusted than other children with LD. The results of our study suggest that being included in the general education classroom and not having comorbid conditions such as ADHD also minimize the risk.

IMPLICATIONS

Although the present study involved a broad investigation of the social and emotional functioning of children with LD, and an in depth analysis of peer relations, there are several, likely important, areas that were not investigated. Studies have shown that self-perception of social support among children with LD is associated with self-concept (Morrison & Cosden, 1997). Therefore, it may be important to identify parenting and teaching styles that may put children with LD at risk or be protective factors. Also, as indicated by Cosden and her colleagues (Cosden, Elliot, Noble, & Keleman, 1999; Rothman & Cosden, 1995), the conceptions of children with LD about their disability, their self-awareness and self-understanding may be related to positive emotional and social adaptation.

This theoretical analysis underlines the position that researchers investigating the social and emotional functioning of children with LD should go beyond comparing children with and without LD on specific variables to examine risk and protective factors. For the most part, these comparisons confirm findings over the past 25 years that children with LD are deficient in comparison to children without LD in the affective and social domain. The postulation of risk and resilience models guides researchers to investigate internal and contextual variables that may mediate varying success at social adaptation and emotional adjustment among individuals with LD.

These within group analyses may enhance practitioners' ability to determine which children with LD are especially at risk for social and emotional difficulties, and in some cases, to enhance protective factors. Nevertheless, being pulled out to a resource room for a short period each day does not appear to have adverse effects. The results of the present study, however, suggest that placement of children with LD in self-contained special education classes for the majority of the school day should be avoided. The risk of peer relationship difficulties is likely to be reduced if children with severe LD are placed in Inclusion programs with intensive support. The results also suggest that we need to intensify our efforts to develop effective interventions for children with LD+ADHD. In addition, it is likely that low self-esteem and depression might be prevented in some children with LD if parents, teachers, and other practitioners help them acquire more mutual friendships, including high quality friendships with children who do not attend their school. Therefore, the identification of risk and protective factors may provide the basis for the development of preventive programs and interventions that will enhance the social and emotional functioning of children with learning disabilities.

REFERENCES

Asher, S. R., Hymel, S., & Renshaw, P. D. (1984). Loneliness in children. *Child Development, 55*, 1456–1464.

Bagwell, C. L., Newcomb, A. F., & Bukowski, W. M. (1998). Preadolescent friendship and peer rejection as predictors of adult adjustment. *Child Development, 69*, 140–153.

Barkley, R. A. (1998). *Attention-deficit hyperactivity disorder: A handbook for diagnosis and treatment* (2nd ed.). New York: Guilford Press.

Berndt, T. J. (1996). Exploring the effects of friendship quality on social development. In W. M. Bukowski, A. F. Newcomb, & W. W. Hartup (Eds.). *The company they keep* (pp. 346–365). Cambridge, England: Cambridge University Press.

Biederman, J., Newcorn, J., & Sprich, S. (1991). Comorbidity of attention deficit hyperactivity disorder with conduct, depressive, anxiety, and other disorders. *American Journal of Psychiatry, 148*, 564–577.

Carlberg, C., & Kavale, K. (1980). The efficacy of special versus regular class placement for exceptional children: A meta-analysis. *The Journal of Special Education, 14*, 25–52.

Coben, S., & Zigmond, N. (1986). The social integration of learning disabled students from self-contained and mainstream elementary school settings. *Journal of Learning Disabilities, 19*, 614–618.

Cosden, M., Elliot, K., Noble, S., & Keleman, E. (1999). Self-understanding and self-esteem in children with learning disabilities. *Learning Disability Quarterly, 22*, 279–290.

Demchuk, L. (2000). *Children's perceptions and attitudes about special education.* Unpublished doctoral thesis, University of Toronto.

DuPaul, G. J. (1990). *The ADHD Rating Scale: Normative data, reliability and validity.* Unpublished manuscript, University of Massachusetts Medical Center, Worcester, MA.

Flicek, M. (1992). Social status of boys with both academic problems and attention-deficit hyperactivity disorder. *Journal of Abnormal Child Psychology, 20*, 353–366.

French, D. C., & Waas, G. E. (1985). Behavior problems of peer rejected and neglected elementary age children: Teacher and parent perspectives. *Child Development, 56*, 246–252.

Fuchs, D., & Fuchs, L. S. (1994). Inclusive schools movement and the radicalization of special education reform. *Exceptional Children, 60*, 294–309.

Garmezy, N. (1983). *Stressors of childhood.* Minneapolis, MN: McGraw-Hill.

Gartner, A., & Lipsky, D. (1987). Beyond special education: Toward a quality system for all students. *Harvard Education Review, 57*, 367–395.

Greenham, S. L. (1999). Learning disabilities and psychosocial adjustment: A critical review. *Child Neuropsychology, 5*, 171–196.

Gresham, F. M., & Elliot, S. N. (1990). *The Social Skills Rating System.* Circle Pines, MN: American Guidance Service.

Heath, N. L. (1995). Distortion and deficit: Self-perceived versus actual academic competence in depressed and non-depressed children with and without learning disabilities. *Learning Disabilities Research and Practice, 10,* 2–10.

Hoosen, S., & Wiener, J. (1996). *Gender differences in friendship selection and friendship quality of children with and without learning disabilities.* International Society for the Study of Behavioral Development. Quebec, Canada.

Juvonen, J., & Bear, G. (1992). Social adjustment of children with and without learning disabilities in integrated classrooms. *Journal of Educational Psychology, 84,* 332–330.

Keogh, B. K., & Weisner, T. (1993). An ecocultural perspective on risk and protective factors in children's development: Implications for learning disabilities. *Learning Disabilities Research and Practice, 8,* 3–10.

Kovacs, M. (1992). *Children's Depression Inventory.* Toronto: Multi-Health Systems Inc.

Kuhne, M. (1999). *Friendship patterns of children and adolescents with learning disabilities and attention problems.* Unpublished doctoral dissertation, University of Toronto.

Kuhne, M., & Wiener, J. (2000). Stability of social status of children with and without learning disabilities. *Learning Disabilities Quarterly, 23,* 64–75.

Larie, M., & Wiener, J. (2001). *The emotional functioning of children with learning disabilities and ADHD symptomatology.* Canadian Psychological Association, Quebec, Canada.

Morrison, G. M., & Cosden, M. A. (1997). Risk, resilience, and adjustment of individuals with learning disabilities. *Learning Disability Quarterly, 20,* 43–60.

Newcomb, A. F., & Bagwell, C. L. (1996). The developmental significance of children's friendship relations. In W. M. Bukowski, A. F. Newcomb, & W. W. Hartup (Eds.), *The company they keep.* Cambridge, England: Cambridge University Press.

Parker, J. G., & Asher, S. R. (1993). Friendship and friendship quality in middle childhood: Links with peer group acceptance and feelings of loneliness and social dissatisfaction. *Developmental Psychology, 29,* 611–621.

Pires, P., & Wiener, J. (2001). The friendship quality of children with learning disabilities: Association with loneliness and self-perception. Canadian Psychological Association, Quebec, Canada.

Power, S. (1999). *Psychological adjustment of children with learning disabilities: Do friends make the difference?* Unpublished doctoral dissertation, University of Toronto.

Renick, M. J., & Harter, S. (1988). *The Self-Perception Profile for Learning Disabled Students.* CO: University of Denver.

Richards, C., & Wiener, J. (1996). *Friendship stability of children with and without learning disabilities.* International Society for the Study of Behavioral Development. Quebec, Canada.

Rothman, H. R., & Cosden, M. (1995). Self–perception of a learning disability: self-concept and social support. *Learning Disability Quarterly, 18,* 203–212.

Roff, M., Sells, S. B., & Golden, M. M. (1972). *Social adjustment and personality development in children.* Minneapolis: University of Minnesota Press.

Rutter, M. (1983). Stress, coping and development: Some issues and some question. In N. Garmezy & M. Rutter (Eds.), *Stress, coping, and development in children* (pp. 1–41). New York: McGraw Hill.

San Miguel, S. K., Forness, S. R., & Kavale, K. A. (1996). Social skills deficits in learning disabilities: The psychiatric comorbidity hypothesis. *Learning Disability Quarterly, 19,* 252–261.

Schneider, B. H., Wiener, J., & Murphy, K. (1994). The giant step beyond peer acceptance. *Journal of Social and Personal Relationships, 11,* 323–340.

Schumm, J., Vaughn, S. R., Gordon, J., & Rothlein, L. (1994). General education teachers' beliefs, skills, and practices in planning for mainstreamed students with learning disabilities. *Teacher Education and Special Education, 17,* 22–37.

Swanson, H. L., & Malone, S. (1992). Social skills and learning disabilities: A meta-analysis of the literature. *School Psychology Review, 21,* 427–443.

Stanovich, P. J., & Jordan, A. (1998). Canadian teachers' and principals' beliefs about inclusive education as predictors of effective teaching in heterogeneous classrooms. *The Elementary School Journal, 98,* 221–238.

Tardif, C., & Wiener, J. (2001). *Social and emotional functioning of children with learning disabilities: The impact of special education placement.* Minneapolis, MN: Society for Research in Child Development.

Tur-Kaspa, H., Margalit, M., & Most, T. (1999). Reciprocal friendship, reciprocal rejection, and socio-emotional adjustment: The social experiences of children with learning disorders over a one-year period. *European Journal of Special Needs Education, 14,* 37–48.

Vandell, D. L., & Hembree, S. E. (1994). Peer social status and friendship: Independent contributors to children's social adjustment. *Merrill Palmer Quarterly, 40,* 461–477.

Vaughn, S., & Elbaum, B. (1999). The self concept and friendships of students with learning disabilities: A developmental perspective. In R. Gallimore (Ed.), *Developmental perspectives on children with high-incidence disabilities* (pp. 81–107). Mahwah, NJ: Lawrence Erlbaum Associates.

Vaughn, S., Elbaum, B. E., & Schumm, J. S. (1996). The effects of inclusion on the social functioning of students with learning disabilities. *Journal of Learning Disabilities, 29,* 598–608.

Vaughn, S., & Haager, D. (1994). Social competence as a multifaceted construct: How do students with learning disabilities fare? *Learning Disability Quarterly, 17,* 253–266.

Vaughn, S., McIntosh, R., Schumm, J. S., Haager, D., & Callwood, D. (1993). Social status, peer acceptance, and reciprocal friendships revisited. *Learning Disabilities Research and Practice, 8,* 82–88.

Wang, M. C., Reynolds, M. C., & Walberg, H. J. (1990). *Special education research and practice: Synthesis of findings.* Oxford, England: Pergamon Press.

Wenz-Gross, M., & Siperstein, G. N. (1997). Importance of social support in the adjustment of children with learning problems. *Exceptional Children, 63,* 183–193.

Wiener, J. (1987). Peer status of learning disabled children and adolescents: A Review of the literature. *Learning Disabilities Research, 2,* 62–79.

Wiener, J. (1998a). *Friendship patterns of children with learning disabilities: Does special education placement make a difference?* International Academy for Research in Learning Disabilities, Padua, Italy.

Wiener, J. (1998b). The psychiatric comorbidity hypothesis: A response to San Miguel, Forness & Kavale. *Learning Disability Quarterly, 21,* 195–201.

Wiener, J., Harris, P. J., & Duval, L. (1993). Placement, identification and subtype correlates of peer status and social behaviour of children with learning disabilities. *Exceptionality Education Canada, 3,* 129–155.

Wiener, J., Kuhne, M., & Schneider, B. H. (1996). *Friendship selection and friendship quality in children with and without attention deficit disorder.* Society for Research in Child and Adolescent Psychopathology, Santa Monica, CA.

Wiener, J., & Schneider, B. H. (1999). *Gender and developmental correlates of friendship in children with learning disabilities.* Society for Research in Child Development, Albuquerque, NM.

Wiener, J., & Schneider, B. (2002). A multisource exploration of friendship patterns of children with learning disabilities. *Journal of Abnormal Child Psychology, 30,* 127–141.

Wiener, J., & Sunohara, G. (1998). Parents' perceptions of the quality of friendship of their children with learning disabilities. *Learning Disabilities Research and Practice, 13,* 242–257.

Chapter 7

Preparing Prospective Teachers to Work in the Social and Emotional Worlds of Students With Learning Disabilities

Mary Bay
University of Illinois at Chicago

> *As the United States moves from a simpler society dominated by a manufacturing economy to a much more complex world based largely on information technologies and knowledge work, its schools are undergoing a once-in-a-century transformation. Never before has the success, perhaps even the survival, of nations and people been so tightly tied to their ability to learn. Consequently, our future depends now, as never before, on our ability to teach.*
> —L. Darling-Hammond (1997, pp. 1–2)

For the last decade, our "ability to teach" has been in the educational community's spotlight. Researchers, administrators, teachers, and policymakers have paid particular attention to a wide array of teacher learning and teacher education issues: identifying and assessing teachers' knowledge and skills, developing ways to advance teachers' abilities, describing the relationships among teachers' actions and students' performance, and setting a policy agenda for how to improve the quality of America's teaching force (Holmes Group, 1986; National Commission on Teaching and America's Future, 1996).

A major impetus for the attention has been the national discourse on the "failure" of our nation's schools to educate all of our students at challenging levels. An obvious solution has been to focus on and attempt to improve teaching and the ways in which individuals are prepared to teach (e.g., The Association of Teacher Educators, 1986; Carnegie Task Force, 1986; and the National Commission on Teaching and America's Future,

115

1996). As Cochran-Smith and Lytle (1999a, 1999b) pointed out, "blaming" teachers for schools' problems promoted the idea that teachers could be powerful agents in the educational scene, capable of making a difference as a result of the day-to-day decisions they make. The logical next step has been the implementation of a wave of reform efforts that are intended to transform the ways in which teachers are prepared and to create a more qualified teaching force, one that is capable of creating challenging learning environments for all students (Holmes Group, 1986; The National Board for Professional Teaching Standards, 1988; The National Commission on Teaching and America's Future, 1996).

These efforts to transform teacher education programs are fueled by the growing body of evidence that supports the idea that the teacher *does* matter (Cochran-Smith & Lytle, 1999a; Darling-Hammond, Wise, & Klein, 1995; Darling-Hammond, 1997; Fuller, 1999). That is, what teachers know, what they are able to do, the decisions they make, the actions they take in the classroom are, in fact, critical ingredients for advancing students' academic and social and emotional growth.

Studies in Texas, North Carolina, and California support these findings. After controlling for students' socioeconomic status, teacher experience, and school wealth, students in districts with fully licensed teachers were significantly more likely to pass the Texas state achievement tests (Fuller, 1999). Teachers' average scores on the National Teacher Examinations, which measure subject matter and teaching knowledge, had a large effect on students' pass rates on North Carolina's state competency examinations (Strauss & Sawyer, 1986). Reporting on California high school students' scores in mathematics, Fetler (1999) found a strong negative correlation between these scores and the percentage of math teachers on emergency certificates, after controlling for student poverty rates. Studying the effects of repeated exposure to poor teaching, Sanders and colleagues (e.g., Sanders & Horn, 1998; Sanders & Rivers, 1996) found that groups of students with comparable abilities and initial achievement levels have vastly different academic outcomes as a result of the teachers to whom they are assigned. Furthermore, the deleterious effects of underperforming teachers are both additive and cumulative, with little to suggest that these effects may be overcome by exposure to more effective teachers in later grades. *Hence, within the research and policy community, the agenda emphasizes the critical role of teachers' knowledge and teachers' actions in advancing students' learning. This gives the current interest in teacher learning and teacher education a broad appeal, one that has resulted in a national-level movement to re-examine conceptions of teacher learning and to reform preparation programs.*

A second impetus for the attention to teacher learning and teacher education is the critical shortage of teachers. Our nation faces a crisis of extraordinary proportions in terms of the anticipated need for teachers. It is estimated that half of the current teachers will leave the profession in the decade that started in 1996. Most of these individuals are "baby boomers" who will soon reach retirement age. At the same time, educators, parents, and policymakers' demand for smaller classes means expanding staffs beyond current numbers. Some estimate that approximately 1.25 million teachers, more than half the current teaching force, will be needed by 2010 to work with future generations of children and youth (Griffin, 1999; Kantrowitz & Wingert, 2000).

In special education, teacher shortages are chronic and severe. The 1995–1996 school year serves as an example. Approximately 26,000 less-than-fully qualified special education teachers were employed in American schools; an additional 3,700 special education positions were vacant (U.S. Department of Education, 1998). Nowhere is the need for teachers greater than in large, urban school districts like Chicago. Large systems are confronted with a sharp rise in student enrollments, plagued by teacher attrition, and challenged by prospective teachers' reluctance to accept positions in communities characterized by poverty and violence. On any day of the academic year, the Chicago public school district needs 300-plus special educators (Gamm, personal communication, April, 2000). Because of the shortage, school districts are increasingly forced to hire less-than-qualified teachers.

With this type of shortage, who teaches our nation's children? Recent data reveal that well over one fourth of all new teachers have either no license or hold a substandard license for the area in which they are employed to teach (National Commission on Teaching and America's Future, 1996). These same data further indicate that the problem is at its worst in urban schools and classrooms serving the most educationally vulnerable students (Darling-Hammond, 1992). "Students are too often taught by inexperienced beginning teachers, short-term substitutes, and uncredentialed teachers." (Sindelar & Rosenberg, 2000, p. 191).

Because of the evidence that demonstrates teachers make a difference, it is critical to maintain high professional standards. Yet, as we work to design and offer rigorous programs, school districts are forced to hire less-than-qualified teachers. These converging factors create an extremely challenging dilemma for the education community. How can teacher educators, simultaneously, prepare individuals who are qualified to enter the profession *and* address the extreme teacher shortage that confronts school districts? The purpose of this chapter is to address this question for a particular case of teacher education: the preparation of special educators who are well qualified to advance the social and emotional learning of children with learning disabilities. The issues are discussed within the conundrum of maintaining professional standards in light of the critical need for special educators. In the first section, I examine the special education community's teaching standards to determine the extent to which the profession thinks special educators must demonstrate knowledge and skills pertaining to the social dimensions of learning disabilities. Given that teachers' knowledge and abilities are related to students' learning, it is important to examine what the profession thinks are the standards for beginning teachers in this domain. How does the special education profession define "qualified" special educator with respect to the social and emotional learning of students with learning disabilities?

In the next section, I propose several ways in which teacher preparation programs might be improved in an effort to graduate qualified individuals who will remain in teaching. Many schools of education, often in partnership with school districts, have begun to reform their teacher education programs. This work has resulted in a growing body of evidence indicating that the type and quality of preparation can make a difference in the novice's abilities to advance students' learning (Ashton & Crocker, 1986; Darling-Hammond, 2000; Fetler, 1999; Fuller, 1999; Goodlad, 1994) and in the novice's satisfaction with teaching and interest in remaining in the profession (Andrew, 1990; Andrew & Schwab, 1995; Shin, 1994). Specifically, I focus on three program features: (a) replacing a "knowledge for practice" perspective with a "knowledge in practice" stance; (b) remembering that prospective teachers do not enter teacher education programs as "blank slates"; and (c) supporting and guiding special educators in the initial year of teaching. Although the chapter focuses on preservice teachers' opportunities to learn, many of the ideas are relevant to the learning of experienced teachers as well.

To What Extent Are Prospective Teachers Expected to Know and Understand How to Advance Students' Social and Emotional Learning?

Regardless of the various ways in which individuals want to improve schooling in America (e.g., strengthen basic skills, promote character, prevent violence), everyone wants to graduate elementary and secondary students who become knowledgeable, responsible, and caring adults. As Elias, Zins, Weissberg, and their colleagues (Elias et al., 1997) remind us, behind each word—knowledgeable, responsible, caring—lies an educational challenge. For students to become knowledgeable, they must be motivated and ready to learn. For students to become responsible, they must understand social contexts, and be able to choose actions that serve not only their interests, but also those of others. For students to become caring, they must be able to read the social setting and appreciate the concerns of others. Many students with mild disabilities demonstrate difficulties in social relationships and emotional development (see e.g., Farmer & Farmer, 1996; Pavri & Monda-Amaya, 2001). It is critical that prospective and practicing teachers understand that students' growth in these domains can be advanced with thoughtful, sustained, and systematic attention to social and emotional learning.

To address the question pertaining to expectations regarding social and emotional learning, I examine the teacher standards that have been developed by the Council for Exceptional Children (CEC) for beginning special education teachers. These standards represent the profession's thinking regarding the minimum essential knowledge and skills necessary for the beginning practitioner. They establish what some would call the "knowledge base" for those entering practice and, therefore, directly address the issue of "quality." What these standards include and what they ignore is critical because the standards movement dominates discussions about teaching and learning, curriculum for teacher education programs, the design of teacher assessment systems, and teacher certification. Prompted by changes in the standards of professional organizations and accrediting agencies, teacher education institutions nationwide are shifting from input-based models (e.g., requiring certain courses) to standards-based (or outcomes-based) ones (Dietz, 1998).

To create the standards, CEC established committees, subcommittees, and working groups in the United States and Canada. According to the document entitled *What Every Special Educator Must Know: The International Standards for the Preparation and Certification of Special Education Teachers*, thousands of special educators and others (parents and policymakers, for example) worked across a 6-year period to develop the standards and guidelines. The standards are classified into two categories: (a) the Common Core of Knowledge and Skills Essential for Beginning Special Education Teachers; and (b) Specialized Knowledge and Skills for the area in which the individual is being certified to teach. The abilities represented in the second category are designed to supplement those abilities reflected in the Common Core. In addition, the Council recommended that each beginning special education teacher complete a 1-year mentorship. In the following paragraphs, I review the Common Core standards and those focused specifically on the teaching of students with learning disabilities to determine the standards' attention to social and emotional learning.

Before I analyze these standards, it is important to discuss origins. Shulman (1987) identified four major sources of teaching knowledge that typically influence the design of standards: (a) educational and content-area scholarship; (b) educational agencies (licensure structures, state policies); (c) educational materials for both teachers and their students (e.g., teaching materials, assessment strategies, tests); and the (d) wisdom of practice (including the codified and yet to be codified understandings that guide the practice of able teachers). With respect to the CEC standards, the document states:

> The subcommittee gathered materials from literature; state, provincial, and local governments; institutions of higher education; and elsewhere. The subcommittee then identified and organized thousands of competencies into major categories, culled them down to 195 statements, and determined the importance of each by surveying a 1,000-person sample of CEC's membership. Based on the response, the Subcommittee reduced the number of statements to 107. (Council for Exceptional Children, 1996, p. 9)

There are eight Common Core statements that describe the knowledge and skills expected of all beginning special educators. The first focuses on the philosophical, historical, and legal foundations of special education and addresses such topics as definitions and identification procedures, due process rights, rights and responsibilities of parents, and the ability to formulate a personal philosophy of special education.

The second Common Core focuses on knowledge and abilities related to the characteristics of learners. Here there is direct attention to the social and emotional domains as well as to communication. Beginning special educators are expected to understand social and emotional development as well as normal, delayed, and disordered communication patterns of individuals with exceptional learning needs. They are expected to understand the influence of the environmental milieu (e.g., culture, socioeconomic status) on development and to know the effects of medications on the social and emotional behavior of individuals.

The third Common Core attends to the assessment, diagnosis, and evaluation of persons with exceptionalities. Attention is given to basic terminology, ethical concerns, legal provisions and regulations, typical procedures used for screening, pre-referral, referral, and classification. Beginners are expected to know how to calculate scores, maintain records, gather background information (academic, medical and family histories), use various informal and formal assessment procedures, understand the relationship between assessment and placement decisions, and work collaboratively with families and other professionals. Whereas statements pertaining specifically to social and emotional learning are not included in the Standard, reference is made to a variety of assessment approaches and types as well as to understanding the influence of culture and language on assessment results.

The fourth statement in the Common Core pertains to instructional content and practice. Such topics as understanding differing learning styles, knowing the demands of various learning environments, and relating assessment data with the selection of instructional approaches are listed. Specific to social and emotional learning, one knowledge statement addresses the ability to develop curricula for various leaning dimensions, including social and language learning. One of the skills focuses specifically on the social domain by stating "integrating affective, social, and career/vocational skills with academic curricula" (Council for Exceptional Children, 1996, p. 17).

Planning and managing the teaching and learning environment is the focus of the fifth Common Core statement. Topics focus on basic classroom management theories and research-based effective practices for orchestrating life in the classroom. Three skills seem to focus primarily on students' social and emotional learning. The first expects beginning special educators to use approaches that integrate individuals with exceptional learning needs into various settings. The second expects the beginner to design learning environments that encourage active participation of individuals in a variety of individual and group learning activities and, the third, to create an environment that encourages self-advocacy and increased independence.

The sixth Common Core statement focuses specifically on issues of social and emotional learning; it addresses teachers' abilities related to managing student behavior and developing social interaction skills. The beginning special educator is expected to understand the relationship between teacher attitudes and behaviors that positively or negatively influence the behavior of individuals with exceptional learning needs, develop their students' social skills, and prepare individuals to live harmoniously and productively in a multicultural world. They are expected to demonstrate a variety of effective approaches to managing behavior, promoting prosocial conduct, and promoting self-awareness, self-control, and self-esteem.

Common Core statements seven and eight fall within the broad domain of professionalism. The standards in Core #7 focus on the teacher's ability to communicate and collaborate with parents, general educators, and other school and agency-based professionals to promote students' learning. Core #8 emphasizes the importance of each special educator being aware of the influence of his or her personal biases on teaching as well as appreciating his or her responsibility to serve as a model for persons with exceptionalities.

In addition to examining the Common Core statements, it is necessary to review the standards pertaining to the knowledge and skills for all beginning special education teachers of students with learning disabilities. The attention to social and emotional learning is again evident in these standards. For example, the beginning special educator is expected to understand the social–emotional aspects of individuals with learning disabilities and demonstrate the ability to integrate appropriate teaching strategies to advance not only students' academic growth, but also their nonacademic development. Specific mention is made of social imperceptiveness and learned helplessness. Also, novices are expected to understand the impact of language development on the academic and social skills of individuals with learning disabilities.

Clearly, these eight Common Core statements and those specific to teachers of students with learning disabilities attend to the importance of the special educator knowing how to promote their students' social and emotional learning. The expected knowledge and understandings reflected in these standards is quite comprehensive. The statements address characteristics of students, use of appropriate teaching methods, use of approaches that effectively integrate students into various settings, and understanding the relationship between language development and social competence.

Clearly, the impact of Bryan's and her colleagues' research on the social dimensions of learning disabilities (see, e.g., Bryan, 1974, 1998; Donahue & Bryan, 1983; Pearl & Bryan, 1994), as well as the body of work that this research spawned, are reflected throughout these standards. This research moved questions of children's social understandings and competence to center stage in the debate about learning disabilities. It influenced a wide range of issues in the field, including the definition of learning disabilities, the identification process, and how best to work with children to advance their ability to understand and manage the social aspects of their lives in ways that enable learning, foster relationships, and solve everyday problems. The thousands of special education professionals who designed the CEC teacher standards recognized the necessity for future special educators to demonstrate knowledge and abilities in this domain. In summary, at least 8 of the total 16 standards directly reflect the need for attention to students' social and emotional development.

These professional standards can be used as a guide for the preparation, induction, and continued development of new practitioners. As a guide or framework, they are useful in pointing the professional community in the right direction by defining outcomes. In the case of the social and emotional dimensions of learning disabilities and what is expected of beginning teachers, the standards are comprehensive and rigorous. With the outcomes in view, we turn our attention to three recommended features of teacher preparation programs that support teacher learning and foster retention in the profession.

How Can Teacher Education Programs Prepare Individuals Qualified to Address Social and Emotional Dimensions Who Will Remain in Teaching?

For decades, mainstream teacher education programs have been widely criticized as being ineffective. Prospective and beginning teachers report that what they learn in teacher education programs does not easily transfer to the real world of the classroom (Burden, 1986; Lampert & Ball, 1998; Zeichner & Tabachnick, 1982). Teacher educators write about the frustration they experience when their program effects "wash out" as a result of the power of the classroom experience, an experience that often reflects a more conservative stance toward teaching and learning (see, e.g., Zeichner & Tabachnick, 1982). Teachers complain that their preparation was of little value and that they learned about teaching "on the job" (see, e.g., Feiman-Nemser, 1983). According to Sindelar and Rosenberg (2000), the prevailing wisdom regarding teacher education programs tends to be highly critical and dismissive. In contrast, counter evidence has been ignored. Recent efforts show encouraging trends both in terms of preparing qualified individuals and in graduating beginning professionals who want to remain in the profession.

A Stance Toward "Knowledge in Practice." Traditional programs have focused primarily on how teachers should implement, use, or adapt what they have learned of a particular knowledge base for use in the classroom. Lampert and Ball (1998) described this approach in the following way: "One simple model of learning teaching is that the knowledge *goes in* during teacher education and then *comes out* to be used in the classroom. Theory is dispensed in some preservice courses, practical methods of teaching in others, and success in learning to teach is assumed to depend on applying what has been learned on campus" (p. 19). The *what goes in* is usually in the form of a program that lacks coherence. The typical program contains a mix of formal knowledge and firsthand experience, theory and practice divided both conceptually and within the program's structure. In special education programs, fragmentation often occurs by the common practice of separating the study of the characteristics of learners with disabilities from pedagogy from classroom management. This fragmentation leaves the prospective teacher with the difficult task of integrating what has been learned and then trying to figure out how to apply it during the field component.

Drawing on the work of Cochran-Smith and Lytle (1999a) and Lampert and Ball (1998), a shift away from this "knowledge for practice" approach to a "knowledge in practice stance" is recommended. A knowledge in practice approach focuses on the prospective teachers' ability to observe instances of teaching and learning, interpret the events, and take deliberate actions. One needs to spend only 10 minutes in a classroom to realize the complex and challenging demands placed on the teacher. The dynamics can lead to multiple interpretations, which, in turn, can lead to a wide range of responses and actions. For example, in the midst of attempting to advance a student's social learning, what the teacher should do next depends on numerous interactive factors: where the student is in understanding the social context; who is involved in the situation; what the student is doing; the student's level of interest and motivation; the extent to which the student is understanding the situation and the teacher's response; the relationship between the student and the teacher; the relationship between the student and other students; the teacher's understandings of the social dimensions of development; the teacher's ability to create a scaffold to move the student to the next step; and so on. Hence, the relationship between knowledge (what the teacher should know and do) and context is highly interdependent.

> Teachers need to know things that one cannot know in advance of any particular encounter . . . Knowing in teaching depends fundamentally on being able to observe in the moment of classroom interaction, interpret the situation, and act "deliberately." It depends on being able to use what one can learn from textbooks, experts, and colleagues as one makes reasoned judgments in the context of action. (Lampert & Ball, 1998, p. 29)

As teacher educators, we must encourage prospective teachers to see that their responsibility is to restructure knowledge about teaching and learning in conditions of use. Several program design features help prospective teachers develop knowledge and appreciate what it takes to use it wisely in context. First, prospective teachers need the opportunity to work with competent professionals (special educators, social workers, general educators, school psychologists) to learn how these professionals conceptualize and describe classroom dilemmas—how they set the problem or frame the situation. Future teachers need to hear how these competent professionals name and select what is important to attend to, what sources of knowledge they draw from, how they choose among alternative strategies, what influences their thinking and decision making, and how they improve their practice (see Koeppen, Huey, & Connor, 2000; McIntyre & O'Hair, 1996). Next, prospective teachers need to engage in activities that foster their abilities to think and reason in similar ways. Analysis of written and videotaped cases is useful; creation of portfolios that require description, analysis, and evaluation of artifacts that reflect decisions made and actions taken is also beneficial; and working with prospective and experienced teachers in collaborative arrangements (dyads, teacher groups, teams) that support teachers' working together to reflect in and on practice is critical (see Lieberman, 2000; Nevarez-La Torre & Rolon-Dow, 2000). From this perspective, it is acknowledged that prospective teachers need to construct problems out of the complexity of practice, make sense of situations by connecting them to previous ones, and enhance and restructure the knowledge they have gained from multiple sources to manage the learning environment (Cochran-Smith & Lytle, 1999a; Schon, 1987).

A Recognition That Prospective Special Educators Are Not Blank Slates.
One often cited reason for teacher education programs' weak effects is
that prospective teachers are treated as "blank slates," that is, teacher educators deliver information and teacher candidates are expected to absorb
it and then implement it in the classroom. Yet, because of their many years
of schooling—years that provided an abundance of opportunities to observe and absorb what teachers do and say—prospective teachers enter
teacher education programs not with blank slates but with powerful images, understandings, and beliefs about teaching, learning and schooling
(Lortie, 1975). They enter programs having constructed deeply-rooted
ideas about good teaching, how learning occurs, what is worth knowing,
and who can learn (Bennett & Carre, 1993; Calderhead & Robson, 1991;
Holt-Reynolds, 1992).

This means that future special educators have spent a long apprenticeship watching their teachers respond to the social and emotional needs of
their students. Filled with preconceptions, they are often ready to re-enact
their teachers' behavior—to rely on prior experience and common sense
to guide their decisions and actions. Particularly when confronted with the
day-to-day challenges of beginning teaching, challenges that at times
seem overwhelming, this overreliance on common sense and prior experience is powerful in predicting actions. Prospective and beginning teachers
may not be aware of these deep seated beliefs and should be encouraged
to make them explicit, to challenge their soundness, and to replace them,
when needed, with professional knowledge and understandings.

Our challenge as teacher educators is to engage future special educators in experiences that will guide them in making explicit their beliefs
and understandings about the role of the teacher in advancing children's
social learning. A wide range of experiences might be included in the
preparation program. For example, as they progress through the program, teacher candidates could write and re-write a philosophy of education statement or a position paper regarding teaching and learning for
the purpose of examining their beliefs and how they change over time.
Teacher educators could provide teacher candidates with realistic school
situations to consider and reflect upon to allow them to articulate and
make explicit their beliefs about schooling and the role of the teacher.
And, teacher candidates can view videotapes of themselves teaching for
the purpose of identifying their actions and describing the beliefs about
teaching and learning that guided their actions.

Describing belief structures is only the first step, however. Teacher candidates must then examine them through multiple lenses. Such lenses
would include the profession's standards, empirically based evidence from
the field, theoretical perspectives, competent professionals' wisdom of
practice, and evidence from their own practice in their field placements. It

is critical that prospective teachers begin to see beyond their own perspectives and experiences, particularly in special education, where learners' experiences are quite different from prospective teachers' experiences. To see beyond one's own perspective, one needs to have a clear understanding of his or her own beliefs about teaching and learning.

Replace the "Sink or Swim" Model With Support and Guidance. The initial year of teaching can be challenging, intimidating, and confusing. Nationally, 22% of all new teachers leave the profession in the first 3 years (Darling-Hammond, 1997). Dissatisfied first-year teachers are exiting the profession in record numbers and leaving a significant portion of the teaching force with little professional experience. The exodus contributes significantly to the critical shortage of teachers.

Where beginning teachers have received support during their first years of teaching, attrition has been dramatically arrested (Colbert & Wolf, 1992; Odell & Ferraro, 1992; Williams & Bowman, 2000). Receiving support, however, is the exception, not the rule. Even though 21 states have established teacher-induction programs and some 5 more are planning initiatives, nearly 50% of beginning teachers still do not participate in anything more substantive than brief school orientations (DePaul, 2000). In the information age where increasingly people are members of teams, working collaboratively and pooling their knowledge, it is striking that a teacher in one classroom often has no idea what the teacher in the next classroom is doing. In special education, the situation is often exacerbated by the fact that there may be only one special educator in the school. This isolation not only denies a new teacher the chance to improve performance by learning from experience, but also fosters a debilitating isolation that leads to stress and burn-out (Cochran-Smith & Lytle, 1999a; Lieberman, 2000; McLaughlin & Talbert, 1993).

Early attempts at supportive induction were little more than an orientation to the school building and indoctrination into the bureaucracy by the building principal (Wilkinson, 1994). Subsequent research efforts disclosed an array of problems frequently encountered by beginning teachers that focused on relational, cultural, logistical, and organizing dilemmas (Veenman, 1984). As a result, induction programs have been structured to assist beginning teachers in solving common first-year problems.

As our knowledge of the needs of beginning teachers accumulates, it is clear that support must move beyond merely survival and into the realm of continued professional growth and development. Although social support that ameliorates the demands and stresses experienced by beginning teachers is necessary, it is not sufficient. The professional support needed to advance their knowledge and skills is even more critical (Field, 1994). This is especially pertinent to beginning special educators who are expected to demonstrate knowledge and abilities across a wide age range of students, across multiple areas of exceptionality, and across various learning settings (resource room, general classroom, etc.). In Illinois, for example, current special educators are eligible to teach students in Grades K through 12 in the specialty area in which the teacher is certified. New legislation (effective 2002) may result in a licensure structure that makes special educators eligible to teach students ranging in age from 3 years to 21 years, all areas of exceptionality (with the exceptions of hearing impairment, visual impairment, and speech or language disorders), and all levels of severity. The breadth and depth of knowledge required for this work demands extensive continued professional studies in the initial years of teaching.

Summary

The special education community is confronted with conflicting demands regarding the recruitment, preparation and retention of a quality teaching force. On the one hand, there is a national movement to provide every student with a qualified, caring teacher who is well prepared to advance students' learning. On the other hand, the critical shortage of teachers, especially in specialty areas like learning disabilities, is causing districts to hire less-than-qualified teachers to fill classrooms.

A first step in addressing the need to educate and retain qualified teachers is to identify the minimum standards for beginning special educators. This review indicated that the Council for Exceptional Children's standards include specific knowledge and skill statements pertaining to the social and emotional dimensions of learning disabilities. Issues of social cognition, social competence, motivation, language in social contexts, assessment of social functioning, instructional approaches that advance social and emotional learning, and other dimensions are reflected in the Common Core standards and in the Specialized Standards for teachers of students with learning disabilities.

To prepare individuals well and to create conditions that promote retention, three features of teacher preparation programs were highlighted. Teacher preparation programs need to be focused on the central tasks of teaching. They need to engage prospective teachers in identifying and framing classroom problems, drawing on knowledge from multiple sources to manage instances of teaching and learning, enhancing and recombining that knowledge when necessary, and conducting inquiries into one's own practice to continue to learn *from* teaching. This approach is in contrast to a common conception of teacher learning that supports an "application of theory to practice" or the "enactment of technical skills" (Lampert & Ball, 1998). The proposed conception of teacher learning fosters preparation that is better aligned with the complexities of classroom teaching and the moment-to-moment decision-making required of teachers.

Another important feature of programs is to place prospective teachers at the center of programs and not to ignore the knowledge, beliefs, and images of teaching, schooling and learning that they bring with them. They come to their studies with strong images and beliefs about good teaching, how learning happens, who learns, and what knowledge is of worth. These beliefs are powerful and prospective teachers need to identify their biases, make them explicit, and examine them against theoretical perspectives, research-derived knowledge, and the wisdom of practice. When programs take a knowledge in practice perspective and keep prospective teachers at the center of the educational experience, the knowledge and abilities that are attained and the disposition to learn from teaching are more easily "transferred" to the initial years of teaching.

The frequency with which beginning special educators are supported and guided during the initial year of teaching and the nature of that interaction are critical in influencing novices' abilities to expand their understandings of teaching and to enhance their professional development. Given the wide range of knowledge and abilities that special educators must demonstrate, it is critical that teacher educators continue to work with beginning special educators beyond entitlement to the certificate and into the first years of teaching. Additionally, the support novices receive, or lack thereof, has an impact on their level of satisfaction with their chosen profession and their willingness to remain in teaching. For these reasons, the special education community must design and offer ways to support and guide those entering the profession—those who are prepared to work in the complicated and exciting world of the classroom.

REFERENCES

Andrew, M. (1990). The differences between graduates of four-year and five-year teacher preparation programs, *Journal of Teacher Education*, *41*(3), 45–51.

Andrew, M., & Schwab, R. L. (1995). Has reform in teacher education influenced teacher performance? An outcome assessment of graduates of eleven teacher education programs. *Action in Teacher Education, 17*, 43–53.

Ashton, P., & Crocker, L. (1986). Does teacher certification make a difference? Florida *Journal of Teacher Education, 3*, 73–83.

Association of Teacher Educators (1986). *Visions of reform: Implications for the education profession*. Reston, Virginia: Author.

Bennett, N., & Carre, C. (1993). *Learning to teach*. London: Routledge.

Bryan, T. (1974). Peer popularity of learning disabled children. *Journal of Learning Disabilities, 7*, 621–625.

Bryan, T. (1998). Social competence of students with learning disabilities. In B. Y. L. Wong (Ed.), *Learning about learning disabilities*. New York: Academic Press.

Burden, P. R. (1986). Teacher development. In W. R. Huston, M. Haberman, & J. Sikula (Eds.), *Handbook of research on teacher education* (pp. 311–328). New York: Macmillan.

Calderhead, J., & Robson, M. (1991). Images of teaching: Student teachers' early conceptions of classroom practice. *Teaching and Teacher Education, 7*(1), 1–8.

Carnegie Task Force on Teaching as a Profession. (1986). *A nation prepared: Teachers for a 21st century.* Washington DC: Carnegie Forum on Education and the Economy.

Cochran-Smith, M., & Lytle, S. L. (1999a). Relationships of knowledge and practice: Teacher learning in communities. In A. Iran-Nejad & P. D. Pearson, *Review of Research in Education* (pp. 249–305). Virginia: American Educational Research Association.

Cochran-Smith, M. & Lytle, S. L. (1999b). The teacher research movement: A decade later. *Educational Researcher, 28*(7), 15–25.

Colbert, J. A., & Wolf, D. E. (1992). Surviving in urban schools: A collaborative model for a beginning teacher support system. *Journal of Teacher Education, 43*(3), 193–199.

Council for Exceptional Children. (1996). *What every special educator must know: The international standards for the preparation and certification of special education teachers.* Reston, Virginia: Council for Exceptional Children.

Darling-Hammond, L. (1992). Teaching and knowledge: Policy issues posed by alternative certification for teachers. *Peabody Journal of Education, 67*(3), 123–154.

Darling-Hammond, L. (1997). *The right to learn.* San Francisco: Jossey-Bass.

Darling-Hammond, L. (2000). How teacher education matters. *Journal of Teacher Education, 51*(3), 166–173.

Darling-Hammond, L, Wise, A. E., & Klein, S. R. (1995). *A license to teach: Building a profession for 21st-century schools.* San Francisco: Westview Press.

DePaul, A. (2000). *Survival guide for new teachers.* U.S. Department of Education, Office of Educational Research and Improvement, Washington, DC.

Dietz, M. (1998). *Changing the practice of teacher education: Standards and assessment as a lever for change.* Washington, DC: AACTE.

Donahue, M., & Bryan, T. (1983). Conversational skills and modeling in learning disabled children. *Applied Psycholinguistics, 4,* 251–278.

Elias, M. J., Zins, J. E., Weissberg, R. P., Frey, K. S., Greenberg, M. T., Haynes, N. M., Kessler, R., Schwab-Stone, M. E., & Shriver, T. P. (1997). *Promoting social and emotional learning: Guidelines for educators.* Virginia: Association for Supervision and Curriculum Development.

Farmer, T. W., & Farmer, E. M. Z. (1996). Social relationships of students with exceptionalities in mainstream classrooms: Social networks and homophily. *Exceptional Children, 62,* 431–450.

Feiman-Nemser, S. (1983). Learning to teach. In L. Shulman & G. Sykes (Eds.), *Handbook of teaching and policy* (pp. 150–170). New York: Longman.

Field, B. (1994). The new role of the teacher: Mentoring. In B. Field & T. Field (Eds.), *Teachers as mentors: A practical guide* (pp. 63–77). London: Falmer.

Fetler, M. (1999, March 24). High school staff characteristics and mathematics test results. *Education Policy Analysis Archives, 7* [Online] Available: http://epaa.asu.edu.

Fuller, E. J. (1999). *Does teacher certification matter? A comparison of TAAS performance in 1997 between schools with low and high percentages of certified teachers.* Austin: Charles A Dana Center, University of Texas at Austin.

Goodlad, J. (1994) *Educational renewal: Better teachers, better schools.* San Francisco: Jossey-Bass.

Griffin, G. (1999). *The education of teachers.* Chicago: The National Society for the Study of Education.

Holt-Reynolds, D. (1992). Personal history-based beliefs as relevant prior knowledge in course work. *American Educational Research Journal, 29*(2), 325–349.

Holmes Group. (1986). *Tomorrow's teachers.* East Lansing, Michigan: Author.

Kantrowitz, B., & Wingert, P. (2000). *Teachers wanted.* Newsweek, October 2, pp. 37–42.

Koeppen, K. E., Huey, G. L., & Connor, K. R. (2000). Cohort groups: An effective model in a restructured teacher education program. In D. J. McIntyre & D. H. Byrd (Eds.), *Research on effective models for teacher education* (pp. 136–152). Thousand Oaks, CA: Corwin Press.

Lampert, M., & Ball, D. (1998). *Mathematics, teaching, and multimedia: Investigations of real practice.* New York: Teachers College Press.

Lieberman, A. (2000). Networks as learning communities: Shaping the future of teacher development. *Journal of Teacher Education, 51*(3), 221–227.

Lortie, D. C. (1975). *Schoolteacher: A sociological study.* Illinois: University of Chicago Press.

McIntyre, D. J., & O'Hair, M. J. (1996). *The reflective roles of the classroom teacher.* Boston: Wadsworth.

McLaughlin, M. W., & Talbert, J. W. (1993). *Contexts that matter for teaching and learning.* Palo Alto, CA: Context Center on Secondary School Teaching.

National Board for Professional Teaching Standards. (1988). *Toward high and rigorous standards for the teaching profession.* Detroit: Author.

National Commission on Teaching and America's Future. (1996). *What matters most? Teaching for America's future.* New York: Teachers College, Columbia University.

Nevarez-La Torre, A., & Rolon-Dow, R. (2000). Teacher research as professional development. In D. J. McIntyre & D. H. Byrd (Eds.), Research on effective models for teacher education (pp. 78–96). Thousand Oaks, CA: Corwin Press.

Odell, S. J., & Ferraro, D. P. (1992). Teacher mentoring and teacher retention. *Journal of Teacher Education, 43*(3), 200–204.

Pavri, S., & Monda-Amaya, L. (2001). Social support in inclusive schools: Student and teacher perspectives. *Exceptional Children, 67*(3), 391–411.

Pearl, R., & Bryan, T. (1994). Getting caught in misconduct: Conceptions of adolescents with and without learning disabilities. *Journal of Learning Disabilities, 27,* 193–197.

Sanders, W. L., & Horn, S. (1998). Research findings from the Tennessee Value-added Assessment System data-base: Implications for educational evaluation and research. *Journal of Personnel Evaluation in Education, 12*(3), 227–235.

Sanders, W. L., & Rivers, J. C. (1996). *Cumulative and residual effects of teachers on future academic achievement.* Knoxville: University of Tennessee Value-Added Research and Assessment Center.

Schon, D. (1987). *Educating the reflective practitioner: Toward a new design for teaching and learning in the professions.* San Francisco, CA: Jossey-Bass.

Shin, H. S. (1994). *Estimating future teacher supply: An application of survival analysis.* Paper presented at the annual meeting of the American Educational Research Association, New Orleans, LA.

Shulman, L. (1987). Knowledge and teaching: Foundations of the new reform. Educational Researcher, *15*(2), 4–14.

Sindelar, P., & Rosenberg, M.S. (2000). Serving too many masters: The proliferation of ill-conceived and contradictory policies and practices in teacher education. *The Journal of Teacher Education, 51*(3), 188–193.

Strauss, R. P., & Sawyer, E. A. (1986). Some new evidence on teacher and student competencies. *Economics of Education Review, 5*(1), 41–48.

U.S. Department of Education (1998). *20th annual report to congress on the implementation of the individuals with disabilities education act.* Washington, DC: Author.

Veenman, S. (1984). Perceived problems of beginning teachers. *Review of Educational Research, 54*(2), 143–178.

Wilkinson, G. A. (1994). Support for individualizing teacher induction. *Action in Teacher Education, 16*(2), 52–61.

Williams, D. A., & Bowman, C. L. (2000). Reshaping the profession one teacher at a time: Collaborative mentoring of entry-year teachers (pp. 173–187). In D. J. McIntyre & D. M. Byrd (Eds.), *Research on effective models for teacher education*. Thousand Oaks, CA: Corwin Press.

Zeichner, K., & Tabachnick, B. (1982). The belief systems of university supervisors in an elementary student teaching program. *Journal of Education for Teaching, 8*, 34–54.

Chapter 8

Parental Understanding of Children With Language/Learning Disabilities and Its Role in the Creation of Scaffolding Opportunities

C. Addison Stone
University of Michigan

Kathleen Bradley
Jordi Kleiner
Northwestern University

Scholars and educational practitioners interested in helping children with language and learning disabilities (L/LD) have understandably focused their primary energies on identifying learning challenges and opportunities for these children in school settings. However, the premise of this chapter is that a richer appreciation of these issues can be obtained by a simultaneous focus on the family. Children with L/LD are often first identified as such in the formal educational setting, and intervention programs are centered on that setting. However, as the literature on multicultural issues in special education has made abundantly clear, family dynamics constitute an essential backdrop against which to view educational issues (Harry & Kalyanpur, 1994). In addition, the developmental psychology literature highlights the role of routine parent–child interactions in the child's development of strategic behaviors such as planning, remembering, and categorizing (Rogoff, 1990) and in the development of coping behaviors such as delay of gratification and attributions for success and failure (Maccoby & Martin, 1983). These dynamics are no less important in the case of children with L/LD, regardless of their cultural or economic background or their specific disability. Indeed, a strong case can be made that parental understanding and support for children with atypical developmental patterns is a particularly important prerequisite for the child's successful adaptation to challenge.

Early research on the family context of children with L/LD painted a somewhat pessimistic picture of parents' attributions and expectations (e.g., Bryan, Pearl, Zimmerman, & Matthews, 1982; Chapman & Boersman, 1979; Owen, Adams, Forrest, Stolz, & Fisher, 1971; Sigel, McGillicuddy-De Lisi, Flaugher, & Rock, 1983; Wulbert, Inglis, Kriegsmann, & Mills, 1974; for reviews, see Bryan, 1991; Stone & Conca, 1993). Although some authors reported few, if any, group differences, the majority of the authors concluded from their results that the parents of children with L/LD had lower expectations for their child's future success. In addition, these parents more often attributed child success to luck and child failure to low ability, or exhibited patterns of interaction characterized by greater directiveness and reduced opportunities for child learning.

These conclusions were quite sobering; however, they were based on a still-emerging research base. Also, with the benefit of hindsight, we can identify significant conceptual and methodological shortcomings in many of the early studies. For example, appropriate comparison groups were not always available, and some of the tasks that were used have been criticized as unrepresentative of everyday situations (Schneider & Gearhart, 1988; Stone & Conca, 1993). In addition, parental interaction patterns were often studied without an eye to the child's preceding and subsequent activity, and in isolation from the parallel research on broader parental perceptions and expectations. Finally, data speaking directly to the validity of the implied long-term consequences of reduced parental perceptions and interaction patterns were not available. As a result, these early conclusions about the potential implications of observed patterns of parental perceptions and interactions should be considered with caution.

Clearly, there is a need for a new look at the issues raised by this literature. A significant number of new studies have been conducted. In addition, it is possible to view this work on parent–child interaction with an eye to broadening the picture by integrating work on parental beliefs and perceptions. Parental perceptions of their children's capabilities and needs undoubtedly play a role in shaping parent–child interaction. In addition, parents' beliefs about causal influences on development, and their beliefs about causes and consequences of disabilities, have also been cited as shaping interaction patterns. Yet these issues were largely ignored in earlier research. In this chapter, we hope to highlight such interactive influences on the developing child with L/LD. Our goal for the chapter is to review recent research regarding the extent to which the parents of children with L/LD provide an optimally supportive interactive environment for their children's early learning and development within the context of the broader issues of parental perceptions and beliefs. Our major focus is on parents' perceptions of their child's needs and on the nature of the parental guidance provided in potential learning situations. Because of the availability of earlier reviews, we concentrate primarily on studies published since the 1990's. Our hope is that this review contributes to the development of a richer, multidimensional understanding of the needs and opportunities for enriching the learning of children with L/LD.

A FRAMEWORK FOR CONSIDERING PARENTAL INFLUENCES ON THE CHILD WITH L/LD

In our comments about the early research on parental influences on the child with L/LD, we alluded to the need to consider multiple, interactive factors. Indeed, patterns of parent–child interaction must be viewed in the context of parental perceptions of the child's needs, while, in turn, these perceptions must be viewed in the context of how they influence family dynamics. At a broader level, both parental perceptions and patterns of interaction must be considered within a sociocultural context regarding conceptions of appropriate child activities, education, and the role of experience in learning.

Stratton (1988) provided a useful discussion of these interactive influences. As a family systems theorist, Stratton placed greater emphasis on family members' conceptions of self and other (e.g., the parents' views of failure or disability) and on their implicit 'decisions' regarding how to behave in particular situations than he did on the role of parent–child interactions in fostering or hindering the development of a child's cognitive–linguistic skills. Still, his discussion provided a good feel for the complex, mutually influential dynamics involved.

The dynamics at issue in a comprehensive account of parental influences on children's learning are illustrated in Fig. 8.1, which is adapted from a figure in Stratton (1988). The multiple arrows in the diagram suggest the complex, bi-directional nature of the dynamics involved in the types of parent-child interactions to be discussed below. The darker arrows represent causal pathways that we assume to be particularly important. It is these pathways that are the primary focus of our discussion in the following pages.

As the complexity of the diagram suggests, we feel, as do many others (e.g., Schneider & Gearhart, 1988), that the focus on any one piece of the whole in isolation from the others is inherently limiting, and potentially distorting. Nonetheless, we found it necessary to take such an approach in the early sections of this chapter. This approach was dictated in part by the need to simplify the discussion, but it was necessitated in large part by the nature of the existing literature, which often considered one piece of the overall set of issues in isolation. Thus, we discuss in turn the literature on parent–child interactions, followed by the literature on parental per-

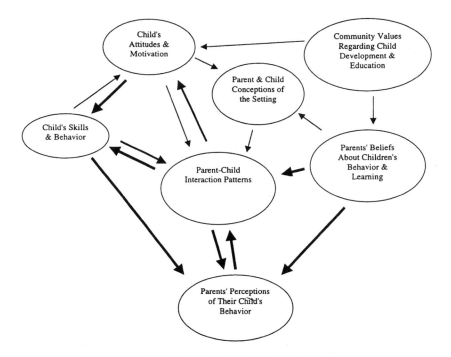

FIG. 8.1. Parental perceptions and interactions in context.

ceptions. As we emphasize in our final discussion, however, the conclusions of each individual section should be considered in reference to each other, as well as in the broader context of parental belief patterns.

PARENT–CHILD INTERACTIONS INVOLVING CHILDREN WITH L/LD

Teaching interactions between a child and parent play a primary role in many current theories of children's early cognitive and linguistic development. Different elements of such interactions have been examined, depending upon researchers' theoretical orientations and the developmental domain in question. The literature on language learning, for example, has explored the impact of semantically contingent replies (e.g., Lasky & Klopp, 1982; Nelson et al., 1984) or syntactic expansions or recasts (Conti-Ramsden, Hutcheson, & Grove, 1995), whereas sociocultural studies have addressed the internalization or 'appropriation' of patterns of adult guidance (e.g., Rogoff, 1990). As is generally the case, research with the L/LD population has lagged behind the literature on parent–child interactions with normal populations, but studies including atypical learners have uncovered important dimensions of communication, such as maternal directiveness, which potentially impact the development of all learners.

With the inclusion of atypical populations come a number of methodological issues. The first is the question of the appropriate contrast group in comparative designs. Research teams have compared children with L/LD to chronologically age-matched normally developing children, to younger normally developing children matched by cognitive or language skills, or to other disability groups. Each of these choices has both advantages and shortcomings, and the choice must be made with careful attention to the questions at hand (Conti-Ramsden, 1994; Schneider & Gearhart, 1988). As a complement to group-comparison designs, recent studies have begun to examine subgroups within the target population, such as children with LD who have a discrepancy between verbal and performance IQ versus those who exhibit no such discrepancy (Poikkeus, Ahonen, Narhi, Lyytinen, & Rasku-Puttonen, 1999), or children with communication delays identified as 'responders' or 'nonresponders' to remediation (Sigel, 1998).

The methodology for examining the interactions between children with L/LD and their parents varies widely across studies. Settings range from free-play tasks in the literature on language learning to more structured problem-solving tasks in the scaffolding literature. Most designs are cross-sectional in nature, but there is an increased interest in follow-up studies (Sigel, 1998), and some noteworthy studies have utilized prospective longitudinal designs (Menyuk, Liebergott, & Schultz, 1995; Scarborough & Fichtelberg, 1993). The value in measuring evolving interactions and children's development over time is the possibility of unraveling the complex causal relationship between hypothesized interactive anomalies and delayed skill development.

The units of analysis used in studies of parent–child interaction vary widely. Recent methodologies have favored coding semantic and pragmatic features of both parents' and children's moves in efforts to capture the transactional nature of linguistic and teaching interchanges (Rasku-Puttonen, Lyytinen, Poikkeus, Laakso, & Ahonen, 1994; Wertsch, McNamee, McLane, & Budwig, 1980). In the language development literature, there has been a shift from examining structural elements of language (e.g., sentence length, type of sentence) to more pragmatic, discourse and conversational aspects of input (Menyuk et al., 1995).

The last decade of research on parent–child interactions with atypical learners has focused primarily on four themes: maternal directiveness, the "communicative clarity" of parents' speech when interacting with their children, the cognitive "demands" of parents' questioning strategies, and the contingent scaffolding of activities in the child's zone of proximal development. In the following sections, we consider each of these themes in turn.

Directiveness

Since the 1970s, one of the consistent findings of research on typical and atypical development is that parents of atypical learners are more directive than parents of age-matched normally developing children (Marfo, 1990). Greater directiveness was originally proposed as one source for children's language delay. For example, longitudinal studies of 1-year-olds revealed that the frequency of maternal imperatives (e.g., "Look here!" "Push it this way!") was negatively correlated with children's gains in syntactic development (Furrow, Nelson, & Benedict, 1979; Newport, Gleitman, & Gleitman, 1977).

In contrast to the early interpretations of the implications of directiveness, a number of recent discussions have suggested that greater directiveness may be appropriate or even beneficial for the needs of many atypical learners. Directiveness has been found, for example, to be correlated with the mental age of a child, regardless of the presence of a disability (Marfo, 1990). In this context, directiveness has been seen as an appropriate way in which to compensate for many atypical learners' unresponsiveness and lack of engagement (Schneider & Gearhart, 1988; Siegel, Cunningham, and van der Spuy, 1985). Parents' directive moves have also been discussed in terms of "conversational buffering" (Bryan, Donahue, Pearl, & Herzog, 1984; Stanhope & Bell, 1981). Because many atypical learners are less adept at initiating and sustaining control of conversations with their parents (Bryan et al., 1984), parents are often left with the seeming need to take more conversational turns, to elicit nonverbal responses ("Give me the red piece"), or to shift their child's attention to the task at hand, in order to avoid a break down of the conversation. In support of the hypothesized functional need for directiveness, directive questions have been found to elicit more responsiveness in children with mental retardation who showed low responsiveness in general to mothers' questions (Liefer & Lewis, 1984).

Recently, the notion of maternal directiveness has also become more differentiated in the literature, due to the realization that the term encompasses many different behaviors (Marfo, Dedrick, & Barbour, 1998). One such differentiation is that directiveness is an independent dimension from insensitivity (Marfo, 1990). Whereas directiveness can be understood as parents' degree of control in an activity, sensitivity is an index of parental awareness of the child's needs. Marfo and Kysela (1988) found, for example, that mothers of children with mental handicaps issued two times as many instructions to their children as did mothers of chronological age matches and mental age matches; however, they showed equal degrees of responsiveness to the child's gestures and visual attention, and equal amounts of imitation and positive reinforcement.

Directiveness has also been conceptualized as having both attentional and behavioral dimensions (Marfo et al., 1998). It is difficult to make general statements about the effect of each dimension because they may well serve different roles depending on the nature of the child's disability (e.g., ADHD vs. SLI) or age (Landry, Smith, Swank, & Miller-Loncar, 2000). However, parents' behavioral directives ("throw the ball") are generally seen as providing needed structure within an on-going stream of behavior, whereas attentional directives ("Look over here") are seen as potentially interrupting the child's on-going focus (Marfo et al., 1998). Akhtar, Dunham, and Dunham (1991) found, for example, that mothers' attentional directiveness at their child's age of 1;1 was negatively correlated with the child's vocabulary development at 1;10, but mother's behavioral directiveness was positively correlated with the same measure. This suggests that mother's directiveness can be beneficial when it follows and does not disrupt the child's current focus.

Together, the foregoing studies demonstrate the importance of differentiating directiveness and sensitivity, as well as the attentional and behavioral components of directiveness. In doing so, these studies highlight the adaptive relevance of parental directiveness when it is properly operationalized. This work is a welcome refinement of the earlier unidimensional emphasis on directive behavior as inherently counterproductive. However, it does not obviate the need for greater understanding of the frequency and consequences of parental directiveness.

Communicative Clarity

Parental communication that contains a high proportion of semantic or pragmatic errors may impede the transmission of meaning from parent to child. Language containing disruptions, inconsistencies, or ambiguous references could serve as a poor language model, or it could leave the child with an unclear focus of attention. Such interaction patterns have been found in several studies to occur significantly more often for parents of children with L/LD. Ditton, Green, and Singer (1987), who were the first to report such evidence, argued that repeated interactions of this sort can lead to a pattern of communication with others in which the child would be unassertive and less likely to request clarification for ambiguous messages.

In a more recent study, Rasku-Puttonen et al. (1994) examined mothers' speech to their children with or without LD on a Rorschach card arrangement task. Mothers of children with LD provided less orientation to the task, less-accurate descriptions of the cards and their location, and less overall information. Despite the incomplete or inaccurate input, the children with LD did not request more clarification than controls of the ambiguous statements (a finding that echoes earlier findings of Donahue, Pearl, & Bryan, 1980). Rasku-Puttonen et al. (1994) interpreted their findings in terms of an interactional framework in which children's language problems negatively impact the clarity of parents' communication, as well as the reverse.

To pursue this hypothesis, the same research team (Poikkeus et al., 1999) re-analyzed the data, comparing two subgroups of the LD children: those with significantly weaker Verbal than Performance IQ scores (VIQ < PIQ) and those with similar scale scores (VIQ = PIQ). The authors found that children in the low VIQ group were less successful on the task, and that their mothers exhibited less communicative clarity. An interesting interaction effect revealed that mothers of the low VIQ children used less communicative clarity in a "dialogue" condition (in which mothers and children were free to converse) than in a "monologue" condition (in which children could not respond to their mother's comments), whereas the opposite pattern was found for the VIQ = PIQ group. Thus, the opportunity for feedback regarding the effectiveness of their communications appeared to aid the parents in the VIQ = PIQ group, but may have resulted in even less effective interactions for the children with lower VIQ.

Although the findings in studies of communicative clarity have been generally accepted, there is much debate regarding the interpretations of such findings. One possible explanation is that parents' entrenched maladaptive patterns of communication create a suboptimal learning environment for the child (Green, 1989). It is also possible, however, that the communication challenges of children with L/LD disrupt parental communication patterns (Poikkeus et al., 1999), or that both parents and children share the same genetically based linguistic difficulties (Leonard, 1998; Poikkeus et al., 1999). The resolution of this issue must await further research. Although the issue of causality cannot be resolved, these findings do suggest the presence of greater communicative anomalies in parent–child interactions for children with language-learning weaknesses, compared to the interactions involving children with other types of learning disabilities.

Cognitive Demands of Parents' Directives

Another dimension of the parent–child interactions involving children with L/LD relates to the cognitive demands of parents' directives. In general, parents of children with L/LD have been found to be less demanding

than parents of age-matched controls in terms of the abstraction and reasoning solicited from their children. This phenomenon was initially documented with parents of "communicationally handicapped" (CH) children
on book reading and paper-folding tasks (Pellegrini, Brody, & Sigel,
1985). Both the mothers and fathers of 60 4-year-old children with diagnosed language or communication disorders were videotaped as they assisted their child with the two tasks. The interactions were coded in terms
of number of interaction turns, frequencies of questions, verbal structuring, nonverbal structuring, verbal emotional support, and the cognitive
demand of each parental utterance. These interactions were compared to
those of parents with their normally developing children, matched for age
and socioeconomic status (SES). Although the findings varied somewhat as
a function of parent gender and task, the parents of the CH children spent
longer at the activities, engaged in more interactive turns, asked more questions, and used an interaction style characterized by lower cognitive demands (labeling, describing, demonstrating). In contrast, the parents of the
normally developing children engaged in less activity management and
made significantly more medium (comparisons, sequences, classifications)
and high (evaluations, cause–effect, transformations) cognitive demands.

A more recent study by another research team revealed a similar pattern in a sample of children identified as LD. Lyytinen Rasku-Puttonen,
Poikkeus, Laakso, and Ahonen (1994) asked mothers of 30 8 to 11 year-
old children with LD and 30 age-matched children without LD to teach
their children five pseudo foreign-language words in a simulated home-
work task. The two groups of children attended the same schools, and the
groups were matched on SES. Despite the comparability of backgrounds,
the teaching strategies for the two groups of mothers differed significantly. Mothers of the children with LD were more likely to ask the child
to look at the word, repeat it, and recite it from memory. In contrast, the
control mothers sought associations between words, linked the words to
the child's environment, constructed narratives with the words, and used
them in playing a game. The authors also examined variation of maternal
style within the LD group and found differences between those mothers
who used more high-level (conceptual) strategies and those who used
more low-level (perceptual) strategies. They found that mothers using the
high-level strategies were rated as showing involvement in the task, ex-
pressing more emotion and cooperation, and smiling more during the
task. The children receiving this pattern of guidance learned significantly
more words.

Although not involving children diagnosed as L/LD, a study by Donahue and Pearl (1995) reported similar characteristics in the interactions
of preterm and full-term preschool children and their mothers. Donahue
and Pearl asked the mother–child dyads to negotiate which snack they

wanted as a reward for participating in an earlier activity. The mothers of the preterm children utilized the interaction as an occasion to teach the names of the snack options with relatively little elaboration. In contrast, the mothers of the full-term preschoolers were more likely to emphasize reasoning in considering the options. These findings are all the more striking if one considers the fact that the two groups of children did not differ on a battery of cognitive and language measures. Such differences in maternal teaching style suggest that children identified as at risk, like those identified as L/LD, may be exposed to less cognitively challenging linguistic interchanges with their mothers than are typical learners. We return later to consider alternative explanations for these findings.

Analyses of Contingent Support for Children With L/LD

Although the foregoing studies highlight a potentially important set of interaction patterns differentiating parents of children with and without L/LD, there are two notable shortcomings of many of these studies. First, they do not address possible changes in the teaching dynamic that unfold as the session progresses. Second, these studies have not evaluated the appropriateness of the parents' teaching strategies by linking them directly to indices of the child's task success. One way of assessing the appropriateness of parents' demands on their children is to code the behaviors of the child and determine the contingency of parents' moves to the child's successes and setbacks.

The contingency of parents' support for children's learning has been addressed in increasing depth in terms of the metaphor of "scaffolding" (Wood, Bruner, & Ross, 1976). Based on the theoretical notion of Vygotsky's (1978) zone of proximal development, this approach examines instructional interactions in terms of several components. The most important component of a scaffolded interaction is that of *contingency*, or the extent to which parents follow the child's failure with a more helpful or directive move, and the child's success with the gradual withdrawal of support. A second component is that of *microgenetic development*, by which parents take increasingly less responsibility as the activity progresses. A third critical component of scaffolding is the implicit notion of *interdependence of participants*. Neither the child nor the parent is entirely responsible for the scaffolding that takes place; rather, each individual move (M) is intricately reliant on their partner's previous move (P), and their own previous move (M-1), which was, in turn, affected by their partner (P-1), and so on.

Recent empirical work has demonstrated the potential utility of scaffolding analyses for describing interactions with atypical learners. Levine (1993), for example, analyzed interactions between mothers and their developmentally delayed 3-year-old children as they attempted to put shoes away in pairs. Levine defined a hierarchy of parental moves ranging in level of explicitness. He then defined parental moves as scaffolding consistent or inconsistent, depending on their relation to the child's successful or unsuccessful previous move. Scaffolding-consistent moves were more than twice as frequent as scaffolding-inconsistent moves, suggesting sensitivity to the child's activity; however, more than half of the parents' moves were at the same level of explicitness as the preceding move, and were therefore presumed by Levine to underchallenge the child. Levine concluded that the mothers did not take advantage of opportunities to link their actions to the child's prior knowledge or to the overall goal of the activity. Unfortunately, no control group was included in the study, so there is no reference point for drawing a conclusion regarding the typicality of such parental behavior in the specific task setting.

A second study of the scaffolding of atypical learners was an analysis of mothers and their children with specific language disorders (Wertsch and Sammarco, 1985). Both the target children and age-matched peers worked with their mothers to copy a model of an airport scene. In examining who was responsible for the placement of the pieces, Wertsch and Sammarco (1985) found that mothers of the children with language disorders took more responsibility than the comparison mothers. The interactions involving children with language disorders included briefer chains of mothers' contingent assistance, and the mothers more often placed the pieces themselves. Wertsch and Sammarco argued that by aborting the sequence of assistance, the mothers of children with language disorders were providing less contingent instruction and offering fewer opportunities for the child to take responsibility for the task.

The studies by Levine and by Sammarco and Wertsch are the only ones to date utilizing the full features of the scaffolding paradigm to analyze the interactions of parents and children who exhibit atypical cognitive or linguistic development. However, a number of additional studies have made use of the specific notion of contingent responses in studies of parent–child interaction in this population. A series of studies by Conti-Ramsden and colleagues (Conti-Ramsden, 1990; Conti-Ramsden et al., 1995), for example, provides evidence regarding possible short-comings in the contingency of parental responses to the utterances of their children with language impairments. In an initial study, Conti-Ramsden (1990) observed mothers interacting with their preschool children during a free-play activity. The results indicated that mothers of children with language impairments provided fewer "recasts" (i.e., syntactic rephrasings) of the utterances than did the mothers of younger normally developing children at the same level of language development (as indexed by mean length of utterance). Such a finding suggests that the mothers of children with language impairments may be missing opportunities to provide their children with contingent models of more complex syntax. Conti-Ramsden et al. (1995) replicated this finding and extended it to a comparison of interactions between mothers of their language disabled child and those same mothers' interactions with the target child's younger normally developing sibling. This design feature of the study allowed the authors to demonstrate a within-parent contrast in the frequency of contingent recasts. The same mothers used more recasts with their younger, normally developing child than they did with the older sibling with language impairments, who was at the same level of language development and thus seemingly equally poised to benefit from the recasts.

In contrast to the findings from the studies by Levine, Sammarco, and Wertsch, and Conti-Ramsden, another set of studies suggests that parents of children with L/LD do modify their assistance to their children's needs. In general, the analyses in these studies focus less on group comparisons in the frequency of specific interaction patterns and more on the correlations between measures of the child's skills or task success and measures of the parents' interaction patterns. In a study involving the same families of 4-year-old children studied in Pellegrini et al. (1985; described earlier), Pellegrini, McGillicuddy-De Lisi, Sigel, and Brody (1986) focused on those characteristics of parents' behavior that best predicted the child's task engagement. On a book-reading task, the engagement of the CH children was best predicted by low-level parental demands, whereas the engagement of the age-matched comparison children was best predicted by high-level demands. The authors interpreted these findings as evidence that the low-level demands of the parents of the CH children were actually appropriately attuned to the child's needs.

McGillicuddy-De Lisi (1992) reached similar conclusions in a study involving 44 families consisting of a 6-year-old child with CH (called here the "target" child) as well as an older sibling. The data from these families were compared to data from a matched set of 42 families containing a normally developing target child. Both mothers and fathers were asked to read two books with the target child, and each parent's contributions to the interactions were coded along three dimensions, including level of cognitive demands. The results showed that the target child's abilities (vocabulary and nonverbal reasoning) were a significant predictor of mothers' and fathers' frequency of use of low-level cognitive demands for children with CH; however, there was only limited evidence of such a relation for the normally developing children. In addition, in the families of the normally developing children, the abilities of the older sibling were a better predictor overall of mothers' interaction style with the younger, target child than were the abilities of the target child him or herself, suggesting that the mothers were applying a generic "scheme" for assisting young children, a scheme acquired while raising the older child. In contrast, only the target child's abilities predicted maternal behavior in the families with a CH child, suggesting that these mother's behaviors were fine-tuned to their child's specific needs, rather than merely following a generic scheme. The authors interpreted their findings as indicating that the parents' interactions were sensitively attuned to the needs of the CH child.

As this summary indicates, the research on the contingency of parents' interactions with atypical learners presents a mixed picture. In some studies, these parents appear to be less contingent than parents of normal controls; in other studies, parental interactions seem appropriately attuned to the child's cognitive–linguistic needs. The inconsistencies may be due in part to the heterogeneity of the population and in part to the methodology employed by the researchers. Studies including subgroups of disabilities (e.g., Poikkeus et al., 1999; Sigel, 1998) may hold promise for identifying specific interaction patterns. In addition, comparison of multiple methods for measuring "contingency" in the same dataset may serve to highlight differential sensitivity of the measures. Unfortunately, work in this tradition is still limited, and the volume of studies does not yet exist to reach a clear conclusion. The preliminary findings do, however, appear to justify the need for more studies using the notion of contingency of parental support.

The Challenges of Teaching Interactions Involving Children With L/LD

We have proposed four elements that distinguish the interactions of parents and their children with L/LD. Relative to the parents of age-matched, normally developing children, the parents of children with L/LD are more directive, exhibit reduced communicative clarity, use lower-level teaching strategies, and are potentially less contingent in their scaffolding. Our earlier discussions have, in part, explained these differences in terms of the additional challenge of interacting with atypical learners. Maternal directiveness is more common with children who are less responsive and initiate fewer exchanges (Schneider & Gearhart, 1988). Also, parents' lower levels of communicative clarity are found more commonly in interactions with children who have a significantly lower Verbal IQ than Performance IQ (Poikkeus et al., 1999), suggesting the possibility that these children's own communications are less clear regarding their understanding or needs. Finally, parents' lower-level questioning strategies are at least partially appropriately fine tuned to maintain their children's involvement (Pellegrini et al., 1986).

As the summary suggests, the recent research on parent–child interactions serves in part to reinforce the conclusions of earlier research. However, it also serves to highlight the need for continued analyses of the contingent nature of the pattern of interactions evident in families with children exhibiting L/LD. In addition, there is a need for greater understanding of the role of parents' perceptions and beliefs regarding the child's needs. This latter issue is the focus of the following section.

PARENTAL ESTIMATIONS, EXPECTATIONS, AND ATTRIBUTIONS

The greater demands of interacting with children exhibiting atypical patterns of language and cognitive development suggest that parents of such children must be particularly sensitive to the needs and performance levels of their children. Is there evidence for unique patterns of perceptions and expectations on the part of parents of children with L/LD? In this section, we review evidence relevant to these issues. The following studies fall into two broad categories: those focused on parents' estimations of their child's skills and their expectations for the child's future performance, and those focused on parents' assumptions regarding the reasons for their child's performance.

Parental Estimations and Expectations

Some of the earliest work in the LD field on parental perceptions was conducted by Tanis Bryan and her colleagues. These early studies suggested that parents of children with LD tended to have lower expectations for their children than did the parents of their normally achieving peers. Bryan et al. (1982) found that these lower expectations were evident across assessments of parents' direct estimations of the child's current strengths and weaknesses, parents' evaluations of their child's skills relative to those of his or her peers, and parents' predictions for future performance. These findings are notable because the children in this study had not been identified as LD by their schools, and thus the parents' perceptions were not influenced by the existence of a special education label. Alternatively, it is, of course, possible that the parents had been influenced by their children's classroom teachers. We return to this issue at a later point.

It is important to note that the findings of Bryan et al. (1982) were similar to those of other researchers (Chapman & Boersma, 1979; Hiebert, Wong, & Hunter, 1982). Consistent with this pattern, Epstein, Berg-Cross, and Berg-Cross (1980) found that parents of children with LD were more likely to underestimate their child's performance on an academic task when compared to that same parent's estimate of the academic performance of a normally achieving sibling. It is important to note, however, that early research did not always support this pattern. For example, Adelman, Taylor, Fuller, and Nelson (1979) found that parents of children with LD tended to *over*estimate their child's ability levels in academic areas when compared to teachers' ratings.

By the mid to late 1980s, a sufficient number of studies had been undertaken to allow a systematic examination of the relative "accuracy" of parental perceptions of students with disabilities. Achenbach, McConaughy, and Howell (1987) performed a meta-analysis, comparing the correlations between ratings of parents, other observers, and the children themselves. Looking across disability groups (emotional disorders, mental retardation, learning disabilities), the researchers found the highest correlations between the ratings of similar observers or informers, such as two parents ($r = .60$), while the ratings across informer groups, such as parent and teacher, tended to have a lower correlation ($r = .28$). The lowest correlations were found between the children's self-ratings and those of any other informer group ($r = .22$), although children and parents showed a slightly higher correlation ($r = .25$). The results suggested that parental perceptions of the skills of their child are not in line with the perceptions of other adults or of the children themselves.

Stone and his colleagues conducted several studies of parents' estimations of children's skills in the school-aged and adolescent years. Boynton-Hauerwas and Stone (2000) analyzed parents' estimations of the language skills of their 5- to 7-year-old children. Twenty-six children had been diagnosed with specific language impairment (SLI), with an additional 60 children serving as control subjects. Parents were asked to rate their child's language in eight areas, using the children's peers as a comparison group. Judgments of accuracy were made by comparing the parental responses to both teacher ratings and standardized test results. When the parent ratings were compared to those of the teachers, the parents of normally achieving children were found to overestimate their children's language ability level. This pattern echoed Miller's (1988) findings from a review of the literature on parental estimations of the language and cognitive skills of their normally developing children. On the other hand, parental ratings of children with specific language impairment were lower than those of the children's teachers. Although this difference was not statistically reliable, the existence of a trend toward *under*estimation reflected the findings from earlier studies showing parents of children with LD as more negative in their ratings. In addition, the parent ratings of the normally achieving children correlated significantly with standardized test results, whereas the parent ratings of the target children did not. In contrast to these indications of less accurate perceptions, however, the parents of children with language disorders were found to be *more* accurate than parents of normally achieving peers from the perspective of comparisons to actual test performance of their children. Thus, the picture with respect to parental accuracy was mixed.

Stone (1997) asked 26 ninth- to twelfth-grade students with LD, their parents, and their teachers to rate the student in 21 academic, social, and sociomotivational skill areas. Similar to the study described earlier for elementary school-aged children, parents' ratings were lower than teachers' ratings on 17 of the 21 skills (although significantly so in only 5 areas). The adolescents were generally the most optimistic appraisers of their skills, showing significantly higher assessments than their parents in 11 of the skill areas. Despite this discrepancy between adolescent and parent ratings, the family members demonstrated a high correlation across skill areas in relative ratings, suggesting strong agreement regarding the student's *relative* strengths and weaknesses ($r = .8$). A similar set of findings was evident in a more recent study involving the parents of 50 adolescents with LD and a similar number of normally achieving students (Stone & May, in press).

Since 1985, then, studies have shown that parents' ratings of their children with L/LD have tended to be lower than those of the parents of normally developing children. In addition, those studies allowing such a comparison have also found parents' ratings of children with L/LD to be lower than the child's self-ratings or the teacher's ratings as well. One exception to this pattern was reported by Hadley and Rice (1992). These authors compared parent and teacher ratings of the language skills of preschool children with ($N = 20$) and without ($N = 14$) SLI. In this study, the parent ratings were significantly higher than the teacher ratings for both child groups.

One important question raised by the studies just summarized relates to the accuracy of the parental ratings. Unfortunately, the data with respect to this issue are far from clear, as is highlighted by the findings of Boynton-Hauerwas and Stone (2000). An interesting perspective on the potential implications of lowered parental perceptions for students with LD was provided by Feagans, Merriwether, and Haldane (1991). These authors investigated how the perceptions of mothers regarding "desirable" and "undesirable" qualities in children in general related to their evaluation of their own child. Participants in the study were 63 families of grade school students with LD, who were matched on age, gender, and race with a family of a student without LD; students were followed over a 3-year period. Mothers were asked to identify their candidates for the five most-favored and five least-favored child characteristics. Later in the study, the mothers were asked to rate the degree to which their own child possessed the selected characteristics.

The authors assumed that children would show a "poor" fit in the family when the undesirable behaviors they displayed were the very ones that their mothers found particularly unacceptable. Results indicated that students, both with and without LD, who evidenced a "poor fit" displayed more problem behavior in the classroom and had lower academic performance over the 3 years covered by the study. Additionally, children who were both LD and a poor fit showed significantly more off-task behaviors in school than any of the other groups. Therefore, it would appear that a mismatch between maternal perceptions and child characteristics might serve to exacerbate the learning disability.

A study by Patrikakou (1996) provided another perspective on the implications of parental expectations for students with LD. The author used an existing database from the National Education Longitudinal Study, a study of approximately 5,000 adolescents and their families, which included a group of 269 adolescents self-identified as LD. Using path analysis, Patrikakou predicted student achievement using a model that included student–family descriptors; parental involvement, communications, and expectations for academic achievement; the student's perceptions of the parent variables; and student self-concept, effort, and expectations for academic achievement. In separate analyses, the model accounted for approximately 70% of the variance in achievement for both the students with LD and their peers. Student expectation for academic success was one of the most robust predictors of achievement for both student groups. Additionally, the student's perception of parental expectations showed an indirect effect, and parental expectations showed a significant effect (as did student expectations). Moreover, the effect of parental expectations was strong enough that path analysis showed not only an effect on the student's perceptions of parental expectations, but also a direct effect on the student's perceptions themselves, and on the student's self-concept as well. The impact of these results on student achievement was evident even after controlling for prior achievement. Although large database studies may lose some of the precision of subject identification and measurement that are possible in smaller studies, this study does serve as an initial step toward tying parental perceptions and expectations to subsequent student performance.

As the studies described in the preceding paragraphs make clear, one crucial question regarding the evidence of lowered parental expectations and perceptions for children with L/LD relates to the impact of such perceptions on the child. One possibility is that such perceptions and expectations may be self-fulfilling, resulting in adverse effects on students' self-beliefs and future performance. An alternative possibility is that such perceptions may allow the child to set realistic goals for both short-term and long-term performance. Careful research regarding such consequences is sorely needed.

Parental Attributions

A second aspect of parental perceptions that has been investigated in the
LD literature relates to parents' explanations for their child's difficulties.
Pearl and Bryan (1982) provided the seminal research to document that,
like children with LD themselves, the parents of children with LD displayed a maladaptive attribution pattern with respect to academic performance. In a study of children with LD and their mothers, the researchers
demonstrated that mothers tended to attribute their children's successes
to luck rather than ability, while viewing their child's failures as due to lack
of ability (Pearl & Bryan, 1982). These results were replicated by Bryan et
al. (1982) and others (e.g., Lewis & Lawrence-Patterson, 1989; see review
by Bryan, 1991).

Other researchers have explored the determinants or consequences of
the attribution patterns of the parents of children with LD regarding their
child's performance. In one such study, Dembo and Vaughn (1989) explored the role of parental observations of the child's performance on
their explanations for their child's success and failure. The authors compared the attributions of mothers of school-aged children with LD who
either watched their child perform two tasks (one academic, and one nonacademic) or were merely informed of the results of the child's performance. There were no differences between mothers who were present or ab-
sent during the tasks with respect to their attributions for the child's
success; however, mothers who actually saw their children fail on the tasks
were more likely to assume that their child had not tried as hard. Although
mothers' attribution of failure to lack of effort appears to suggest the
mothers believed that greater success may be within the child's control, a
second finding suggests the need for caution. The mothers in the viewing
condition rated their child's future performance as *lower* than did the
mothers who were not observing. Thus, mothers' presence during their
child's seemingly poor performance on a task may have a negative influence on their perceptions regarding future performance.

Dohrn, Bryan, and Bryan (1993, in Dohrn & Bryan, 1998) conducted a
10-week intervention study with parents of students with LD. In the context of a family math activity, one group of parents was instructed to provide only strategy statements to their child; the second group was asked to
provide causal attribution statements related to ability and effort in response to accurate student responses, while responding with comments
about the need to try alternative strategies in response to inaccurate responses. The researchers found that mothers in the attribution plus strategy group viewed their children as improving more, not only on academic
measures but in social skills and behavior as well. Children in the attribu-

tion plus strategy group were also more likely to view their successes as re-lated to ability or effort. These findings suggest a direct link between pa-rental attributions and the child's own attributions. Such a link is often assumed to exist, but direct causal evidence for such a link is still meager.

Some authors have argued that parental attributions regarding their child's difficulties may also have an impact on the parents' future efforts to aid their child. Green (1989), for example, has discussed the potential im-plications for parents who felt that the academic progress of their child with LD was not under their control. Green hypothesized that in such cases the parents would be prone to feelings of helplessness and failure, possibly transmitting those attributional patterns of helplessness to their children. Although it was not focused specifically on families with LD, a re-cent study by Reimers, Wacher, Derby, and Cooper (1995) provided evi-dence of just such a link between parental attributions and parents' will-ingness to help their child. Looking at families of students with behavior problems, Reimers et al. (1995) found that parents who attributed their child's behavior problems to intrinsic child factors were reluctant to invest in behavioral treatments for their children. These results, similar to those of the Dembo and Vaughn (1989) study, suggest a link between parental attributions and expectations for future performance, and hence, poten-tially, an impact on future interaction patterns. Similar research focused on the parents of children with LD has promise to help us understand par-ents' readiness to help their child, both directly and indirectly through ad-vocacy efforts.

PARENTAL INTERACTIONS AND PERCEPTIONS
IN A BROADER CONTEXT

In the preceding sections, we have attempted to provide an overview of re-search findings regarding the perceptions, expectations, and interaction styles of the parents of children with L/LD. Given the nature of the exist-ing literature, we found it necessary to treat the various issues in relative isolation. However, as we stressed in the introduction to this chapter, we feel that these issues must eventually be considered in a more inclusive framework, such as that sketched in Fig. 8.1. Such a framework should look not only at how parental perceptions and behavior interact with each other, but also at how they are situated within a broader context. In this section, we return to these integrative issues, both to contextualize the findings summarized above and to assist us in identifying unresolved is-sues that should be the focus of future research.

Interplay of Parental Perceptions and Behavior

In our review of research on parent–child interaction, we identified general patterns in the interaction styles demonstrated by the parents of children with L/LD as they attempted to assist their children with complex activities. In doing so, we noted the on-going controversy regarding the appropriateness of the unique patterns of structure and challenge evident in the behaviors of these parents. This issue of appropriateness centers in large part on the question of whether parental interactions are accurately calibrated to the child's needs. This question, in turn, raises the issue of the accuracy of parental perceptions of their child. With few exceptions, however, this latter issue has been addressed in relative isolation from questions regarding interaction patterns.

Similarly, findings on parental perceptions, expectations, and attributions regarding their child's skills are often discussed in terms of the potential impact of such perceptions on the child's future progress without consideration of how that impact is mediated. As we suggested earlier, one important mediating link in this chain may be the degree of parental motivation to seek assistance for their child. However, another potentially important mediating link is the role of parental perceptions in guiding on-going interactions with their child.

Unfortunately, we have relatively little information about how parental perceptions and expectations influence interaction patterns, or about how patterns of interaction lead parents to insights regarding their child's skills and needs. The studies by Pellegrini et al. (1986), and McGillicuddy-De Lisi (1992) discussed before, plus a study by Donahue, Pearl, and Herzog (1997) discussed shortly are an important start in this direction. The findings in all of these studies suggest that the interaction patterns of the parents of children with L/LD, although "directive" and relatively low in cognitive demand, are attuned to the child's current task needs. However, these conclusions are based on correlations among summary measures of child and parent behavior, and they should be verified with direct analyses of the moment-by-moment contingency of parental assistance.

The Impact of Belief Structures on Parental Perceptions and Behavior

Although the relation between parental perceptions and behavior represents an important piece of the puzzle, this relationship must be considered in a yet broader context, a context that considers how such dynamics impact, or are impacted by, the set of beliefs by which parents and children live. Issues such as attributions are related to broader assumptions about disability and the social institutions that intersect with the family in providing care for people with disabilities.

Whether parents view disability as malleable, for example, and therefore responsive to special care, can vary widely with cultural background (Danesco, 1997). Additionally, the attributions that parents make regarding the cause of the disability may affect the adjustment and well-being of the parent (Mickelson, Wroble, & Helgeson, 1999; Shapp, Thurman, & DuCette, 1992), which in turn may influence patterns of parent–child interaction. The potential influence of parental beliefs regarding children's learning and development on family interactions is evident in two recent studies involving children with L/LD. Sigel (1998), in a 5-year follow-up of 78 of the 120 children involved in his research group's original study of CH and normally developing children (Pellegrini et al., 1985), reported that the parents of the CH children ($N = 38$) were significantly more likely to express a belief in children as passive learners, and in need of more explicit direction and control. These findings mirrored unpublished findings from the total sample in the original study (Sigel et al., 1983). Unfortunately, the relationships between parents' beliefs and their interaction styles were unclear.

A second study of the influence of parents' beliefs on interaction patterns was reported by Donahue et al. (1997). This study involved a subset of the mother–child dyads participating in an earlier study by Donahue and Pearl (1995; described earlier). Donahue et al. (1997) found that mothers' beliefs that a child's early experiences can effect positive change in development did not differ as a function of whether or not the children had been born prematurely ($N = 19$) or at term ($N = 19$). However, in contrast to Sigel's (1998) negative findings, Donahue et al. found that mothers who believed in the power of the environment to influence development asked significantly more questions during the interactions with their child in a referential communication task.

Another potential influence of beliefs on parental treatment of the child relates to parents' readiness to use community resources. Unless parents believe that a disability is amenable to remediation, therapeutic efforts may be hindered. Also, parents must see the locus of control for change as existing not only in the family, but also in professionals and the school system. However, differences in how these authority figures are viewed vary significantly among subcultures. Indeed, some authors suggest that the advocacy expectations for parents inherent in federal law are in conflict with the beliefs and values of some parents, potentially leading to low participation rates or ineffective communication with school personnel (Danesco, 1997; Kalyanpur, Harry, & Skrtic, 2000).

CONCLUSIONS AND QUESTIONS
FOR THE FUTURE

Our review of research related to the role of parents in fostering cognitive and linguistic development in children with L/LD has led us to some general conclusions regarding the quality of parental interactions and the nature of parent perceptions and beliefs about their child's performance. However, in the process of making sense of these findings, we also find ourselves with a number of questions. In this final section, we highlight the major conclusions cutting across the various issues reviewed in the preceding sections. In addition, we highlight what we see as the most important questions for future research.

Consistent with the conclusions drawn from earlier research, research since 1990 has confirmed that the behavioral patterns of parents when interacting with their children with L/LD can be characterized as more directive than those of the parents of age-matched children. Such parents present their children with fewer cognitive challenges and engage in more perceptually or factually oriented exchanges than do the parents of same-aged peers. In addition, several studies have concluded that the interactions involving children with L/LD contain a greater frequency of incomplete or ambiguous parental directives. Also, there are some indications that parents' efforts at guidance in goal-directed tasks may be less sustained or systematic. The parents of children with L/LD are also less likely to demonstrate the typical pattern of parental overestimation of their child's performance, and to have lower expectations for the child's future performance. Finally, several studies have reported that the parents of these children are less likely to explain their child's successes in terms of ability and are more likely to invoke limitations in ability to explain their child's failures.

It is important, however, to qualify this brief summary in three ways. First, there is considerable variation across studies and across families within the same study with respect to these patterns. Second, this same body of research has pointed to several factors suggesting that this general pattern of interactions and beliefs may be, at least in part, an adaptive adjustment to the child's needs. Parents who are directive are, nonetheless, rated as exhibiting sensitivity to the child's needs, for example, particularly in studies involving children with mental retardation. In addition, parental behaviors have been shown to correlate with reduced level of initiative on the child's part, and thus may represent attempts to sustain the interaction. Third, none of the studies reviewed here includes long-term follow-up data regarding the child's progress, and thus conclusions regarding the functional significance of the parental behaviors cannot be reached.

As this brief summary hopefully makes clear, we have learned a good deal more about parental interaction patterns over the last decade, but we still are a long way from clear conclusions about the role of such parental behavior in fostering or hindering the cognitive and linguistic development of children with L/LD. Thus, although we have made progress in this regard, much more needs to be learned. Indeed, the preceding discussion raises a number of important questions. In the following paragraphs, we highlight some of the more pressing questions.

One unresolved issue relates to the generality of the observed patterns and to possible sources of variability across and within families. Although general trends were evident across studies, the findings reviewed earlier were by no means consistent. Research is needed to establish the extent to which such variability is related to socioeconomic or ethnic status, for example. In addition, we know relatively little about consistency across parents in two-parent families. Studies by McGillicuddy-De Lisi and Sigel (McGillicuddy-De Lisi, 1992; Sigel, 1998) and by Conti-Ramsden et al. (1995) suggested that mothers and fathers may well exhibit different interaction patterns. Finally, there are some indications that family constellation may be an important moderator of parental behavior. Individual studies suggest that birth order (Epstein et al., 1980) and number of children (Sigel, 1998) are related to patterns of parental behavior. These findings need replication, and the reasons for any stable influences need careful analysis.

A second set of questions relates to the need for a finer grained understanding of the factors influencing the patterns of parental behaviors highlighted earlier. Do parental perceptions and expectations play themselves out in interactions, and, if so, how? To what extent are on-going interactions governed by: current or earlier observations of child performance; or explicit or implicit beliefs about the nature of child learning or disability?

A third fruitful set of questions for future research relates to the nature of the on-going pattern of parental interactions that fosters resilience in children with L/LD. Follow-up studies of children with LD who were successful as adults (i.e., felt in control of their lives, accepted their learning disability, and had realistic goals) suggest a key role for parental support (Spekman, Goldberg, & Herman, 1993; Werner, 1993). Receiving practical and emotional support, particularly from supportive parents, has been shown to be a protective factor (Morrison & Cosden, 1997; Werner, 1993). Interestingly, the relative protective importance of these factors may change with the age of the child. Although support may always be a factor, structure in the home environment may be more important through adolescence, and issues such as an internal locus of control may take prominence in adolescence and adulthood (Werner, 1999).

A fourth question relates to the issue of the "realism" of parental perceptions and expectations. Although it is indeed often realistic to acknowledge that a child with L/LD may have reduced academic success, and that the child's failures are, at least in part, related to inherent cognitive or linguistic limitations, such a perspective runs the distinct risk of becoming a self-fulfilling prophecy. On the other hand, unrealistically high expectations may also be counterproductive. Thus, a key question relates to the optimal degree of expectation or challenge necessary to foster positive growth in children with L/LD (Stone, in press).

One final question relates to the nature of the broader contextual factors impinging on the family that may influence parental beliefs and behaviors regarding the child with L/LD. We know nothing, for example, about how school policies and teacher communications with parents influence the parents' assumptions about their child's needs and about appropriate responses to their child's behaviors and expressed needs. How do teachers' conceptions of language and learning disabilities influence parental beliefs and behaviors? How do the special education bureaucracy and procedures color parents' assumptions about their role in their child's learning?

To address questions such as those discussed earlier, we need increased research on the role of parental beliefs and behavior in the lives of children with L/LD, and on the societal context of parental beliefs. Multimethod studies combining interview/questionnaire methodology with fine-grained analyses of parent–child interaction may prove useful in shedding light on such questions. Hopefully, the next decade will provide answers to many of these questions.

REFERENCES

Achenbach, T., McConaughy, S., & Howell, C. (1987). Child/adolescent behavioral and emotional problems: Implications of cross-informant correlations for situational specificity. *Psychological Bulletin, 101*, 213–232.

Adelman, H., Taylor, L. Fuller, W., & Nelson, P. (1979). Discrepancies among student, parents, and teacher ratings of the severity of a student's problems. *American Educational Research Journal, 16*, 38–41.

Akhtar, N., Dunham, F., & Dunham, P. J. (1991). Directive interactions and early vocabulary development: The role of joint attentional focus. *Journal of Child Language, 18*, 41–49.

Boynton-Hauerwas, L., & Stone, C. A. (2000). Are parents of school-age children with specific language impairments accurate estimators of their child's language skills? *Child Language Teaching and Therapy, 16*(1), 73–86.

Bryan, T. (1991). Social problems and learning disabilities. In B. Y. L. Wong (Ed.), *Better understanding learning disabilities* (pp. 195–229). New York: Academic Press.

Bryan, T., Donahue, M., Pearl, R., & Herzog, A. (1984). Conversational interactions between mothers and learning-disabled or nondisabled children during a problem-solving task. *Journal of Speech and Hearing Disorders, 49*, 58–64.

Bryan, T., Pearl, R., Zimmerman, D., & Matthews, F. (1982). Mothers' evaluations of their learning-disabled children. *Journal of Special Education, 16,* 149–159.

Chapman, J. W., & Boersma, F. J. (1979). Learning disabilities: Locus of control and mother attitudes. *Journal of Educational Psychology, 71,* 250–258.

Conti-Ramsden, G. (1990). Maternal recasts and other contingent replies to language-impaired children. *Journal of Speech and Hearing Disorders, 55,* 262–274.

Conti-Ramsden, G. (1994). Language interaction with atypical language learners. In C. Gallaway & B. J. Richards (Eds.), *Input and interaction in language acquisition* (pp. 183–196). Cambridge, England: Cambridge University Press.

Conti-Ramsden, G., Hutcheson, G., & Grove, J. (1995). Contingency and breakdown: Children with SLI and their conversations with mothers and fathers. *Journal of Speech & Hearing Research, 38,* 1290–1302.

Danseco, E. (1997). Parental beliefs on childhood disability: Insight on culture, child development and intervention. *International Journal of Disability, Development, and Education, 44,* 41–52.

Dembo, M., & Vaughn, W. (1989). Effects of mother presence and absence on LD children's and their mothers' causal attributions for performance outcomes. *Learning Disability Quarterly, 12,* 199–207.

Ditton, P., Green, R. J., & Singer, M. T. (1987). Communication deviances: A comparison between parents of learning disabled and normally achieving students. *Family Process, 26,* 75–87.

Dohrn, E., & Bryan, T. (1998). Coaching parents to use causal attributions and task strategies when reading with their children. *Learning Disabilities: A Multidisciplinary Journal, 9*(2), 33–45.

Donahue, M. L., & Pearl, R. (1995). Conversational interactions of mothers and their preschool children who had been born pre-term. *Journal of Speech and Hearing Research, 38,* 1–9.

Donahue, M., Pearl, R., & Bryan, T. (1980). Learning disabled children's conversational competence: Responses to inadequate messages. *Applied Psycholinguistics, 1,* 387–403

Donahue, M. L., Pearl, R., & Herzog, H. (1997). Mothers' referential communication with preschoolers: Effects of children's syntax and mothers' beliefs. *Journal of Applied Developmental Psychology, 18,* 133–147.

Epstein, J., Berg-Cross, G., & Berg-Cross, L. (1980). Maternal expectations and birth order in families with learning disabled and normal children. *Journal of Learning Disabilities, 13,* 273–280.

Feagans, L., Merriwether, A., & Haldane, D. (1991). Goodness of fit in the home: Its relationship to school behavior and achievement in children with learning disabilities. *Journal of Learning Disabilities, 24,* 413–420.

Furrow, D., Nelson, K., & Benedict, G. (1979). Mother's speech to children and syntactic development: Some simple relationships. *Journal of Child Language, 6,* 423–442.

Green, R. (1989). "Learning to learn" and the family system: New perspectives on underachievement and learning disorders. *Journal of Marital and Family Therapy, 15,* 187–203.

Hadley, P. A., & Rice, M. L. (1992). Parental judgments of preschoolers' speech and language development: A resource for assessment and IEP planning. *Seminars in Speech and Language, 14,* 278–288.

Harry, B., & Kalyanpur, M. (1994). Cultural underpinnings of special education: Implications for professional interactions with culturally diverse families. *Disability and Society, 9,* 145–165.

Hiebert, B., Wong, B., & Hunter, M. (1982). Affective influences on learning disabled adolescents. *Learning Disability Quarterly, 5,* 334–343.

Kalyanpur, M., Harry, B., & Skrtic, T. (2000). Equity and advocacy expectations of culturally diverse families' participation in special education. *International Journal of Disability, 47,* 119–136.

Landry, S. H., Smith, K. E., Swank, P. R., & Miller-Loncar, C. L. (2000). Early maternal and child influences on children's later independent cognitive and social functioning. *Child Development, 71,* 358–375.

Lasky, E., & Klopp, K. (1982). Parent–child interaction in normal and language disordered children. *Journal of Speech and Hearing Disorders, 47,* 7–18.

Leonard, L. B. (1998). *Children with specific language impairments.* Cambridge, MA: MIT Press.

Levine, H. G. (1993). Context and scaffolding in developmental studies of mother–child problem-solving dyads. In S. Chaiklin & J. Lave (Eds.), *Understanding practice* (pp. 306–326). Cambridge, England: Cambridge University Press.

Lewis, S. K., & Lawrence-Patterson, E. (1989). Locus of control of children with learning disabilities and perceived locus of control by significant others. *Journal of Learning Disabilities, 22,* 255–257.

Liefer, J. S., & Lewis, M. (1984). Acquisition of conversational response skills by young Down syndrome and nonretarded young children. *American Journal of Mental Deficiency, 88,* 610–618.

Lyytinen, P., Rasku-Puttonen, H., Poikkeus, A. M., Laakso, M. L., & Ahonen, T. (1994). Mother–child teaching strategies and learning disabilities. *Journal of Learning Disabilities, 27*(3), 186–192.

Maccoby, E., & Martin, J. (1983). Socialization in the context of the family: Parent–child interaction. In P. H. Mussen (Series Ed.) & E. M. Hetherington (Vol. Ed.), *Handbook of child psychology: Vol. 4. Socialization, personality, and social development* (4th ed., 1–101). New York: Wiley.

Marfo, K. (1990). Maternal directiveness in interactions with mentally handicapped children: An analytical commentary. *Journal of Psychology and Psychiatry, 31,* 531–549.

Marfo, K., Dedrick, C. F., & Barbour, N. (1998). Mother–child interactions and the development of children with mental retardation. In J. A. Burack, R. M. Hodapp, & E. Zigler (Eds.), *Handbook of mental retardation and development* (pp. 637–668). New York: Cambridge University Press.

Marfo, K., & Kysela, G. (1988). Frequency and sequential patterns in mothers' interactions with mentally handicapped and nonhandicapped children. In K. Marfo (Ed.), *Parent–child interaction and developmental disabilities: Theory, research, and intervention* (pp. 64–89). New York: Praeger.

McGillicuddy-De Lisi, A. V. (1992). Correlates of parental teaching strategies in families of children evidencing normal and atypical development. *Journal of Applied Developmental Psychology, 13,* 215–234.

Menyuk, P., Liebergott, J. W., & Schultz, M. C. (1995). *Early language development in full-term and premature infants.* Mahwah, NJ: Lawrence Erlbaum Associates.

Mickelson, K., Wroble, M., & Helgeson, V. (1999). "Why my child?" Parental attributions for children's special needs. *Journal of Applied Social Psychology, 29,* 1263–1292.

Miller, S. (1988). Parents' beliefs about children's cognitive development. *Child Development, 59,* 259–285.

Morrison, G. M., & Cosden, M. A. (1997). Risk, resilience, and adjustment of individuals with learning disabilities. *Learning Disability Quarterly, 20,* 2–12.

Nelson, K. E., Denninger, M. M., Bonvillian, J. D., Kaplan, B. J., & Baker, N. D. (1984). Maternal adjustments as related to children's linguistic advances and to language acquisition theories. In A. D. Pellegrini & T. D. Yawki (Eds.), *The development of oral and written language in social contexts* (pp. 31–56). Norwood, NJ: Ablex.

Newport, E., Gleitman, H., & Gleitman, L. (1977). "Mother I'd rather do it myself": Some effects and non-effects of maternal speech style. In C. Snow & C. Ferguson (Eds.), *Talking to children* (pp. 109–149). Cambridge, England: Cambridge University Press.

Owen, R. W., Adams, P. A., Forrest, T., Stolz, L. M., & Fisher, S. (1971). Learning disorders in children: Sibling studies. *Monographs of the Society for Research in Child Development, 36*, No. 144.

Patrikakou, E. (1996). Investigating the academic achievement of adolescents with learning disabilities: A structural modeling approach. *Journal of Educational Psychology, 88*, 435–450.

Pearl, R., & Bryan, T. (1982). Mother's attributions for their learning disabled child's successes and failures. *Learning Disabilities Quarterly, 5*, 53–57.

Pellegrini, A. D., Brody, G. H., & Sigel, I. E. (1985). Parents' teaching strategies with their children: The effects of parental and child status variables. *Journal of Psycholinguistic Research, 14*, 509–521.

Pellegrini, A. D., McGillicuddy-De Lisi, A. V., Sigel, I. E., & Brody, G. H. (1986). The effects of children's communicative status and task on parents' teaching strategies. *Contemporary Educational Psychology, 11*, 240–252.

Poikkeus, A. M., Ahonen, T., Narhi, V., Lyytinen, P., & Rasku-Puttonen, H. (1999). Language problems in children with learning disabilities: do they interfere with maternal communication? *Journal of Learning Disabilities, 32*, 22–35.

Rasku-Puttonen, H., Lyytinen, P., Poikkeus, A. M., Laakso, M. L., & Ahonen, T. (1994). Communication deviances and clarity among the mothers of normally achieving and learning disabled boys. *Family Process, 33*, 71–80.

Reimers, T., Wacher, D., Derby, K. M., & Cooper, L. (1995). Relation between parental attributions and the acceptability of behavioral treatments for their child's behavior problems. *Behavioral Disorders, 20*, 171–178.

Rogoff, B. (1990). *Apprenticeship in thinking*. New York: Oxford University Press.

Scarborough, H. S., & Fichtelberg, A. (1993). Child-directed talk in families with incidence of dyslexia. *First Language, 13*, 51–67.

Schneider, P., & Gearhart, M. (1988). The ecocultural niche of families with mentally retarded children: Evidence from mother–child interaction studies. *Journal of Applied Developmental Psychology, 9*, 85–106.

Shapp, L., Thurman, S. K., & DuCette, J. (1992). The relationship of attributions and personal well-being in parents of preschool children with disabilities. *Journal of Early Intervention, 16*, 295–303.

Siegel, L. S., Cunningham, C. E., & van der Spuy, H. I. J. (1985). Interactions of language delayed and normal preschool boys with their peers. *Journal of Child Psychology and Psychiatry, 26*, 77–83.

Sigel, I. (1998). Socialization of cognition: A family focus. In M. Lewis & C. Feiring (Eds.), *Families, risk, and competence* (pp. 289–307). Mahwah, NJ: Lawrence Erlbaum Associates.

Sigel, I. E., McGillicuddy-De Lisi, A. V., Flaugher, J., & Rock, D. A. (1983). *Parents as teachers of their own learning disabled children*. Princeton, NJ: Educational Testing Service.

Spekman, N., Goldberg, R., & Herman, K. (1993). An exploration of risk and resilience in the lives of individuals with learning disabilities. *Learning Disabilities Research & Practice, 8*, 11–18.

Stanhope, L., & Bell, R. Q. (1981). Parents and families. In J. M. Kaufman & D. P. Hallahan (Eds.), *Handbook of special education*. Englewood Cliffs, NJ: Prentice-Hall.

Stone, C. A. (in press). Promises and pitfalls of scaffolded instruction for students with language learing disabilities. In K. Butler & E. Silliman (Eds.), *Speaking, reading, and writing in children with language learning disabilities: New paradigms for research and practice*. Mahwah, NJ: Lawrence Erlbaum Associates.

Stone, C. A. (1997). Correspondences among parent, teacher, and student perceptions of adolescents with learning disabilities. *Journal of Learning Disabilities, 30*, 660–669.

Stone, C. A., & Conca, L. (1993). The nature and origins of strategy deficiencies in learning-disabled children: A social constructivist perspective. In L. Meltzer (Ed.), *Strategy assess-*

ment and instruction for students with learning disabilities: From theory to practice (pp. 23–59). Austin, TX: Pro-Ed.

Stone, C. A., & May, A. (in press). The relative accuracy of academic self-evaluations in adolescents with and without learning disabilities. *Journal of Learning Disabilities.*

Stratton, P. (1988). Parents' conceptualization of children as the organizer of culturally structured environments. In J. Valsiner (Ed.), *Child development within culturally structured environments. Vol. 1: Parental cognition and adult–child interaction* (pp. 5–29). Norwood, NJ: Ablex.

Vygotsky, L. (1978). *Mind in society.* Cambridge, MA: Harvard University Press.

Werner, E. (1993). Risk and resilience in individuals with learning disabilities: Lessons learned from the Kauai longitudinal study. *Learning Disabilities Research & Practice, 8,* 28–34.

Werner, E. (1999). Risk and protective factors in the lives of children with high-incidence disabilities. In R. Gallimore, L. Bernheimer, D. MacMillan, D. Speece, & S. Vaughn (Eds.), *Developmental perspectives on children with high-incidence disabilities* (pp. 15–31). Mahwah, NJ: Lawrence Erlbaum Associates.

Wertsch, J. V., McNamee, G. D., McLane, J. B., & Budwig, N. A. (1980). The adult–child dyad as a problem-solving system. *Child Development, 51,* 1215–1221.

Wertsch, J. V., & Sammarco, J. G. (1985). Social precursors to individual cognitive functioning: The problem of units of analysis. In R. Hinde & A. N. Perret-Clermont (Eds.), *Social relationships and cognitive development* (pp. 276–293). Oxford, England: Clarendon Press.

Wood, D. J., Bruner, J. S., & Ross, G. (1976). The role of tutoring in problem solving. *Journal of Child Psychology and Psychiatry, 17,* 89–100.

Wulbert, M., Inglis, S., Kriegsmann, E., & Mills, B. (1974). Language delay and associated mother–child interaction. *Developmental Psychology, 85,* 41–70.

Chapter 9

Bibliotherapy: Practices for Improving Self-Concept and Reading Comprehension

Dheepa Sridhar
Sharon Vaughn
University of Texas

Self-concept can be understood as a person's evaluation of him or herself. It provides an estimate of a person's sense of self and emotional well-being (Haager & Vaughn, 1997). Self-concept is considered an important construct to understand for several reasons. First, it is often viewed as the "window" to a person's happiness and self-satisfaction. We consider individuals with a high self-concept as well adjusted and self-satisfied, whereas those with low self-concept are troubled and in need of support. Furthermore, low self-concept is associated with many negative outcomes including delinquency and drug use (Harter, 1993; Jung, 1994; Kaplan, Martin, & Johnson, 1986), depression (Parker & Asher, 1987), low peer acceptance (Li, 1985; Vaughn, McIntosh, & Spencer-Rowe, 1991), and long-term unhappiness (Bednar, Wells, & Peterson, 1989; Harter, 1993). Thus, there are lots of reasons to consider self-concept an important outcome measure, particularly for students with significant learning problems.

This chapter provides a review of self-concept and intervention approaches used to enhance it. One intervention that has historically been linked to self-concept is bibliotherapy. Its use and application are reviewed as well as modifications to bibliotherapy designed to enhance self-concept and text comprehension.

SELF-CONCEPT

The understanding of self-concept has been refined over the years. It was originally regarded, "as the person known to himself, particularly the sta-

161

ble, important, and typical aspects of himself as he perceives them" (Gordon & Combs, 1958, p. 433). Essential to this view of self-concept is the notion that self-perception is the most relevant view and that self-concept is a unitary construct. However, self-concept is now better understood as a multidimensional construct based on the knowledge that individuals of all ages view themselves differently across various (academic, social, athletic, and so forth) domains of functioning (Vaughn & Elbaum, 1999). Hence, self-concept can vary depending on the specific domain assessed. For example, a person who demonstrates low academic and high athletic achievement may report low academic self-concept but a high self-concept regarding their athletic ability. This refined view of the multiple domains that contribute to self-concept has been an important advance and has provided insight into how an individual's overall self-concept may be high despite low abilities in particular areas (Harter & Pike, 1984).

There is a vast amount of literature regarding the importance of a positive self-concept and the effects of positive and negative self-concept on behavior, academic, and social success. Positive self-concept is associated with peer acceptance, and peer acceptance has been consistently identified as a key factor that distinguishes between students who transition successfully from school to adult life and those who do not (Parker & Asher, 1987). Positive self-concept has also been associated with self-confidence, effective coping, and psychosocial well being (Bednar et al., 1989; Harter, 1993). Conversely, students lacking a positive self-concept are vulnerable to a host of emotional, social, and learning problems (Brendtro, Brokenleg, & Van Bockern, 1990).

Self-concepts are formed based on repeated experiences such as repeated academic successes, or failures. For that reason, although self-concept between domains can vary greatly, that is between academic self-perception and self-perception of physical appearance; within domain self-concept is relatively stable over time (Vaughn & Elbaum, 1999). However, self-concept is influenced by factors such as age, gender, achievement, and physical appearance, which are briefly reviewed next.

Factors Influencing Self-Concept

Although self-concept is recognized as being relatively stable, it is influenced by a number of factors such as age, academic achievement, athletic ability, physical appearance, and so forth. In particular, the following factors influence the formation of students' self-concept: achievement, age, and self-awareness.

Achievement.   Achievement and the individual's perception of achievement is positively related to self-concept. High-achieving students demonstrate a higher self-concept than low-achieving peers (Battle & Blowers,

1982; Chapman, 1988). About 70% of students with learning disabilities (LD) demonstrate lower academic self-perceptions when compared to their non-LD peers (Hagborg, 1996). This is not surprising considering that low academic achievement is the defining characteristic of students with LD. Students with poor academic achievement demonstrate similar self-concepts as average-achieving students when academic achievement is statistically controlled (Oliva, 1990). It is not surprising that interventions designed to enhance self-concept often focus on achievement.

Age. Self-concept is influenced by the comparison group used. Students' self-perceptions are influenced by whom they compare themselves to (Renick & Harter, 1989). Thus, students with disabilities in self-contained special education classes who compare themselves with other special education students are more likely to view themselves more favorably than when asked to compare themselves to other students without disabilities in the general education classroom. This influence of social comparison on self-concept appears to be strong around ages 7 to 8. Although students engage in social comparisons at earlier ages, the influence of these comparisons on self-concept is not as strong (Renick & Harter, 1989; Ruble, 1983).

Students start school with a relatively high self-concept and experience a steady decline until eighth grade (Grolnick & Ryan, 1990; Marsh, 1989; Renick & Harter, 1989). According to Marsh (1989), students' self-concept becomes less positive with time before stabilizing around the preadolescent years.

Self-Perception and Self-Awareness. The over time decline in a students' self-concept during the early years has been attributed to exposure to the skills and abilities of the peer group and the understanding that their abilities compare favorably or unfavorably on specific domains (Marsh, 1989). This understanding requires a certain level of understanding of self. A study of the relationship between self-perception, academic achievement and cognitive development among third and fifth graders indicated a higher correlation between self-perception and achievement among third graders. Third graders who perform academically well, also perceived their ability to be high whereas low achieving students demonstrated a comparatively poor correlation between perception and achievement. However, low-and high-achieving fourth and fifth graders were similarly accurate in their self-perceptions (Bouffard, Markovits, Veneau, Boisvert, & Dumas, 1998).

According to Brown and Dutton (1995), inaccurate self-perception is common and may even be beneficial to the individual. The reasoning is that because low self-perception is associated with a host of negative variables a more positive self-perception, even if inaccurate, may be somewhat of a buffer for the other negative variables associated with low self-perception. Self-perception appears to be influenced by the feedback received from significant others (Baumeister, 1999). For example, 9 and 11 year-old students rated as popular by their peers also rated themselves more positively than students rated as average by peers (Boivin & Begin, 1989). Hence, the feedback students receive from teachers, parents, and peers influences self-concept. This is particularly relevant for teachers whose opinions about students likely influence the student directly and then indirectly by influencing peers in the classroom.

APPROACHES TO ENHANCE SELF-CONCEPT

Because self-concept has been identified as such a critical area of concern, interventions designed to enhance self-concept have been developed, implemented, and evaluated. The majority of such interventions adopt one of two methods: focusing on self-awareness, social development, or academic achievement.

Self-Awareness and Social Development

A number of interventions have attempted to enhance students' self-concept by improving their social skills (Larson & Gerber, 1987; McMahon, Wacker, Sasso, & Melloy, 1994; Wiener & Harris, 1997). Social skills interventions often include a self-awareness component such as cognitive training (role play, self-reflection, behavior contracts) to assist students in changing specific behaviors (Conte, Andrews, Loomer, & Hutton, 1995; Larson & Gerber, 1987; McMahon et al., 1994; Omizo & Omizo, 1988). Although many such studies report significant change in the treatment group, a meta-analysis of the positive effects of social skills training found effects of the training were about two tenths of a standard deviation. Moreover, the control groups responded better in 10% of the studies, thus providing little support for the positive effects of social skills training alone (Kavale & Forness, 1996).

A related issue has been the influence of "setting" on the self-concept of students with LD. By setting, we refer to where the student is taught (e.g., resource room, general education classroom, self-contained classroom) and with who other special education students, a mix of special education and general education students, or mostly general education students. Fundamentally, students with LD are perceived as demonstrating improved social development and ultimately self-concept when taught primarily in the general education classroom with their nondisabled peers

(Madge, Affleck, & Lowenbraun, 1990). Mainstreaming of students in the general education classroom is often assumed to enhance self-concept as students will be exposed to and included with peer models. This exposure is then expected to enhance aspects of social development such as peer-acceptance and self-concept. Although some studies suggest improvements in social functioning and peer-acceptance as a result of placement among typically developing students (Madge et al., 1990) there is no converging evidence to indicate such a conclusion. A 1-year study of 16, second to fourth graders compared the peer acceptance of low-achieving students with that of average-achieving students in a general education setting. Findings indicated that peer acceptance of students with LD and low-achieving students was lower than that of average-achieving students (Vaughn, Elbaum, & Schumm, 1996).

A study conducted by Geyer (1985) suggested that the level of mainstreaming (full vs partial) may have no effect on the self-concept of the students. However, the students in the fully mainstreamed condition reported more positive attitudes toward school than the partially mainstreamed group. The nature of instruction provided in the mainstream classroom and the level of support perceived by the target students might have a greater influence on peer acceptance than mere placement of the student in a specific classroom.

Forman (1988) studied the effects of social support on the self-concept of mainstreamed students with LD. According to this study students with higher levels of perceived social support, particularly from classmates, demonstrated higher self-concept regardless of school placement. Students in this study were either in a resource room or in a self-contained special education setting.

Although the specific benefits of various levels of mainstreaming appears to be controversial, the level of social support perceived by the students, demographics of the classroom, and the nature of instruction in the classroom may be predictors of the effect of mainstreaming on the social functioning of the target students.

Academic Achievement

Achievement in any domain (e.g., academic, athletic, social) contributes to an increase in global self-concept (Kobal-Palcic & Musek, 1998). High-achieving students demonstrate higher self-concepts when compared to average-achieving peers (Montgomery, 1994). Students with a learning disability demonstrate lower academic self-concept than their average-achieving peers, but similar to low-achieving peers without a learning disability (Grolnick & Ryan, 1990; La Greca & Stone, 1990). Because academic achievement plays such a significant role in self-concept the influence of improvement in academic achievement on students' self-concept warrants examination.

Academic achievement has been considered a component in interventions designed to enhance self-concept and social functioning (Fox, 1989; Mesch, Lew, Johnson, & Johnson, 1985; Oscarsson, 1992; Smilon, 1985). A study comparing the effects of a social and an academic intervention on peer acceptance demonstrated significantly increased peer acceptance ratings for students in both treatment groups compared to control groups (Fox, 1989). These findings suggest that both academic and social interventions can be associated with improved outcomes in self-concept. A similar study comparing the effects of social skills training with academic remedial instruction and remedial math or reading instruction reported no significant gain in total self-concept between the groups. However, the group receiving social skills training demonstrated significant gains in social self-concept (Smilon, 1985). The academic self-concept among students in the other two groups was not reported.

Studies that have examined the effects of interventions designed to enhance self-concept often focus exclusively on either academic or social interventions. However, a combination of academic and social interventions may be more effective in enhancing self-concept, particularly among low-achieving students. Bibliotherapy appears to be one such intervention that meets the academic and social needs of students (Sridhar & Vaughn, 2000). In recent years, the effects of bibliotherapy on self-concept and reading and writing (Oscarsson, 1992) or self-concept and text comprehension (Sridhar, 2000) have been studied and present promising results. It is beyond the scope of this chapter to focus on all possible interventions designed to enhance self-concept, so we have targeted bibliotherapy plus text comprehension instruction as one intervention that simultaneously meets social and academic needs of students. Hence, the rest of this chapter focuses on bibliotherapy and the modification of bibliotherapy to include certain validated text comprehension strategies (bibliotherapy+) as means to enhance both reading comprehension and self-concept.

BIBLIOTHERAPY: AN OVERVIEW

Bibliotherapy is the use of books to help people gain insight into their behavior and feelings (Cornett & Cornett, 1980). It has been most often used to enhance self-concept or modify specific behaviors (Cornett & Cornett, 1980). According to Wolverton (1988), bibliotherapy helps solve personal problems through the use of books; develops life skills and improves self-concept while creating a dynamic interaction between readers' personality and literature.

The term bibliotherapy indicates a method of choosing, reading, and analyzing text in which the main characters experience problems similar to those of the readers. Students engage in guided discussions and activities after reading to express their reactions and to engage in problem solving of the challenges faced by the characters (Keats, 1974).

Bibliotherapy underscores the importance of the student's emotional response to literature. Its focus is typically not on checking the student's academic skills per se, but on helping individuals recognize, sort out, and evaluate their emotional responses to the literature (Schlichter & Burke, 1994). The effectiveness of bibliotherapy rests on the mental process experienced by the student. The use of multiple mediums of self-expression such as art (e.g., painting, drawing), dramatization (McCarty & Chalmers, 1997; Pardeck, 1990), and so forth are known to facilitate the student in this process. Multiple mediums of self-expression may be helpful as many students find it easiest to communicate about themselves and their environment through displacement or metaphor, particularly in the form of stories (Gardner, 1971; Mills & Crowley, 1986). Through reading and discussion of selected books, a person can see how others in similar situations as themselves have confronted their problems. Furthermore, a person can see how others have responded to emotions such as anxieties, frustrations, hopes and disappointments, and then apply this insight to real life situations he or she may be facing (McCarty & Chalmers, 1997). A support person such as a teacher, parent, or therapist can help individuals process the book and gain insight into their behavior through discussion (Pardeck, 1990).

THE PROCESSING OF TEXT IN BIBLIOTHERAPY

For bibliotherapy to be effective, the reader needs to progress through the interdependent stages of identification, catharsis, and insight (Afolayan, 1992; Shrodes, 1949). Theoretically the process follows a consistent pattern in which the reader or listener initially senses a common bond with the story's character, and finally, by sharing in the dilemma of the story character, the reader reflects upon personal circumstances and internalizes some of the coping mechanisms (Jalongo, 1983). Features of the three mentioned processes are elaborated next.

Identification

The identification process begins by establishing a relationship between the reader and a story character. This relationship facilitates in expanding the perspective of the reader and helps them view their situations from different perspectives. This process enables the readers or listeners to realize that their situation is not a unique or isolated problem and that others experience or have experienced similar situations. Through identification, individuals are less likely to consider themselves different in a negative manner (Afolayan, 1992). For example, Sarah, a student with a learning disability considered her academic abilities and peer relations negatively. However, while reading and discussing the book "Thank you Mr. Faulker" (Polacco, 1998) Sarah thought, "this character is like me." She realized that her situation is not unique and that other students have had similar experiences.

Catharsis

Following identification with a story character, readers start to relate to the situations and events in the story and begin to experience emotional ties with the characters. Often the reader is able to understand the motives and behavioral options available to the story character (Afolayan, 1992). When readers become emotionally involved, literature may have the effect of purging their emotional status (Cianciolo, 1965). This release of emotions may facilitate the reader to look for solutions to the story character's problem (Nickolai-Mays, 1987), thereby engaging in problem solving of situations similar to his or her own. For example, while discussing the character, events, and solutions in the book Sarah suggested that the character may not be included by peers in games. A discussion of such a situation led to the generation of problem-solving strategies from Sarah and her classmates. Sarah's peers suggested that the character may not participate in games and talk to the other classmates. Sarah mentioned that the character may find it difficult to socialize with her peers and noted that the character was probably ashamed of her academic performance. The group decided that the character needed to talk to her classmates. The group also mentioned that the character was extraordinarily good at certain other things such as drawing. This helped Sarah value her strengths such as drawing.

Insight

At this stage readers become aware that the problems they are experiencing can be changed (Russell, & Russell, 1979). Insight allows the reader to analyze the character and situation, and subsequently develop opinions regarding behaviors adopted by the characters in their attempts to deal with problems. This may help readers critically analyze their own situations and behaviors. As readers place themselves in positions to interpret the decision making and options of the characters in the story, they begin to view themselves in control of the situations in terms of the story outcome. The goal is that the feelings of control and the ability to problem solve will be transferred to the individual's real life situations. Thus, insight may be viewed as maturation from a sense of helpless submission to that of hopeful objectivity (Cornett & Cornett, 1980) with an expanded repertoire of behavioral responses to a given situation. For example, Sarah realized that her peers did not view her as negatively as she had imagined. The solutions generated by the group and Sarah's expanded view of the various events helped her gain new insight into her situation. Awareness of the perceptions and reactions of her peers helped Sarah generate a variety of problem-solving solutions to different situations.

BIBLIOTHERAPY, SELF-CONCEPT, AND ACADEMIC ACHIEVEMENT

A review of research on the effectiveness of bibliotherapy to determine the extent to which it was successful in enhancing self-concept with adults, adolescents, and children (Piercy, 1996) revealed that bibliotherapy yielded a medium effect sizes in enhancing self-concept (Elbaum & Vaughn, in press). See Table 9.1 for a description of various studies. For those studies that had self-concept as an outcome and a comparison sample effect sizes were calculated.

The effects of bibliotherapy in practice can be seen in The Special Education and Treatment Program in Frederick County, Maryland, where bibliotherapy was used with elementary-age students with serious emotional disturbances. This program has demonstrated an increase in academic and emotional development of students (Bauer & Balius, 1995).

A study of the effects of bibliotherapy on self-concept, reading, and writing skills among Haitian students learning English as a second language indicated an increase in reading skills and in the number of words used in written reconstruction of stories. However, there was no change in self-concept (Oscarsson, 1992). Self-concept may have remained stable as the students demonstrated a high self-concept at pre test. Miller (1993) used bibliotherapy specifically to improve reading skills in students. This study used books selected by matching the book to the students based on experiences of the students and the story in the novel. The teacher administered the intervention following the principles of bibliotherapy: The teacher first read the books and marked the material to be read each day; then developed activities that reinforced the concepts covered in the reading for each day, and the students were provided time and opportunity for discussion of the material (Miller, 1993). The results suggested bibliotherapy was effective in motivating adolescent females to read (Miller, 1993).

Study/Participants/ Purpose	Intervention/Books	Outcome Measure/Results	Effect Sizes	Mean Effect Size
Bauer (1977) 32 seventh-grade remedial readers. Intervention conducted for 45-minutes, once a day for two consecutive days. Purpose: To study effects of folk-tales on changing attitudes.	Folk tales at seventh-grade reading level aimed at changing specific attitudes were read silently by the students and aloud by the researcher or teacher followed by a discussion of the story meanings and messages.	Researcher designed attitude measure. Attitude toward parental punishment, advice, greed, selfishness, younger siblings and animals was measured. No significant change in attitude after the intervention.	Mean and SD not provided	
Beardsley (1981) 136 third graders with and without disabilities. Duration of intervention not reported. Purpose: To study effects of selected reading materials on the acceptance of peers with disabilities.	The researcher read selected books to: Group 1 every other day who had contact with students with LD, MR, and PH.	Researcher designed attitude measure. No significant change in attitude after the intervention.	Mean and SD not provided	
Blake (1988) 6 sixth graders with various levels of reading ability. Intervention conducted for 45-minutes a week for six weeks. Purpose: To study effects of bibliotherapy on self-esteem.	Involved individual and group reading of a novel emphasizing consequences of decisions. Events in the novel and the character's behavioral responses were discussed. Personal reactions to the same events and behaviors were drawn from the group.	Culture-Free Self-Esteem Inventory for Children Form A. Students made modest but not statistically significant gains from pre to post test.	Single-Subject design	

(Continued)

DeFrances, Dexter, Leary, and MacMullen (1982) 33 male adolescents with behavior disorders. Intervention conducted for 12 weeks. Purpose: To study effects of bibliotherapy and videotaping on the self-concept in adolescents.	Group 1 received bibliotherapy (group directed reading of school designed personal growth literature emphasizing personal experiences/situation followed by discussion). Group 2 received videotaping (students were taped during regular class sessions and the tape was played back for class review and discussion). Group 3 received bibliotherapy and videotaping (students were videotaped during the therapy and discussion sessions and the video was reviewed and discussed). Group 4 was a no contact control group.	Self Observation Scales (SOS) and Harmony Hill Self-Concept Rating Scale (school designed). No significant differences between the treatment and control groups on the SOS scales. Observable behavioral changes were noted by researchers for all treatment groups.	Mean and SD not provided
Garrett (1984) 108 high school students from the White's institute, IN. Intervention conducted in 45-minute sessions twice a week for 11 weeks. Purpose: To study effects of bibliotherapy on self-concept.	Stories at appropriate age and interest levels relating to an aspect of self-concept were presented to students through reading aloud, films, and tapes. Each story presentation was followed by a discussion structured around areas of interest and concern expressed by students.	The modified Piers-Harris Children's Self-Concept Scale. No significant difference between the groups on global self-concept at post-test. Males showed a significantly higher score on the popularity subscale.	T boys vs C boys= .14 T girls vs C girls= .26 ES= .20

(Continued)

TABLE 9.1
(Continued)

Study/Participants/ Purpose	Intervention/Books	Outcome Measure/Results	Effect Sizes	Mean Effect Size
Green (1988) 44, 10 and 11 year old Mexican-American students. Intervention conducted in 45-minute sessions five times a week for 27 weeks. Purpose: To study effects of bibliotherapy on self-concept.	Students learnt about bibliotherapy and were allowed to read age appropriate books with therapeutic value independently. Teacher read books aloud to students followed by guided discussions relating the content of the books to students' lives and personal problems. Awards were given to students reading and discussing the most. Students also watched bibliotherapeutic films and completed a worksheet discussing each film.	The Piers-Harris Children's Self-Concept Scale, Teacher and Student Rating Scales from the Behavior Rating Profile, and a Sociometric Test from the Behavior Rating Profile. The treatment group demonstrated a significant increase in self-concept at post-test. Treatment group demonstrated significantly enhanced relations with peers.	SD not provided	
Greenwald (1984) 93 sixth graders from general education classrooms. Intervention conducted in 30-minute sessions twice a week for 15 sessions. Purpose: To compare effects of rational emotive education (REE); REE plus rational emotive imagery (REI); and REE plus bibliotherapy on self-concept, responsibility, and anxiety.	Groups 1–3 received REE; REE plus bibliotherapy; REE plus REI respectively. Group 1 learnt that feelings are derived from self-talk, selective perceptions affect emotions, and specific methods for examining maladaptive beliefs. Group 2 received the above intervention and read and answered questions from an age appropriate book. Group 3 received the same intervention as group 1	The Idea Inventory, The Piers-Harris Children's Self-Concept Scale, Intellectual Achievement Responsibility Scale, and the trait scale of the State-Trait Anxiety Inventory for Children. Group 3 was significantly more effective in enhancing rational thinking and self-concept.	The Piers-Harris Children's Self-Concept Scale Group1= comparison1 (CM1) Group2= treatment (T) Group3= comparison2 (CM2) Group4= control (C) T vs CM1 = .57 T vs CM2 = .11 T vs C = .04	ES= .24

Lenkowsky, Barowsky, Dayboch, Puccio, and Lenkowsky (1987) 96 adolescents with LD and emotional handicaps. Intervention conducted in 30-minute sessions twice a week for 15 sessions. Purpose: To study effects of bibliotherapy on self-concept.	plus imagery (visualizing adapting to problematic situations). Group 4 received a mental health program. Groups 1 and 2 received 3 weekly sessions of book report on books of general interest. Group 2 also received one weekly session of discussion about feelings, emotional experiences and school related problems. Groups 3 and 4 had three weekly sessions of reading literature related to problems students with disabilities often face. Group 4 also engaged in a directed weekly discussion.	Piers-Harris Children's Self-Concept Scale. Groups 3 and 4 improved significantly compared to groups 1 and 2. No significant differences between groups 3 and 4.	Group1= control (C) Group2= treatment (T1) Group3=treatment2 (T2) Group4=treatment2 (T3) T1 vs C=. 00 T2 vs C= 1.47 T2 vs T1= 1.43 T3 vs C= 1.91 T3 vs T1= 1.88 T3 vs T2= .56 ES= 1.13
Oscarsson (1992) Elementary age Haitian ESL students. Intervention conducted in 30-minute sessions every school day for 12 weeks. Purpose: To study the effects of Haitian folktales on self-concept, reading and writing skills.	Intervention conducted in 6 steps. 1. researcher read age appropriate, culturally relevant stories to students and discussed it. 2. researcher retold the story acting out each character's role with focus on characters, plot, and story details. 3. students retold the story and engaged in choral reading and self-reflection. 4. students retold the story as a class. 5. students wrote the story and created illustrations. 6. students visited other classes as "storyteller" and shared the story and their books.	Chapter I Informal Reading Assessment. A researcher designed self-concept survey. The quantity of words students used in the written reconstruction of stories. Students enhanced their reading skills and increased the number of words used in written reconstruction of stories. No change in self-concept which was high during both pre and post tests.	Means and SD not provided

(Continued)

TABLE 9.1
(Continued)

Study/Participants/Purpose	Intervention/Books	Outcome Measure/Results	Effect Sizes	Mean Effect Size
Porter (1993) 120 at-risk first graders. Intervention conducted daily for 10 weeks. Purpose: To study effects of bibliotherapy using self-concept related books on academic self-concept and achievement.	Teachers in group 1 read aloud books related to self-concept followed by a 15–20-minute discussion on issues related to self-concept. Teachers in group 2 read aloud books chosen for information or entertainment and discussion did not focus on the self-concept of the students.	Bickley Assessment of Self-Esteem (BASE). The Boehm Test of Basic Concepts-Revised (Boehm-R). Both groups significantly enhanced their academic achievement. No significant differences between the groups on self-concept and interpersonal factors.	SD not provided for the Boehm-R. BASE Group1= treatment (T) Group2= control (C)	ES= .112
Pruett (1980) 183 high school students enrolled in Basic English III classrooms. Duration of intervention not mentioned. Purpose: To study effects of bibliotherapy through adolescent novels in changing attitudes towards self, family, and responsibility.	Students signed a contract to read a minimum of 25 pages a day of adolescent novels related to issues of self-concept, family, and responsibility. Reading time was allowed once a week and students answered study/discussion questions on the main character and his/her problems for each story and answers were discussed along with certain theme-related activities.	The California Comprehensive Tests of Basic Skills, The Family Scale, Acceptance of Self and Others Test, and Attitude Scale for Clerical Workers. No significant differences between treatment and control groups on any measure.	T vs C on attitude towards family= .19 T vs C on self-concept= –.03 T vs C on responsibility= .20	ES= .12
Ray (1983) 233 elementary students reading at the first grade level. Intervention conducted for about five months. Purpose: To study the relation between bibliotherapy, self-concept, reading and general readiness.	Teachers followed instructions from a handbook on bibliotherapy. Teachers read aloud books on self-concept to students, students retold the story, discussions and activities followed retelling.	Stanford Early School Achievement Test and I Feel . . . Me Feel: Self-Concept Appraisal. Treatment group gained significantly in self-concept and in four of the five readiness measures (sounds and letters, word reading, listening to words and stories, and environment).	SD not provided	

Robinson (1980) Five seventh graders with poor reading skills and self-concept. Intervention conducted in 45-minute sessions for a year. Purpose: To study effects of bibliotherapy on self-concept.	Treatment group received a combination of stories focussing on aspects of self-concept and anger, poems, and music. They were expected to identify with the main character and experience catharsis and insight at each session.	Teacher report only. Students realized that they had "some alternatives to their behavioral patterns". Intervention had "helped the students to better accept themselves and their difficulties". Means and SD not provided
Saltzberg (1980) 30 college students with poor self-concept. Intervention conducted once a week for two hours over five weeks. Purpose: To compare the effectiveness of bibliotherapy with rational-emotive group therapy (RET) and bibliotherapy alone on self-concept.	Group 1 received RET along with a bibliotherapy book. Group 2 received RET and placebo bibliotherapy. Group 3 received a prescribed bibliotherapy (read a prescribed book and submitted a weekly progress report on their reading). No information on book selection provided.	The Spielberger State-trait Anxiety Inventory, the Rational Behavior Inventory, the Rotter Internal-External Control Scale, the Es Scale and the Tennessee Self-Concept Scale. No significant differences between the three groups at post-test on any of the measures. Tennessee Self-Concept Scale. Group1=treatment (T1) Group2=comparison (CM) Group3= treatment (T2) T1 vs CM= .14 T1 vs T2= .16 T2 vs CM= .06 ES= .12
Shafron (1983) 98 seventh and eighth graders from remedial reading classes. Intervention conducted in 40-minute sessions everyday for a school year. Purpose: To study the effects of bibliotherapy on self-concept.	Age appropriate books focusing on adolescent development with a therapeutic aspect were either read aloud by teacher or students. Discussion took place throughout reading and after reading with attention to the affective or developmental issues raised by students. Control group received the school curriculum.	Self-Esteem Inventory (SEI), the California Tests of Basic Skills, and the Short Form Test of Academic Ability. No significant differences were found between the groups on any of the measures. SD not provided

(Continued)

TABLE 9.1
(Continued)

Study/Participants/ Purpose	Intervention/Books	Outcome Measure/Results	Effect Sizes	Mean Effect Size
Sheridan (1982) 48 eighth and ninth graders from changing families. Intervention conducted in 12, 45-minute sessions for group 1; 5, 45-minute sessions for group 2; and on an as-needed basis for group 3. Purpose: To compare the effectiveness of group counseling, standard counseling, and in-school bibliotherapy in preventing problems.	Group 1 received structured group counseling with emphasis on trust, catharsis, caring, acceptance, and confidence. Group 2 received bibliotherapy (students were assigned an age appropriate materials [book and video] focusing on changing families followed by a discussion about the book and the video in a group setting). Group 3 received the standard school counseling.	Survey of feelings about treatment, test of knowledge of problems of the changing family, count of behavioral referrals to the assistant principal, students' school attendance, GPA, survey of behavior at home and the Piers-Harris Children's Self-Concept Scale. Groups 1 and 2 felt significantly better about the treatment than the control group. No significant between group differences on self-concept or any other measure.	Group1=comparison (CM) Group2=treatment (T) Group3=control (C) T vs CM= .26 (self-concept) T vs C= .09 (self-concept) T vs CM= .01 (academic achievement) T vs C= −.38 (academic achievement)	ES=.18 ES= −.19
Taylor (1982) 92 students from single-parent families in a kindergarten program. Intervention conducted for six weeks. Purpose: To study effects of bibliotherapy on self-concept.	Treatment group read books focusing on issues of single-parent families during the regular story time. Reading was followed by retelling, discussion, and questioning to facilitate identification with story characters, and introspection followed by activities such as dramatizing stories, making family stories from pictures, and developing stories about family members.	Primary Self-Concept Inventory. Treatment group enhanced self-concept significantly at post-test compared to the control group.	T vs C	ES= 1.45

Study	Description/Purpose	Intervention	Measures/Results	Effect Size
Taylor (1993) 30 low SES Mexican-American families (110 individuals). Intervention conducted for five weeks. Purpose: To study effects of a metaphorical story on self-concept.	Families in the treatment group received 4 weeks of counseling. In the fifth week, a taped metaphorical story focused around issues experienced by most low SES Mexican-American families was played to each of the families. Control group received counseling without the metaphorical story.	The Family Relationship Inventory (FRI). Treatment group adults significantly enhanced self-concept compared to control group. No significant differences were found between children in treatment and control groups.	Means and SD for pre-test scores not provided	ES= .45
Walters (1981) 7 primary age students with neurological impairments. Intervention conducted three times a week for 11 weeks. Purpose: To study effects of bibliotherapy on self-concept.	2 film strips focusing on issues of self-concept and problems students may have encountered from the "who am I" series were shown daily followed by a group discussion for a week. Similar books were read to students followed by a group discussion.	Piers-Harris Children's Self-Concept Scale and The Self-Concept Picture Inventory. No significant differences from pre to post test on either measure. A positive change found on mean individual scores in self-concept.	Piers-Harris Children's Self-Concept Scale Pre-test vs Post-test ES= .74 The Self-Concept Picture Inventory Pre-test vs Post-test ES= .16	
Yellin (1982) 36 second and third grade boys. Intervention conducted in 45-minute weekly sessions for 10 weeks. Purpose: To compare effects of folk fairy tales and issues specific literature in bibliotherapy on self-concept, attitude, and behavior.	Groups 1 and 2 selected any story from the researcher's cassette library and listened to them. After the story, they drew a picture of their most and least favorite parts of the story. Group 1 was provided with a library of folk tales while group 2 was provided with a library of issues specific literature. Group 3 was a no contact control.	The Winnetka Scale for Rating School Behavior and Attitudes, Coopersmith Self-Esteem Inventory, and the Missouri Children's Picture Series. No significant between group differences were found on self-concept, attitude, and behavior.	Coopersmith Self-Esteem Inventory Group1= treatment1(T1) Group2= treatment2 (T2) Group3= control (C) T1 vs C= .05 T2 vs C= .44 T1 vs T2= .58	ES= .25

LD = learning disability; MR = mentally retarded; PH = physically handicapped.

We modified traditional bibliotherapy to include certain validated text comprehension strategies such as accessing prior knowledge, focusing on story grammar features, summarization, and retelling (Sridhar & Vaughn, 2000). This modified bibliotherapy is referred to as bibliotherapy+. The process of bibliotherapy+ and its effects on text comprehension are discussed next.

PROCESS OF BIBLIOTHERAPY+

In this subsection strategies that have empirical support in improving text comprehension are reviewed in order of implementation during bibliotherapy. The process of implementing comprehension strategies as part of bibliotherapy can be divided into three stages: prior to reading, during reading, and after reading. It should be noted that these strategies can be used at all times during the reading process. However, they are presented sequentially depending on when the particular strategy will be introduced and emphasized.

Prior To Reading

A number of studies indicate that: eliciting prior knowledge, formulating questions, and generating predictions based on information in the text and prior knowledge can increase comprehension of text (Gillespie, 1990; Van den Broek, Fletcher, & Risden, 1993). Zwaan and Brown (1996) suggested that the connections among text elements that are formed in working memory are based on a situational model that integrates information from the text with situational information from prior knowledge (Fletcher & Chrysler, 1990). Generating questions and making predictions based on prior knowledge and text can increase reading comprehension (Gillespie, 1990; Gillis, 1990). The effectiveness of each of these three strategies has been extensively documented (Fletcher & Chrysler, 1990; Foley, 1993; Rosenshine & Meister, 1994).

Books in which the main character experiences problems similar to those of the students were selected. Some typical problems experienced by students include low academic achievement, poor peer acceptance, or a specific disability. A brief introduction regarding the main character and some events is first provided to enable students to access their prior knowledge regarding such characters and events. At this stage students begin to identify with the main character, share similar experiences and make predictions regarding the book, character, events, solutions, and outcome. See Table 9.2 for a review of story features that students will focus on. This table can also be used throughout the reading process to write students'

TABLE 9.2

Story Features to Focus on: Thank You Mr. Faulker

Story Features	Prediction (What do you think will happen?)	Verification (What has happened?)	Identification (Are you like that? how?)
1. Who is the story about?			
2. What is different about Trisha?			
3. What are some things that could happen? What are some things that have happened?			
4. How does Trisha feel about himself? Why?			
5. What would Trisha like to be like?			
6. What happens to help Trisha?			
7. In the end, how does Trisha feel about himself?			

predictions, verifications, and so forth. Student generated predictions are written on the form provided in Table 9.2. The specific story features are provided as prompts to remind students of the important elements.

During Reading

During reading, students and teachers use the strategy of generating and answering questions. Through the use of questioning, commenting, and paraphrasing, the teacher supports students as they attempt to construct a theme (Au, 1992; Wong & Jones, 1982; Wong, Wong, Perry, & Sawatsky, 1986).

The teacher could read the book aloud while students follow along with their copy. Students are asked to generate questions and answers, share similar personal experiences, problem solve, and revise their predictions based on new information from the book. About half way through the book, students are asked to retell the story in their own words. The teacher could model this process and answer as many questions as possible.

Throughout the reading process, students infer the emotions of characters based on behaviors. For example, if the text mentions that the character cried, students are asked to infer how the character must have felt. When students share personal experiences such as, "my sister shouted" they could be asked how the person must have felt.

After Reading

After reading, students engage in retelling and discussion of the text and process the text further by incorporating personal experiences and prior knowledge. At this stage students are encouraged to recount relevant personal experiences, respond to other students' comments, generate reasons for various incidents described in the text, and discuss how outcomes can be changed by the characters in the text.

The teacher might model retelling to facilitate students learning and understanding this process. Students could also be prompted (story feature questions could be used as prompts) while retelling during reading. See Figure 9.1 for a representation of a bibliotherapy+ lesson.

CONCLUSION

The importance of self-concept to happiness and life satisfaction is well known. The influence of academic achievement on self-concept has also been supported. However, there is a paucity of interventions that simultaneously meet the academic and social needs of students. Bibliotherapy has

Instructional lesson plan

Name of story:_____ Date:_____

Class/Name of student_____ Age:_____

| Prior to reading | Selection of an age appropriate book where the main character demonstrates problems similar to those of the students. Introduction to the story/main character. | Students make predictions based on the introduction and prior knowledge using table 1. Teacher asks questions to facilitate student predictions. | |

↓

| During reading | Students discuss story events and consequences and share similar personal experiences. Teacher helps students infer emotions of characters based on behaviors. | Students revise predictions using table 1 and based on information from text. | Students retell the story using table 1 and cover as many questions as covered by the reading. |

↓

| After reading | Students discuss the book and share insights and personal experiences. | Problem-solving solutions are generated to specific personal problems shared by students. | Students retell the entire story. They may initially use table 1 till they remember the sequence and information to be included in the retell. |

FIG. 9.1. Representation of a bibliotherapy+ lesson.

been shown to enhance self-concept, change attitudes toward reading, and enhance writing and reading skills. The inclusion of certain validated text comprehension strategies into bibliotherapy (bibliotherapy+) has been shown to enhance text comprehension (Sridhar, 2000) and it could be a viable tool for simultaneously improving self-concept and text comprehension.

Research in this area points to the effects of matching the purpose and characters in books with the needs of students. Books in which the main character is similar to the students, and experiences similar difficulties are typically chosen to help students realize that their problems are not unique. Future research needs to focus on the extent to which matching specific features of books and characteristics of students yields more effective outcomes. The effects of using books in which the main character, although similar to the student, overcomes his or her challenges and leads a successful life needs to be studied. Such books could provide role models for students and may influence self-concept. Although processing the central theme of the story between the teacher and student plays an important role in the bibliotherapeutic process, the way in which this process was implemented varies across research. Hence, effects of specific kinds of discussions (e.g., written answers to questions or generating alternative behaviors to problem events) could be studied along with attention to the duration and intensity of the intervention. We think there are opportunities to capitalize on the characters and stories in text to teach children with learning and behavior problems both ways to interact more effectively with others as well as how to better comprehend what they hear and read.

It is simply not possible to discuss the social functioning of students with learning disabilities without mentioning the seminal work of Dr. Tanis Bryan. Her initial work conducted in the 1970s (Bryan, 1974) was the first empirical work examining the social functioning, peer relations, and adjustment of students with LD. Her ongoing pursuit of better understanding of factors that are associated with the social functioning of students with LD yielded insights that have fueled the work of other researchers and assisted educators and parents in better understanding their students and children. Furthermore, she has been a generous research leader who has assisted others like myself (Vaughn) in identifying questions of importance and providing guidance with our work.

REFERENCES

Afolayan, J. A. (1992). Documentary perspective of bibliotherapy in education. *Reading Horizons, 33*, 137–148.

Au, K. H. (1992). Constructing the theme of a story. *Language Arts, 69*(2), 106–111.

Battle, J., & Blowers, R. (1982). A longitudinal comparative study of the self-esteem of students in regular and special education classes. *Journal of Learning Disabilities, 15*, 100–102.

Bauer, R. C. (1977). *Effects of folktales as bibliotherapeutic aids in changing attitudes of seventh grade remedial readers*. Masters thesis, State University of New Jersey, Rutgers. (ERIC Document Reproduction No: ED 137 728).

Bauer, M. S., & Balius, F. A., Jr. (1995). Storytelling: Integrating therapy and curriculum for students with serious emotional disturbances. *Teaching Exceptional Children, 27*, 24–28.

Baumeister. R. F. (1996). Should schools try to boost self-esteem? Beware the dark side. *American Educator, 20*(2), 14–19, 43.

Beardsley, D. A. (1981). Using books to change attitudes towards the handicapped among third graders. *Journal of Experimental Education, 50*(2), 52–55.

Bednar, R. L., Wells, M. G., & Peterson, S. R. (1989). *Self-esteem: Paradoxes and innovations in clinical theory and practice*. Washington, DC: American Psychological Association.

Blake, S. M. (1988). *The effect of bibliotherapy on the self-esteem of sixth graders*. Masters thesis, Kean college, (ERIC Document Reproduction No: ED 293 101).

Boivin, M., & Begin, G. (1989). Peer status and self-perception among early elementary school children: The case of the rejected children. *Child Development, 60*, 591–596.

Bouffard, T., Markovits, H., Vezeau, C., Boisvert, M., & Dumas, C. (1998). The relation between accuracy of self-perception and cognitive development. *British Journal of Educational Psychology, 68*(3), 321–330.

Brendtro, L. K., Brokenleg, M., & Van Bockern, S. (1990). *Reclaiming youth at risk: Our hope for the future*. Bloomington, IN: National Education Service.

Brown, J., & Dutton, K. A. (1995). Truth and consequences: The costs and benefits of accurate self-knowledge. *Personality & Social Psychology Bulletin, 21*(12), 1288–1296.

Bryan, T. S. (1974). An observational analysis of classroom behaviors of children with learning disabilities. *Journal of Learning Disabilities, 7*(1), 35–43.

Chapman, J. W. (1988). Learning disabled children's self-concepts. *Review of Educational Research, 58*, 347–371.

Cianciolo, P. J. (1965). Children's literature can affect coping behavior. *Personnel and Guidance Journal, 43*, 897–903.

Conte, R., Andrews, J. W., Loomer, M., & Hutton, G. (1995). A classroom-based social skills intervention for children with learning disabilities. *The Alberta Journal of Educational Research, 41*(1), 84–102.

Cornett, C. E., & Cornett, C. F. (1980). *Bibliotherapy: The right book at the right time*. Fastback 151. (ERIC Document Reproduction Service No: 192380).

DeFrances, J., Dexter, K., Leary, T. J., & MacMullen, J. R. (1982, April). The effect of bibliotherapy and videotaping techniques on collective and self-concept formation in behaviorally disordered youth. *Paper presented at the Annual International Convention of the Council for Exceptional Children, Houston*. (ERIC Document Reproduction No: ED 218 885).

Fletcher, C. R., & Chrysler, S. T. (1990). Surface forms, textbases, and situation models: Recognition memory for three types of textual information. *Discourse Processes, 13*(2), 175–90.

Foley, C. L. (1993). Prediction: A valuable reading strategy. *Reading Improvement, 30*(3), 166–70.

Forman, E. A. (1988). The effects of social support and school placement on the self-concept on LD students. *Learning Disability Quarterly, 11*, 115–124.

Fox, C. L. (1989). Peer acceptance of learning disabled children in the regular classroom. *Exceptional Children, 56*(1), 50–59.

Gardner, R. (1971). *Therapeutic communication with children: The mutual storytelling technique*. New York: Science House.

Garrett, J. E. (1984). *The effects of bibliotherapy on self-concepts of children and youth in an institutional setting*. Unpublished doctoral dissertation, Ball State University, Muncie, IN.

Geyer, M. A. (1985). Mainstreaming and its relationship to attitude toward school and self concept among learning disabled adolescents. *Dissertation Abstracts,* AAT 8510386.

Gillespie, C. (1990). Questions about student-generated questions. *Journal of Reading, 34*(4), 250–257.

Gillis, M. K. (1990). *Applying comprehension strategies to K–3 tradebooks.* ERIC Document Reproduction No: 322484.

Gordon, I. J., & Combs, A. W. (1958). The learner: Self and perception. *Review of Educational Research, 28,* 433.

Green, D. A. (1988). *A study of the impact of bibliotherapy on the self-concept of Mexican-American children ten and eleven years of age.* Unpublished doctoral dissertation, University of Northern Colorado, Greeley, Colorado.

Greenwald, E. K. (1984). *Effects of rational emotive education, imagery and bibliotherapy on self-concept, individual achievement responsibility, and anxiety in sixth grade children.* Unpublished doctoral dissertation, Long Island, Hofstra University, NY.

Grolnick, W. S., & Ryan, R. M. (1990). Self-perceptions, motivation, and adjustment in children with learning disabilities: A multiple group comparison. *Journal of Learning Disabilities, 23,* 177–184.

Hagborg, W. J. (1996). Self-concept and middle school students with learning disabilities: A comparison of scholastic competence subgroups. *Learning Disability Quarterly, 19,* 117–126.

Harter, S. (1993). Causes and consequences of low self-esteem in children and adolescents. In R. Baumeister (Ed.), *Self-esteem: The puzzle of low self-regard* (pp. 18–37). New York: Plenum.

Harter, S., & Pike, R. (1984). The Pictorial Scale of Perceived Competence and Social Acceptance for Young Children. *Child development, 55,* 1969–1982.

Jalongo, M. (1983). Bibliotherapy: Literature to promote socioemotional growth. *The Reading Teacher, 36,* 796–802.

Jung, J. (1994). *Under the influence: Alcohol and human behaviors.* Pacific Grove, CA: Brooks/Cole.

Kaplan, H., Martin, S., & Johnson, R. (1986). Self-rejection and the explanation of deviance: Specification of the structure among latent constructs. *American Journal of Sociology, 92,* 384–441.

Kavale, K., & Forness, S. R. (1996). Social skill deficits and learning disabilities: A meta-analysis. *Journal of Learning Disabilities, 29*(3), 226–237.

Keats, D. (1974). The effect of language on concept acquisition in bilingual children. *Journal of Cross-Cultural Psychology, 5,* 80–99.

Kobal-Palcic, D., & Musek, J. (1998). *Self-concept and academic achievement of central and western European groups of adolescents. Slovenia.* (ERIC Document Reproduction No: ED 427841).

La Greca, A., & Stone, W. (1990). Children with learning disabilities: The role of achievement in their social, personal, and behavioral functioning. In H. L. Swanson & B. Keogh (Eds.), *Learning disabilities: Theoretical and research issues* (pp. 333–352). Hillsdale, NJ: Lawrence Erlbaum, Associates.

Larson, K. A., & Gerber, M. M. (1987). Effects of social metacognitive training for enhancing overt behavior in learning disabled and low achieving delinquents. *Exceptional Children, 54*(3), 201–211.

Lenkowsky, R. S., Barowsky, E. I., Dayboch, M., Puccio, L., & Lenkowsky, B. E. (1987). Effects of bibliotherapy on the self-concept of learning disabled, emotionally handicapped adolescents in a classroom setting. *Psychological Reports, 61*(2), 483–488.

Li, A. K. F. (1985). Early rejected status and later social adjustments: A 3-year follow-up. *Journal of Abnormal Child Psychology, 13,* 567–577.

Madge, S., Affleck, J., & Lowenbraun, S. (1990). Social effects of integrated classrooms and resource room/regular class placements on elementary students with learning disabilities. *Journal of Learning Disabilities, 23*(7), 439–445.

Marsh, H. W. (1989). Age and sex effects in multiple dimensions of self-concept: Preadolescence to early adulthood. *Journal of Educational Psychology, 81,* 417–430.

McCarty, H., & Chalmers, L. (1997). Bibliotherapy: Intervention and prevention. *Teaching Exceptional Children, 29,* 12–13, 16–17.

McMahon, C. Wacker, D. P., Sasso, G. M., & Melloy, K. J. (1994). Evaluation of the multiple effects of a social skill intervention. *Behavioral Disorders, 20*(1), 35–50.

Mesch, D., Lew, M., Johnson, D. W., & Johnson, R. (1985). Isolated teenagers, cooperative learning, and training of social skills. *The Journal of Psychology, 120*(4), 323–334.

Miller, D. (1993). *Teaching adolescents with behavioral/emotional disorders, adolescent offenders, and adolescents at-risk: A literature-based approach.* (ERIC Document Reproduction No: ED 361972).

Mills, J. C., & Crowley, R. J. (1986). *Therapeutic metaphors for children and the child within.* New York: Brunner/Mazel.

Montgomery, M. S. (1994). Self-concept and children with learning disabilities: Observer-child concordance across six context-dependent domains. *Journal of Learning Disabilities, 27*(4), 254–262.

Nickolai-Mays, S. (1987). Bibliotherapy and the socially isolated adolescent. *School Counselor, 35*(1), 17–21.

Oliva, A. H. (1990). *The social status of learning disabled children: An in-depth analysis.* Unpublished doctoral dissertation, University of Miami, Coral Gables, FL.

Omizo, M. M., & Omizo, S. A. (1988). Group counseling's effects on self-concept and social behavior among children with learning disabilities. *Journal of Humanistic Education and Development, 26,* 109–117.

Oscarsson, K. L. (1992). *Haitian folktales as a literary strategy for elementary Haitian ESOL students.* Masters thesis, Nova University. (ERIC Document Reproduction No: 355 821).

Pardeck, J. (1990). Using bibliotherapy in clinical practice with children. *Psychological Reports, 67,* 1043–1049.

Parker, J. G., & Asher, S. R. (1987). Peer relations and later personal adjustment: are low-accepted children at risk? *Psychological Bulletin, 102,* 357–389.

Piercy, B. A. (1996). *A content analysis and historical comparison of bibliotherapy research.* Kent State University. (ERIC Document Reproduction No: ED 413–930).

Polacco, P. (1998). *Thank you Mr. Faulker.* New York: Scholastic Books.

Porter, E. E. (1993). The effects of storysharing on the self-esteem and achievement of at-risk first grade students. *Doctoral Dissertation,* University of South Carolina.

Pruett, L. M. (1980). A study of the effectiveness of bibliotherapy in conjunction with adolescent novels in altering attitudes of students in a basic English III classroom. *Doctoral Dissertation,* University of South Carolina.

Ray, R. D. (1983). The relationship of bibliotherapy, self-concept, and reading readiness among kindergarten children. *Doctoral Dissertation,* Ball State University, Muncie, IN.

Renick, M. J., & Harter, S. (1989). Impact of social comparisons on the developing self-perceptions of learning disabled students. *Journal of Educational Psychology, 81,* 631–638.

Robinson, D. J. (1980). A bibliotherapy program with special education students. *Top of the News, 36*(2), 189–193.

Rosenshine, B., & Meister, C. (1994). Reciprocal teaching: A review of the research. *Review of Educational Research, 64*(4), 479–530.

Ruble, D. M. (1983). The development of social comparison processes and their role in achievement-related self-socialization. In E. T. Higgins, W. W. Hartup, & D. N. Ruble (Eds.), *Social cognition and social development: A sociocultural perspective.* Cambridge, England: Cambridge University Press.

Russell, A. E., & Russell, W. A. (1979). Using bibliotherapy with emotionally disturbed children. *Teaching Exceptional Children, 11*(4), 168–169.

Saltzberg, L. H. (1980). *A comparison of RET group therapy, RET group therapy with bibliotherapy, and bibliotherapy only treatments.* Unpublished doctoral dissertation, Texas A&M University.

Schlichter, C. L., & Burke, M. (1994). Using books to nurture the social and emotional development of gifted students. *Roeper Review, 16,* 280–283.

Shafron, P. W. (1983). *Relationship between bibliotherapy and the self-esteem of junior high school students enrolled in remedial reading classes.* Unpublished doctoral dissertation, Dekalb, Illinois.

Shrauger, J. S., & Schoeneman, T. J. (1999). Symbolic interactionist view of self-concept: Through the looking glass darkly. In R. F. Baumeister et al (Eds.), *The self in social psychology* (pp. 25–42). Philadelphia: Psychology Press/Taylor & Francis.

Sheridan, J. T. (1982). *Structured group counseling or explicit bibliotherapy as an in-school strategy for preventing problems in children from changing families.* Unpublished doctoral dissertation, Pennsylvania State University.

Shrodes, C. (1949). *Bibliotherapy: A theoretical and clinical experimental study.* Unpublished doctoral dissertation, University of California, Berkeley.

Smilon, R. (1985). The effect of social skills training on self-concept and teacher ratings of adolescents. Dissertation Abstracts, AAT 8502523.

Sridhar, D. (2000). *Effects of bibliotherapy on text comprehension and self-concept in students with ADD.* Unpublished doctoral dissertation, University of Texas, Austin, TX.

Sridhar, D., & Vaughn, S. (2000). Bibliotherapy for all. *Teaching Exceptional Children, 33*(2), 74–82.

Taylor, E. R. (1993). *A metaphorical story to raise relational esteem in Mexican-American families of low socioeconomic status.* Unpublished doctoral dissertation, St. Mary's University, San Antonio, TX.

Taylor, V. W. (1982). *An investigation of the effects of bibliotherapy on the self-concepts of kindergarten children from one-parent families.* Unpublished doctoral dissertation, Jackson State University.

Van den Broek, P., Fletcher, C. R., & Risden, K. (1993). Investigations of inferential processes in reading: A theoretical and methodological integration. *Discourse Processes, 16,* 169–180.

Vaughn, S., & Elbaum, B. E. (1999). The self concept and friendships of students with learning disabilities: A developmental perspective. In R. Gallimore, L. Bernheimer, D. L. MacMillan, D. L. Speece, & S. Vaughn (Eds.), *Developmental perspective on children with high incidence disabilities* (pp. 81–110). Mahwah, NJ: Lawrence Associates Erlbaum.

Vaughn, S., Elbaum, B. E., & Schumm, J. S. (1996). The effects of inclusion on the social functioning of students with learning disabilities. *Journal of Learning Disabilities, 29*(6), 598–608.

Vaughn, S., McIntosh, R., & Spencer-Rowe, J. (1991). Peer rejection is a stubborn thing: Increasing peer acceptance of rejected students with learning disabilities. *Learning Disabilities Research and Practice, 6*(2), 65–132.

Walters, D. A. (1981). *The effects of bibliotherapy on the self-concept.* Masters thesis, Kean College of New Jersey. (ERIC Document Reproduction No: 204 736).

Wiener, J., & Harris, P. J. (1997). Evaluation of an individualized, context-based social skills training program for children with learning disabilities. *Learning Disabilities Research and Practice, 12*(1), 40–53.

Wolverton, L. (1988). *Classroom strategies for teaching migrant children about child abuse.* Las Cruces NM. (ERIC Document Reproduction Service No. ED 293 681).

Wong, B .Y .L., & Jones, W. (1982). Increasing metacomprehension in learning disabled and normally achieving students through self-questioning training. *Learning Disability Quarterly, 5,* 228–240.

Wong, B .Y .L., Wong, R., Perry, N., & Sawatsky, D. (1986). The efficacy of a self-questioning summarization strategy for use by underachievers and learning disabled adolescents in social studies. *Learning Disabilities Focus, 2*(1), 20–35.

Yellin, M. P. (1982). *Bibliotherapy: A comparison of the effect of the traditional folk fairy tale and "issues specific" imaginative literature on self-esteem, hostile attitudes and the behavior of children.* Unpublished doctoral dissertation, Boston University.

Zwaan, R. A., & Brown, C. M. (1996). The influence of language proficiency and comprehension skill on situation-model construction. *Discourse Processes, 21*, 289–327.

Chapter 10

Children and Adolescents With Learning Disabilities: Case Studies of Social Relations in Inclusive Classrooms

Nancy L. Hutchinson
John G. Freeman
Karin Steiner Bell
Queen's University,
Kingston, Ontario, Canada

> *Friends are what gets me through school I guess you could say. They're always there to support me . . . friends you tell everything and they're always there, so they're very important.*
>
> (Lynn, Grade 11 student with learning disabilities)

> *Ah just sometimes I just don't know how to relate to a lot of the people anymore . . . It's not very important I don't think . . . Maybe they just don't like me or you know they find me annoying.*
>
> (Matt, Grade 11 student with learning disabilities)

Although these two adolescents with learning disabilities attend inclusive classes in the same Canadian high school, they have different views of their social relations in these classes. Lynn is a popular cheerleader with close friends, whereas Matt is socially isolated and cannot find anyone to listen to him talk about Quake (his favorite computer game). If they had been in a study comparing students with learning disabilities to students without disabilities, Lynn and Matt would have been in the same group. But in our research each was a single case in a qualitative study of their school experiences. These are two of the many cases of students with learning disabilities studied by a group of researchers at Queen's University using qualitative approaches to understand social relations in inclusive classrooms.

Mostly with him, I think it's social things that we should be working on . . . he doesn't work well with people. And so partly by insisting that he cooperate with his lab partner, its more than just getting data down . . . it's the whole interaction, teamwork here. (Lauren, Grade 10 advanced science teacher, describing her teaching of a student with learning disabilities)

I often use a jigsaw [method of cooperative learning] because with this method, each child has to be responsible for gathering some kind of information and becomes an expert and becomes valued by the group, and the group can't move forward without their contribution. (Jane, a primary teacher describing her teaching)

These two teachers, Lauren and Jane, work in inclusive classrooms in schools in Ontario, Canada. Each was purposively selected as a case to be studied because her principal nominated her as exemplary at including students with learning disabilities (LD). These are two of the many cases, we have studied, of teachers who excel at teaching that fosters the social relations of students with LD in inclusive classrooms.

The case studies described in this chapter provide detailed information about individual students, teaching practices, and inclusive settings. When compared to other forms of scientific inquiry, case studies offer a means of obtaining "extremely rich, detailed, in-depth information" (Berg, 2001, p. 225). This is especially true when the research is focused on real-life phenomena that are difficult to distinguish from contextual factors (Yin, 1994). Berg (2001) emphasized that a case study is not so much a data-gathering method as an approach that includes many data-gathering techniques, including participant observation, general field studies, and interviews. In addition, case studies can range in complexity from the single-site, single-subject case to the multisite, multisubject study (Bogdan & Biklen, 1998). Traditionally, in education, the case study method has been a method of choice for novice researchers (Bogdan & Biklen, 1998), although experienced researchers in education and in several other fields (including medicine, psychology, and business) employ the case study approach (Berg, 2001). Yin (1994) identified three types of case studies, including exploratory, explanatory, and descriptive; the cases in this chapter are primarily descriptive cases. In other words, the theoretical orientation, research questions, and units of analysis were predetermined by the researchers in each case. Stake (2000) categorized case studies as having different purposes, depending on the type of study. Intrinsic cases highlight the uniqueness of a case, instrumental cases provide insight on an issue, and collective cases offer theoretical value by combining instrumental cases. This chapter, then, highlights the work of graduate-student researchers who collected observational and interview data within single sites and across multiple sites. We summarize a collective of descriptive case studies whose instrumental function has been to depict the social relations of children and adolescents with LD in inclusive classrooms.

SOCIAL RELATIONS AND LEARNING DISABILITIES: WHAT THE LITERATURE TELLS US

Bryan (1991b) pointed out that problems in the social domain have now become central in defining learning disabilities. In addition, there has been a growing interest in the social and emotional life of children with LD (Bryan & Bryan, 1990). Despite the new emphasis on social competence, gaps remain in assessment, in instructional planning in the social domain, and in our knowledge of the social understanding of individuals with learning disabilities. By filling some of these gaps, we may be able to answer Bryan's (1991a) call to "continue to conduct research that challenges our stereotypes, diagnostic assumptions and procedures, and teaching techniques" (p. 301).

Current research on learning disabilities in the social domain has spanned a range of issues from social competence (e.g., Yeates & Selman, 1989) to social cognition (e.g., Bryan's (1991b) review of research on perspective-taking, social perception, and moral development). However, much of the work has focused on two elements of social competence: peer acceptance and social skills. Some researchers have begun examining links between measures of peer acceptance, social competence, and achievement (e.g., Stiliadis & Wiener, 1989; Vaughn, Elbaum, Schumm, & Hughes, 1998; Vaughn & Hogan, 1994; Wiener, Harris, & Shirer, 1990). But over-reliance on peer acceptance as a research construct may not provide the kind of information that teachers need to intervene in inclusive classrooms. Peer acceptance has been described as a "one-way or unilateral construct" (Asher, Parker, & Walker, 1996, p. 367). There is clearly a call for qualitative research that portrays the social perceptions of individuals with learning disabilities themselves to help round out the literature on peer acceptance, and to provide details that might prove critical in developing social interventions.

One expectation of inclusive practice is that students with disabilities will benefit cognitively and socially from the opportunities to interact with their nondisabled peers in regular classrooms. Such an expectation is bolstered by social–constructivist theories that suggest learning or conceptual change occurs in classroom communities where peer interactions are the driving force. Indeed, recommendations for social intervention that emerge from the literature on the peer relations of children with LD often include suggestions for implementing cooperative learning strategies, cross-age peer tutoring, and structured group activities (e.g., Farmer, van

Acker, Pearl, & Rodkin, 1999; Hamre-Nietupski, Hendrickson, Nietupski, & Shokoohi-Yekta, 1994; Wiener & Sunohara, 1998). Such recommendations fall within social–constructivist perspectives (Vygotskian, rather than Piagetian), but it is not clear to what extent students with learning disabilities are benefiting from inclusive environments that have adopted social–constructivist practices.

Trent, Artiles, and Englert (1998) argued in favor of adopting the "social origin of development view" of children with disabilities (p. 298). In so doing, research and practice would be forced to acknowledge individual developmental processes, the role of teachers and peers in learning, and a broader sense of what it means to be different and to be socially competent. These authors traced the history of practice in special education, and they outlined some differences in approach between what was characterized as piecemeal deficit-oriented social skills training and holistic practical activity in a cultural context. Although Trent et al. (1998) recommended a fusion of perspectives, they concluded: "children with [mild] disabilities are especially likely to benefit from collaborative interactions in a social context" (p. 287). Unfortunately, little research has been conducted on the social networks of children with LD (Farmer et al., 1999), or on the links between status and the social behavior of individuals (Bryan & Lee, 1990). Rich descriptions of individuals interacting in social situations, then, could shed light on the possible benefits of inclusive classrooms.

It is likely that current views of the benefits of social–constructivist approaches are naïve. O'Connor (1996) indicated that we cannot assume that discussion or collaboration among peers is an "unproblematic pathway to higher-order thinking practices" (p. 496). Indeed, O'Connor describes one case of a student with language impairments whose views were not valued by his classmates, and she reminded readers that adults do not "expect task-related interactions to be free of hidden agendas and the sequelae of past interpersonal experiences" (p. 507). Social–constructivist approaches emphasize making thinking explicit in collaborative problem solving with peers. However, students with LD who are not accepted by their peers may face obstacles in participating fully in a collaborative process, obstacles that are not necessarily made explicit in class-wide discussions. Even if peer acceptance is present, and even if students are willing tutors and co-participants in inclusive classrooms, Baker and Zigmond (1995) suggested that peers may not be equipped to provide the kind of specific instruction that students with LD require.

Despite lack of peer acceptance among children with learning disabilities, many of these children do have friendships (e.g., Farmer et al., 1999; Wiener & Sunohara, 1998). Therefore, the friendships of children with LD may be the best place to begin examining processes involved in social competence, and studying how to help a child with learning disabilities to participate in inclusive collaborative social interactions in school. A focus on friendship might also provide a way to move beyond issues of social status to ones of social support (e.g., Wenz-Gross & Siperstein, 1997). Asher et al. (1996) distinguished between peer acceptance and friendship, but most research has not used the distinction in examining peer relations. Qualitative research on the friendships of children and adolescents with LD may shed light on some of the distinctions between peer acceptance and friendship and provide clues for intervention. Even if these friendships are found to be impoverished or atypical (e.g., Wiener & Sunohara, 1998), studying them may provide information on how to tap the strengths of the student with LD, especially in a social–constructivist era that aims to use strengths as a foundation for intervention (Trent et al., 1998).

Bukowski, Newcomb, and Hartup (1996) suggested that future directions in the study of friendship focus on links to motivation, social networks, the stability of friendships, cultural differences, age differences, and the diversity of friendship relations. In a similar vein, Asher et al. (1996) offered 10 hypotheses about essential elements in developing friendships. These elements include: committing free time to another person; skills in being perceived as a fun, resourceful, and enjoyable companion; recognition that equality is at the heart of friendship; and self-disclosure skills. Other essential elements include: ability to express caring, concern, admiration and affection; helpfulness when friends are in need; reliability as a partner; ability to manage disagreements and conflict; ability to forgive; and understanding that friendship is part of the peer group experience. These directions for research may guide researchers in understanding the peer relations of individuals with LD and practitioners in developing individually relevant interventions.

Such directions for future research, if taken, may also provide insight on indices of social adjustment, such as the self-concept of students with LD. Vaughn and Elbaum (1999) reported a discrepancy between the lower perceived support from friends as reported by students with LD, and the finding that there are no differences in global self-concept between students with and without learning disabilities. They suggested that friends may not provide the only (or even the most important) support for feelings of self-worth. Other sources of support may be parents, siblings, grandparents, and teachers. Inasmuch as the classroom environment is shaped by the teacher who sets the conditions under which peer relations take place, awareness of the characteristics and actions of teachers who foster friendships between students with LD and their nondisabled peers may also further research on peer relations. Teachers define what peer treatment is acceptable, and they form the groups that sit together and learn together during class. In this sense, then, teachers can provide a zone of proximal development for social relations in the classroom. Qualitative research on exemplary practices in fostering friendships may provide a starting point for research, because, to date, there has been little work to support what Stone and Reid (1994) have called a "balanced model of instruction" that describes the "interplay between social and individual forces in development" (p. 80).

In recent years, veteran researchers in this field have called for qualitative studies (e.g., Bryan, 1991a) that will help teachers to understand the nature of the social relations between students with LD and their peers. What actually takes place during the school day as children and adolescents with LD sit with, talk with, and learn with peers in regular classrooms? How do children and adolescents with LD experience the day-to-day life of the classroom, and what actions do teachers take to shape inclusive environments that enable social relations as well as learning for students with learning disabilities?

At Queen's University in Canada, two researchers (Nancy Hutchinson and John Freeman) and their graduate students have undertaken a series of studies to begin to answer some of these questions. We have begun to assemble a population of cases (Stake, 2000) in which each case probes deeply into the social experiences and peer relations of one student with LD. Most of these cases have been set in regular classrooms, although qualitative data have also been collected about experiences at camp, in extracurricular activities, and in the home. The students have been purposefully selected because they have LD, were willing to take part, and appeared to the researcher to be either a good informant or an intriguing case, or both. For example, Lynn was an articulate informant, whereas Matt was not a good informant but was an interesting young man. Zak provided a multifaceted case and was eager to take part in the study, although he did not provide expansive transcript data. Although we think the population of cases of students is representative of the range of students with learning disabilities, the situation is different for the teachers we have studied. We have conducted case studies of teachers known for enhancing learning and social relations in inclusive classrooms. Thus the teachers were selected because they were reported to be good at including students with LD.

Assembling a Population of Cases

A case can focus on a person, classroom, or program. The phenomena at the center of case studies are thought of as organic and systemic, characterized by purpose and self. In each case, the researcher purposively chooses to study one among many, gradually assembling a population, recognizing that a case cannot be understood without knowledge about

other cases. Stake (2000) argued that we must design each study to opti-
mize understanding of the case rather than generalization beyond the
case. As the population of cases accumulates, comparisons become meaningful and patterns emerge. A collective case study involves jointly studying a number of cases to understand the phenomenon more generally
(e.g., interviewing many youth with LD who left school early) to draw a
composite of the features important to understanding dropping out.

This chapter reports the findings of a program of research committed
to assembling a population of cases on social relations of students with LD
in inclusive classrooms. Because one must focus on the features important
to understanding the case itself (Stake, 2000), the studies have been informed by an array of conceptual frameworks, all emphasizing social relations. We describe three qualitative investigations that contribute five
cases of the social relations of individual students. We also report on a collective case study of students with LD who left high school early and who
are compared to a group who graduated with their classmates. Two qualitative investigations provide cases of seven exemplary inclusion teachers,
four elementary teachers and three high school science teachers. We con-
clude with reflections on the understanding that is emerging from these
cases about the social relations of students with learning disabilities in inclusive settings.

CASES OF STUDENTS WITH LEARNING DISABILITIES AND THEIR SOCIAL RELATIONS

The Cases of Lynn and Matt: Perceptions of Friendships and Peer Groups

This research by Nicole Lévesque (1997) invited two adolescents with
learning disabilities named Lynn and Matt to voice their perceptions of
their friendships and peer relationships at school through open-ended interviews. Observations of the participants' interactions with friends and
peers created a more comprehensive picture of the social relations of
Lynn and of Matt.

Friendship is one of "the most prominent features of the social land-
scape during adolescence" (Hartup, 1993, p. 5). Much of the research on
peer relations of adolescents with LD has used a sociometric approach to
study peer acceptance and social status. These studies suggest that, as a
group, these adolescents are at risk for peer difficulties (Conderman,
1995; Perlmutter, Crocker, Cordray, & Garstecki, 1983; Sabornie & Kauffman, 1986; Vaughn, McIntosh, Schumm, Haager, & Callwood, 1993).

Some adolescents with LD have lower peer acceptance and social status whereas others do not. Researchers have suggested that what is needed are in-depth studies of individual adolescents with LD who have lower peer status and who do not have lower peer status. Such studies would enable researchers to identify the characteristics associated with being at risk of peer difficulties and the characteristics associated with being able to interact successfully with others (e.g., LaGreca & Stone, 1990).

Buhrmester (1996) developed a theory of adolescent friendship in the general population characterized by four elements of interpersonal competence: initiating and sustaining conversation; initiating plans to spend time with friends outside of school; disclosing personal thoughts and empathy; and managing conflict effectively. This framework guided the present study of the views of two adolescents with LD of their friendships and peer relations.

Interviews, observations, and field notes comprised the data sources for this study. After working as a volunteer in a high school resource room for 60 hours and becoming part of the scenery, Lévesque chose two adolescents to study who attended the resource room for one period daily and were in inclusive classrooms for the remainder of the day. She interviewed Lynn on four occasions and Matt on eight occasions over 7 weeks. After each interview she transcribed the tape-recorded conversation and made field notes to fill in contextual gaps that escaped recording. The participants checked the transcripts to ensure they represented the conversations. Lévesque observed Lynn and Matt in the resource room and in their subject classrooms; over 7 weeks, she observed Lynn for 25 hours and Matt for 24 hours. She described any interaction between the participant and another person including situational details. Field notes were written in the school immediately following each observation. Data analysis involved a continual process of categorizing, comparing, synthesizing, and interpreting data from the interviews and observations (McMillan & Schumacher, 1993).

The participants' social experiences differed radically; yet both cases exemplified the significance of peer relations in influencing thoughts about school and shaping psychosocial development. Lynn's close friendships and positive peer relationships enriched her educational experiences and enhanced her self-esteem. Her story illustrates how some exceptional students can thrive academically, socially, and personally in supportive environments. Matt stood alone in the halls, could think of nothing he looked forward to at school, and had difficulty carrying on a reciprocal conversation. He assumed little responsibility for his loneliness at school. His struggles with verbal expression are evident in the following passages where he explains to the interviewer that he has few relationships at school:

"There's not a lot of considerate people that socializes [*sic*] with me like on a real base you know . . . Of you know equals, I guess." Later in the same interview, he said, "A lot of people maybe see me as not a serious person at all you know." The following excerpt shows Matt growing frustrated with his own lack of clarity: "I don't really you know, like, you know [pause] people, like you know, it's just sometimes people just you know, like you know, like I don't know . . . like some people just don't take me too serious you know." (Lévesque, 1997, p. 97)

In most classes, Matt was silent and unaware of what was being taught—he was usually reading his science fiction novel. However, Matt participated and appeared to be engaged in his English class. Matt attributed this to his English teacher's sense of humor. Lévesque observed this class and wrote that the teacher facilitated Matt's participation by establishing a personal relationship in which he showed an interest in Matt. This teacher also extracted the main points of Matt's long-winded, wandering explanations and translated them into meaningful language for the class.

Both cases illustrated a reciprocal link between the quality of peer relations and interpersonal competence as Buhrmester's theory predicted. The participants' social experiences also supported the importance of effective conversational skills, efforts to initiate peer contact, emotional sharing and empathy, and conflict management. However, the data suggested that Buhrmester's theory warrants elaboration to better account for individual differences and to consider the role of adolescent social norms (Evans & Eder, 1989) and reputational bias (Hymel, Wagner, & Butler, 1990). Laursen's (1996) emphasis on reciprocity (including equity and interdependence) helped to interpret the data that show adolescents striving for a balance in friendships between personal gains and responsibilities to each other.

The profiles of Lynn and Matt revealed that learning disabilities are multifaceted and can potentially affect interpersonal competence in singular ways. The nature, pervasiveness, and severity of the exceptionality seemed to influence the extent to which the participants' social lives were affected. In Lynn's case, dyslexia and dysgraphia had no obvious impact on her social life, except that she tried to hide her learning disabilities from all but her close friends. Her positive school experiences and self-concept defied the pattern of dissatisfaction with school and self among preadolescent females with LD that has surfaced in the literature (cf. La-Greca & Stone, 1990). Matt's LD and attention deficit hyperactivity disorder, on the other hand, seemed to impair his ability to learn, attend to, and perform daily tasks, including those involving social interaction. Processing and attention deficits hindered his self-expression, self-control, social awareness, social perception and reasoning, and social metacognition. Complicating matters were the potent forces of adolescent peer norms and reputational bias that thwarted Matt's attempts to make friends.

This study demonstrated that qualitative methodology can contribute studies of individual cases to inform thinking about peer relations and exceptionality education, and showed the power of personal stories to inform. Theories of adolescent friendship offer promise for understanding peer relations of exceptional youth. Practitioners need to foster interpersonal and intrapersonal growth as well as cognitive development of exceptional adolescents.

The Case of Zak: Context Matters

Shari Stoch (2000) used a narrative approach (e.g., Connelly & Clandinin, 1990) to describe Zak, an adolescent with LD, in the contexts of camp, school, and home. Her data sources included interviews with Zak, his mother, his special education teachers, and his camp counselors. She conducted five 30 to 40 minute interviews with Zak and two 45-minute interviews with his mother. The individual interviews with the two teachers and the three counselors lasted from 20 to 30 minutes. Interviews were audiotaped and transcribed verbatim. In addition, Stoch observed Zak informally across the three contexts, although the interview transcripts served as the primary data source. Stoch had known Zak for 2 years before she conducted the case study because she was a staff member at the camp that served as one of the contexts in the study.

Despite Stoch's sympathy for critics of LD research who reject any notion of deficit residing within the individual (e.g., Dudley-Marling & Dippo, 1995; Heshusius, 1989), she adopted a theoretical framework that recognized the interaction of contextual factors with individual characteristics (e.g., Gerber, Ginsberg, & Reiff, 1992; Rueda, Gallego, & Moll, 2000). Using this framework, Zak emerged as a complex individual whose LD manifested differently depending on the context.

For two summers, Zak attended an integrated camp where 75% of the campers have a learning disability. At camp, Zak was a relaxed and comfortable individual. His self-confidence was high, and he felt he had many friends. When asked to name his friends at camp, Zak named 40 children before Stoch asked him to stop. When she requested that Zak name only his five closest friends, he named six other campers. Zak experienced success at camp in physical activities, winning awards for his kneeboarding skills. His counselors reported that he demonstrated social and leadership skills in this inclusive setting.

Zak has participated in three distinct school environments with differences in peer relations. For Grades 1 to 5, he was integrated into a regular classroom, receiving 40 minutes daily of resource support from Grade 2 onwards, after he was formally identified as having a learning disability. According to Zak and his mother, school was difficult for him when he was integrated in the regular elementary classroom. He was continually getting into trouble, and the school was constantly calling Elizabeth. As she stated, "it got so frustrating and so overwhelming and so exhausting for me to constantly have to be there and do the teacher's job" (p. 94).

At the beginning of Grade 6, Zak transferred to a private school for children with LD where he participated more socially and academically. Zak was in Grade 9, his first year of high school, when the case study concluded. He was registered in a learning disabilities program, studying two academic subjects in a class of eight students and taking two other subjects in regular classrooms. Again, he was relating better to peers in the learning disabilities program than in the regular classroom. One teacher said, "Zak's behaviour seems to cause more difficulty in his general education classes" (p. 162).

At home, "Zak's designated family role is of a young boy" (Stoch, 2000, p. 106). Home life was dominated by Zak's mother, Elizabeth. A single parent since Zak was a baby, Elizabeth drove him to friends' houses, ensured that he had the CDs and movies he wanted, and made decisions for him. For example, after Zak was diagnosed as having epilepsy, Elizabeth placed greater restrictions on his sports activities than those suggested by the doctor. She refused to let Zak have Aspartame, insisting it would bring on seizures. When Zak was having difficulty in Grade 7, Elizabeth insisted he repeat the grade, and Zak went along with the decision. He reported to the interviewer, "I kind of wanted to go ahead but knew I had to work harder, so I decided to stay back" (p. 150).

Thus, the picture Stoch (2000) painted of Zak, an adolescent with learning disabilities, was multifaceted. He appeared to thrive in settings where he felt included—relating to and leading his peers; however, he had difficulty relating and tended to engage in unacceptable behavior when he was less comfortable. Stoch concluded her thesis by stating:

> Part of the difference between familiarizing oneself with a character and getting to know a real person lies in the trivial things that people experience together and know about each other. I have tried to give you a glimpse of some of these real-life experiences of Zak, and I hope that you are able to see that he is more than a person with learning disabilities—he is a person with a life. (p. 187)

The Cases of Michael and Kelly: A Participant Observation Study

Janet Chan (2000) observed the social skills of two Grade 6 students with learning disabilities, Michael and Kelly, over an 11-week period across multiple school contexts: structured (highly structured morning, less structured afternoon), semistructured (music, computers/resource center, physical education), and unstructured (lunch, recess). Her participant observations were informed by a three-dimensional model (Haring & Breen, 1989). Social skills were defined as the capacity to initiate and respond to others (Vaughn & Hogan, 1994). Vaughn and Hogan suggested that social competence is made up of social skills combined with positive relations with others, accurate age-appropriate social cognition, and absence of maladaptive behaviors. While Chan focused on social skills, she also noted instances of social skills interacting with the other three components of social competence. Vaughn and Hogan's emphasis on initiations and responses was consistent with Haring and Breen's model of social interaction functions, structure in social contexts, and setting characteristics. The four social interaction functions of Haring and Breen are: initiations, responses, social turns, and length of interaction. A pilot study showed Chan that the utility of each of social turns and length of interaction for data collection in task-focused classrooms was limited. Thus she focused on initiations and responses, looking for social and task functions of each.

At the time of the study, Michael was 11 years old in a Grade 5–6 class. Although Michael had not been formally identified as having LD, his teacher described many characteristics that suggested Michael had a learning disability. In structured classroom settings, Michael made few social or task-oriented initiations and had few initiations directed toward him. For example, during 11 mornings of observations consisting of 42 (15-minute) observational intervals, Michael made eight social initiations and four task-oriented initiations, as well two social responses to peers and two task-oriented responses to peers. He made no initiations or responses to the researcher. In semistructured contexts, Michael tended not to interact with classmates. He participated minimally in music class, went quietly about his work in the computer/resource center, and did not become engaged in physical education activities. In unstructured settings, Michael only exhibited positive social skills at recess. Then, he would engage in physical play with Grade 5 male classmates, generally playing foot hockey or climbing on the Junior Climber apparatus.

Kelly was 12 years old at the time of the study. She had been formally identified as having LD when she was in Grade 3. Unlike Michael, Kelly made frequent initiations in the structured classroom setting. For example, during 12 mornings of observations consisting of 65 (15-minute) observational intervals, Kelly initiated socially with peers 25 times, in a task-oriented manner with peers 9 times, and toward the researcher 11 times. She also made 13 social responses and 4 task-oriented responses to peers, and 1 response to the researcher. However, these social initiations and responses rarely led to extended social turns. When Kelly initiated, the other students usually answered with one word or a smile, making a minimal response to the interruption, and then ignoring her. Kelly's social responses were of similar short duration. Task-oriented initiations focused on procedural issues, such as interrupting students while they worked to borrow classroom materials. Kelly's initiations toward the researcher were attention seeking (e.g., repeatedly asking to leave the classroom).

Outside the structured classroom setting, Kelly was isolated socially from her peers. This isolation was particularly noticeable at recess. She did not associate with the other Grade 6 girls, who spent recess walking around the schoolyard. These girls told Chan that they did not invite Kelly to walk with them because they did not like her. Occasionally, she played with one Grade 5 female student from her class, but their relationship diminished during the months of the study. Usually, Kelly spent recess playing with the Kindergarten children or standing alone.

From her observations, Chan (2000) concluded that both these children had social skills difficulties, although these difficulties manifested themselves in different ways. Michael had trouble initiating and responding verbally. He was much more comfortable when he could express himself in a physical manner, for example, during recess. Kelly had no trouble initiating a conversation, but she did not initiate appropriately, often trying to distract classmates when they were engaged in work. Kelly also did not respond appropriately to other students' academic or social initiations. Kelly was isolated in semistructured and unstructured settings (e.g., recess, lunch, physical education), when one might expect every student to experience frequent interactions with peers.

Although Michael's and Kelly's teacher provided a safe environment where students could interact comfortably (Hutchinson, 2002), she did not appear to recognize that Michael and Kelly were experiencing difficulties in social relations. She took no observable actions to ameliorate their social situations. For example, although the teacher frequently changed the seating arrangement to facilitate classroom management, she did not make these changes to promote greater social interaction for either Michael or Kelly. She also did not deliberately use group or pair work as a social development tool; rather she always allowed students to select their own groups or partners (cf. Hutchinson, 1996). Neither Kelly nor Michael knew how to take advantage of the opportunities that abound in a regular classroom for learning with peers and for making friends (Buhrmester, 1996).

Chan found that participant observation is a challenging form of classroom research. Participating in another role while collecting data is distracting and can prevent one from being thorough, whereas observer reactivity is not eliminated by participant observation as one might hope. It also proved difficult to note the number of initiations and responses in the unstructured contexts. Because many children and adolescents with LD are not articulate, they sometimes make poor informants, and observation may prove to be a complementary research strategy to interviews. However, Chan's experience suggested to her that observations, even extended observations, needed complementary interviews.

Summary of Cases of Five Students
With Learning Disabilities

These five studies of individual cases ranging from Grade 6 to Grade 11 highlight the importance of both individual characteristics and of context in understanding social relations of students with LD. Lynn's written expression was atypical, and almost impossible to decipher. However, her integration into a tightly knit circle of friends who shared her interest in cheerleading was typical of adolescents—she went to school to be with her friends. Matt's inabilities in communication presented similarly in his academic endeavors and in his peer relations—his thoughts were incoherent, frustrating to adolescent listeners, and prevented him from conducting meaningful exchanges. His reputation and adolescents' fear of being judged to be similar to their associates compounded his communication difficulties to render Matt a virtual isolate. Both Lynn and Matt benefited from tutoring and support in a resource room designed to meet their academic needs. Lynn thrived on inclusion while Matt wished he could quit school, although the school prided itself on enabling exceptional students to succeed in inclusive classrooms. Zak, on the other hand, thrived at camp in an environment tailored to minimize the impact of his LD, making people like him the norm rather than the exception. He also fared better in a school setting with students with learning disabilities, although it is not clear that many of his school experiences took place in environments that strove to include exceptional students. Kelly and Michael were in an elementary school, with a teacher who created a safe environment but did not see her responsibilities extending to enhancing the social participation or relations of students with LD. Michael could be described as shy and ignored. Kelly was often inappropriate, interrupting and annoying her classmates who reported actively disliking her. Each case highlights the interaction of individual characteristics and context.

THE CASES OF THOSE WHO LEAVE AND THOSE
WHO STAY: RESILIENCE AND SOCIAL RELATIONS

What happens to high school students with learning disabilities who may experience little of the rewarding friendship that is thought to be one of life's greatest joys? Researchers have suggested that many youth with LD, but by no means all, leave high school early or drop out. Do peer relations play a role in these decisions? We were interested in learning about those who left and those who stayed, so we carried out a collective case study (Freeman, Stoch, Chan, Hutchinson, Mann, & Eady, 2001). Retrospective interviews led us to resiliency factors that contributed to the decisions made by two groups of adults with learning disabilities about dropping out. Resiliency was defined as the "capacity to overcome obstacles to healthy development and the ability to spring back from adversity" (Garnier, Stein, & Jacobs, 1997, p. 398).

Resiliency factors tend to be classified in three ways: (a) social relations, (b) interests, and (c) individual characteristics. Social relations in high school center around significant adults and peers (Freeman & Hutchinson, 1994), although resiliency seems primarily affected by connections students make with adults (McMillan & Reed, 1994). Interest in school subjects and extracurricular activities have been shown to increase student engagement in school and may provide incentives for them to remain (McPhail, Pierson, Freeman, Goodman, & Ayappa, 2000). Extracurricular activities, for example, "provide stability and predictability . . . and give hope of success and the possibility of achievement" (Johnson, 1997, p. 42). Individual characteristics may be crucial in drop-out prevention, although empirical support for this contention is lacking. Benard (1993) listed social competence, problem-solving skills, autonomy, and sense of purpose as the critical factors in resiliency. McMillan and Reed (1994) included six individual factors in their resiliency model: self-efficacy, goals orientation, personal responsibility, optimism, internal expectations, and coping ability.

Resiliency studies emphasize risk factors such as race and socioeconomic status. They tend to ignore learning disabilities as a risk factor. This study, therefore, provided a link between the current research on resiliency and our understanding of the drop-out patterns of persons with learning disabilities. The first group of eight adults (5 males, 3 females, ages 19–43), "the late successfuls," had dropped out and then returned to an adult learning center to finish their high school graduation requirements. The second group of eight (5 males, 3 females, ages 21–35), the "early successfuls," had graduated from high school at the expected age. Identification of learning disabilities was through school records, self-disclosure, and teacher nominations (the adult learning center did not test formally for LD but received student files from their former schools when they were available).

Data collection took place through semistructured interviews with participants, all of whom provided informed consent. Each participant was interviewed once for between 30 and 45 minutes. All interviews were mechanically recorded and transcribed verbatim. Interviews were structured around "open-ended questions" (Seidman, 1991, p. 62). They began with "descriptive" questions, such as "grand tour questions" (Spradley, 1979, p. 87), and continued with "structural" and "contrast" questions (Spradley, p. 60). Questions focused on the resiliency factors identified in the research literature. Questions were altered slightly for the two groups of participants to be consistent with their high school leaving patterns.

There were at least four dimensions on which the high school experiences of the late successful adults (who dropped out) contrasted with the experiences of the early successful adults who completed high school on schedule. First, the parents of the early successful participants provided strong support and encouragement for them to remain in school. As one early successful participant commented, my "family was very supportive. Um. They were always there for me, although being a teenager, you're not always receptive to that form of support." Another said his parents "were always clear to me that the effort that I put in was more important than a grade that I got out at the end. And that a grade didn't necessarily reflect my learning experience." In contrast, the late successful participants did not experience a high level of parental involvement. For example, one participant said: "My parents were too busy with the farm, and all the teachers there they can only support so far because there are other students."

Second, teachers of the late successful individuals with learning disabilities (who had dropped out) tended to push them away from school, according to the students' reports. One student stated, "It was like every little thing I couldn't do right according to the school or the teacher, so I guess that's why I dropped out. Because I could not handle the stress from her." Similarly, for another student, "it was mostly the teacher. He made things very uncomfortable for me. He wouldn't say it in as many words but he made me feel like I was stupid." In contrast, the teachers of the early successful individuals helped them. For example, one student reported "[I] finally hit a teacher who just inspired me. And I don't remember what the mark was, but it was certainly, probably, it was probably a B+ for English, which for me was pretty exceptional. But this teacher just had a way of bringing the words to life and making it interesting."

Third, although both groups of adults reported socializing with friends as a high school interest, the early successful group also enjoyed structured, extracurricular activities, some of which took place in the high school. "My favorite parts of a typical school day . . . lunch, recess, and, of course, any extracurricular rehearsals for band or for choir or for new jazz choir or plays or for anything like that." Other activities were outside the school setting, including church, Scouts, and martial arts. The late successful group reported only participating in activities with friends outside the school environment.

Finally, the early successful group had a sense of purpose that helped to keep them in school, while the late successful group developed long-range, personal goals only after having participated in the work force. When this group of adults with LD discussed the individual characteristics that affected their school decisions, they tended to stress their present reasons for returning to school, with an implicit contrast to their high school experiences as adolescents. Therefore, they told of their current maturity and their setting long-range, personal goals. One stated, "I was tired of menial labor and having people step all over me because I was only getting minimum wage. And I thought, no, no more. I'm worth more than that."

This collective case study suggested that according to retrospective accounts, peer relations played a small role in the buffering of school frustrations for those early successful adolescents with LD who stayed in high school to graduate. School-sponsored activities with peers were one of four factors that appeared to contribute to resiliency in the high school years—the others were a supportive family, supportive teachers, and long-range personal goals or a sense of purpose. Some of the adults interviewed for this collective case had attended school before the days of inclusive school policies whereas others had left school within the past 12 months. However, participants reported the importance of feeling a part of the high school and of seeing "the point of being there" regardless of their ages. Peer relations may contribute to early success, that is, high school graduation on time, for students with LD but so do other buffering forces including teachers.

THE CASES OF TEACHERS WHO SHAPE INCLUSIVE ENVIRONMENTS

We have also been interested in learning what kinds of teachers contribute to the inclusive environments that enable students with LD to participate socially and academically. Two graduate students, Anne Beveridge (1997) and Karol Lyn Edwards (2000), carried out interviews to develop cases of teachers who are seen as exemplary at inclusion, in elementary schools and secondary science classrooms, respectively.

Four Outstanding Elementary Inclusion Teachers: Practices and Beliefs

Anne Beveridge (1997) interviewed four experienced teachers nominated by their principals for their exemplary practices in inclusive education: Perry, Bella, Cait, and Jane. Beveridge's purpose was to uncover the beliefs and practices of these teachers. Beliefs play a major role in organizing teacher knowledge and in task definition (Pajares, 1992). In his review paper, "Teachers: Beliefs and knowledge," Calderhead (1996) contended that teachers hold beliefs in at least five main areas: about learners and learning, teaching, subjects, learning to teach, and self and teaching role. Calderhead and others (e.g., Richardson, 1996) suggested that the link between teachers' beliefs and practices is reciprocal and that one cannot separate the study of the two.

Each teacher Beveridge studied filled a slightly different role in schools with large numbers of students who were homeless and had a variety of learning and behavior disabilities. Perry taught students with learning and behavior disabilities in small groups in a resource room and in their regular classrooms. Bella was also a resource teacher who spent much of her time in regular classrooms. Cait was a classroom teacher at the same school as Bella. Jane was also a classroom teacher, but not in the same school as any of the others. Beveridge's analyses were informed by Calderhead's (1996) framework of teacher beliefs and practices.

Perry described his function as a resource room teacher to enable students with learning and behavior disabilities to succeed in regular classrooms—by supporting both students and their teachers. His central belief was that the teacher's role is to facilitate integration. He saw this as his role and helped all the teachers he worked with to assume this role in the lives of their students. In interviews, he also highlighted the importance of assessing children's needs and communicating these needs to teachers, and of recognizing children's needs to feel they belong to a community. He ensured that exceptional children played on school teams and participated in school clubs; the teams that he coached were inclusive, and he set the standard for the rest of the school. His practice, as he described it to Beveridge, was consistent with his beliefs and much of what he did enabled children with and without disabilities to interact with common purpose, in classrooms, on teams, and in clubs.

Bella's central belief focused on the need and desire of every individual to be successful and feel he or she belongs. She emphasized that the community of the school is experienced in integrated or inclusive classrooms "because it's awfully hard to build more than the academic program in a segregated classroom" (p. 59). In describing her practices, Bella related how she adapted teaching to meet students' needs, helped them to feel they had control over their lives at school, and acted as an advocate for students with learning disabilities. She constantly referred to the social opportunities in belonging to the community of a classroom.

Cait was a regular Grade 5–6 classroom teacher, and Bella often came into her classroom to work with the integrated students with learning and behavior disabilities. Cait valued inclusion because children learned "how to follow routines, and how to get along with their peers" (p. 67). She described the specific actions she took to ensure they learned both—giving all students tasks on which they could be successful, making whatever accommodations were necessary, and teaching so that all children were working with classmates for much of the day.

Jane was a primary teacher who emphasized that she believed all children are "entitled to the most memorable and enriching experience teachers can provide" (p. 75) and that one must respect the dignity of all children. She adapted all activities so they could be done in some way by every student, and done with peers, not just in isolation. She talked about "working toward an inclusive society" through her teaching which allowed all students to "participate to the best of their abilities" (p. 77). This chapter opens with a quotation from Jane about her use of cooperative jigsaw activities, a regular part of her classroom. She returned frequently to the idea that she was modeling relationships with, acceptance of, and valuing of children with LD in her inclusive classroom.

Each teacher emphasized individual themes in his or her interviews about beliefs and practices that contribute to inclusion. Beveridge found patterns across the cases. The best practices of these four teachers included facilitating social integration, building a sense of community, and accommodating individual differences. All four teachers talked about the importance of their beliefs about inclusion to their day-to-day practices. Jane's words capture the essence of their views: "when you've got a set of beliefs, all you believe feeds into what you do" (p. 114). Beveridge argued that, given the strong relationship between teachers' beliefs and practices, effective preservice and inservice teacher education must focus on beliefs and practices simultaneously. It is probably not enough to provide classroom teachers with lists of strategies and practices that have enabled other teachers to include students with learning disabilities. "In light of this relationship, preservice teacher education should focus not only on what can be done in a classroom, but why it is done" (Beveridge, 1997, p. 122).

Three Outstanding High School Science Teachers Known for Inclusive Practices

Karol Lyn Edwards (2000) interviewed and observed three high school science teachers (Ellen, Lauren, and Gary) whose principals and special education coordinators in their schools recommended them as exemplary in their inclusion of students with learning disabilities. She used conceptual frameworks from the literature on practices of exemplary science teachers and from the literature on exemplary practices in inclusion of students with LD. The research suggests that exemplary, secondary science teachers adopt a "hands-on, minds-on" philosophy and use strategies that support this philosophy (e.g., Monk & Osborne, 2000). Effective science teachers understand individual students' needs, interests, and strengths and use this understanding to shape their teaching (Driver, Asoko, Leach,

Mortimer, & Scott, 1994). In a series of studies, Scruggs and Mastropieri identified variables associated with successful inclusion of students with disabilities. These included supportive classroom environments that value diversity, activity-oriented science programs, effective instruction (with structure, clarity, etc.), peer assistance, and disability-specific teaching skills (Mastropieri et al., 1998; Scruggs & Mastropieri, 1994a, 1994b).

In interviews and observations, Ellen showed herself to be an early career teacher who was flexible ("I am more than willing to make exceptions and to help one-on-one") and liked working with individual students with LD. She made her teaching interesting and relevant. She tried to use activity-based lessons, cooperative learning, and inclusive practices in teaching and assessment, but by her own admission these often fell short of making every student feel included and of enhancing the social participation of exceptional students. When asked what worked best for her classes, she replied, "I don't know right now, truthfully. I need more techniques" (p. 54). Her classroom management techniques were not effective enough for Ellen to reach her own goals of every student learning with his or her peers. Ellen expressed her frustration: "So how can I sit or help an individual who's having genuine difficulty when I'm asking these people over here (motions with hand) to sit down, focus and do their work. That's a huge frustration."

Lauren, an experienced teacher, described how she created an inclusive environment from the first day of term by modeling accepting behavior and not tolerating bullying and name-calling. (Edwards used the pseudonym, Lynn, which we have changed to Lauren to reduce confusion with the student Lynn described earlier in this paper). Lauren was positive and firm. "I want everybody to be successful and I try to remind them of that" (p. 62) and "I find you have to be pretty strict at the beginning and really follow through on things cause if you let stuff slide then they realize you're going to let stuff slide. So I'm very strict at the beginning" (p. 66). Edwards observed that Lauren used a variety of teaching approaches to ensure that everyone understood and made adaptations for individuals with learning disabilities. She used classwide discussion and cooperative learning activities so students talked together and learned together. Lauren described how "there is some hands on and there's some discovery based learning and there's some taking down notes, problem solving, seat work, discussion" (p. 69) depending on the group, the content, and individual student needs. Students evaluated themselves and their groups on cooperation and on learning.

This chapter opened with Lauren describing her efforts to help one student with learning disabilities improve in social competence and social acceptance. "Mostly with him, I think it's social things that we should be working on . . . he doesn't work well with people. And so partly by insisting that he cooperate with his lab partner, it's more than just getting data down . . . it's the whole interaction, teamwork here." Lauren's organization and management of the class were exemplary so her teaching matched her high aspirations for inclusion of students with learning disabilities.

Gary, a teacher with many years' experience, used hands-on activities or, as he said, "more experimental, the kids are doing more rather than listening to it" (p. 78). He emphasized that he made class interesting to keep all students engaged and created a safe supportive learning environment so students with LD participated. Although Gary referred to "putting out brush fires" and changing seating arrangements early in the year, Edwards wrote, "From my observations, classroom management was not an issue" (p. 79). Gary demonstrated and discussed many of the ways he changed his teaching so individual students could take part: "I do demonstrations, we do worksheets, we do a lot of different things." Gary described showing videos, "walking students through" his expectations for a complex lab activity, and printing on the board when one student could not read cursive writing (pp. 81–83). Excellent classroom management enabled him to use a variety of creative teaching and assessment approaches, including self-assessment. Gary stressed the importance of teachers enjoying their work and of students learning as much as they could, doing hands-on activities cooperatively in small groups.

Edwards looked for patterns across the practices of the three teachers: their efforts to provide supportive and safe classroom environments in which students with learning disabilities were comfortable to participate and their actions to accommodate individual differences. She also described their similar emphasis on activity-learning in small groups, on students taking responsibility for learning, and on a range of strategies. The key differences were in such aspects as classroom management (effectiveness of practices, rather than beliefs), follow-through (where the two experienced teachers were absolutely consistent), and in reasons for adapting teaching. The two younger teachers (Ellen and Lauren) were knowledgeable about learning disabilities, whereas Gary knew what had worked over the years and had a vision of an inclusive, cooperative, hands-on classroom for all, regardless of identified disabilities. This study showed that exemplary high school science teachers vary in their effectiveness in carrying out a social, active-learning classroom although all three had similar beliefs and practices. Edwards also added to the literature with practices not reported in previous studies. The added practices were self- and peer-evaluation forms for all students to encourage cooperative group work, interactive whole class discussions, and demonstrations, and holistic teaching that included enhancing participation and social skills as well as academic skills.

Summary of Case Studies of Individual Exemplary Inclusion Teachers

The population of cases that we are building suggests that exemplary teachers who include students with learning disabilities pay as much attention to the social aspects of inclusion as to the academic aspects. They express beliefs about the importance of modeling acceptance, creating safe classrooms, and using interactive teaching and learning approaches. Perry taught students with LD in a withdrawal setting and in their regular classroom, and insisted on their inclusion in extracurricular activities with peers without disabilities. Bella advocated the regular classroom because it allowed students to be full members of the school community alongside nondisabled peers. Cait talked about teaching students to get along with peers, and Jane saw herself creating citizens, for an inclusive society, who were fellow learners and friends, regardless of disability status. Ellen's teaching fell short of her aspirations because of difficulties with classroom management, but she advocated cooperative learning. Lauren described, in an example highlighted in the opening of this chapter, how she focused on helping a student with LD to work cooperatively and socially with his lab partner. Although Gary may have lacked detailed knowledge about LD, he knew how to adapt teaching and how to create a social climate where all students learned by working with classmates and felt safe participating. These exemplary teachers focused on the social demands of the classroom and accommodating the social needs of students with LD, as well as on the academic demands of teaching students with learning disabilities.

CLOSING COMMENTS

Our developing body of work—studies of cases—on the social relations of students with learning disabilities and the social practices of the exemplary teachers who teach them shows us how complex this area is. Veteran researchers like Tanis Bryan were perceptive to recommend studies of individual students who are socially more and less successful in regular classrooms. Students like Lynn (Lévesque, 1997) who thrive in social settings and yet hide their learning disabilities from all but their friends show that they can develop social competence but don't feel accepted for who they are. Lynn acknowledged that she would be more comfortable at school if she could trust her acquaintances to accept her the way her close friends did. For a student like Matt (Lévesque, 1997), an intervention might have to target his communication disabilities as well as his lack of awareness of how others perceive him. Cases of students like Zak (Stoch, 2000) show us the significance of context and the interactional nature of learning disabilities. Zak was almost like a different person in different contexts. When he was uncomfortable, he was unable to act appropriately, let alone show the leadership of which he was capable. Kelly's case (Chan, 2000) shows a student, placed in a classroom with norms of social acceptance, but without any of the proactive strategies that characterize the practices of exemplary inclusion teachers. These exemplary teachers report beliefs and practices that include making cooperative groups work and advocating for students with LD to be included in the community of the classroom and in extracurricular activities. However, not every teacher who expressed these beliefs was able to enact effective practices consistent with these high aspirations (e.g., Ellen in Edwards, 2000). Our data suggest that assembling a population of cases will help researchers and practitioners to understand the specific factors contributing to individual social difficulties and the wide range of interventions that might be needed. Effective social interventions might have to be as tailored as effective academic interventions. Our studies also suggest we must enhance both beliefs and practices of preservice and inservice teachers who will spend their careers in inclusive classrooms that include students with LD. Targeting teachers and the context may be just as important as developing interventions that focus on students with learning disabilities.

REFERENCES

Asher, S. R., Parker, J. G., & Walker, D. L. (1996). Distinguishing friendship from acceptance: Implications for intervention. In W. M. Bukowski, A. F. Newcomb, & W. W. Hartup (Eds.), *The company they keep: Friendship in childhood and adolescence* (pp. 366–405). New York: Cambridge University Press.

Baker, J. M., & Zigmond, N. (1995). The meaning and practice of inclusion for students with learning disabilities: Themes and implications from the five cases. *Journal of Special Education, 29*(2), 163–180.

Benard, B. (1993). Fostering resiliency in kids. *Educational Leadership, 51*(3), 44–48.

Berg, B. L. (2001). *Qualitative research methods for the social sciences* (4th ed.). Boston, MA: Allyn & Bacon.

Beveridge, A. (1997). *Successful inclusion of children with disabilities into regular classrooms: The practices and beliefs of four elementary teachers.* Unpublished master's thesis, Queen's University, Kingston, Ontario, Canada.

Bogdan, R. C., & Biklen, S. K. (1998). *Qualitative research in education: An introduction to theory and methods* (3rd ed.). Boston, MA: Allyn & Bacon.

Bryan, T. (1991a). Selection of subjects in research on learning disabilities: A view from the social side. *Learning Disability Quarterly, 14*, 297–302.

Bryan, T. (1991b). Assessment of social cognition: Review of research in learning disabilities. In H. L. Swanson (Ed.), *Handbook on the assessment of learning disabilities: Theory, research, and practice* (pp. 285–311). Austin, TX: Pro-Ed.

Bryan, T., & Bryan, J. (1990). Social factors in learning disabilities: An overview. In H. L. Swanson & B. Keogh (Eds.), *Learning disabilities: Theoretical and research issues* (pp. 131–138). Hillsdale, NJ: Lawrence Erlbaum Associates.

Bryan, T., & Lee, J. (1990). Social skills training with learning disabled children and adolescents: The state of the art. In T. E. Scruggs & B. Y. L. Wong (Eds.), *Intervention research in learning disabilities* (pp. 263–278). New York: Springer-Verlag.

Buhrmester, D. (1996). Need fulfilment, interpersonal competence, and the developmental contexts of early adolescent friendship. In W. M. Bukowski, A. F. Newcomb, & W. W. Hartup (Eds.), *The company they keep: Friendship in childhood and adolescence* (pp. 158–185). New York: Cambridge University Press.

Bukowski, W. M., Newcomb, A. F., & Hartup, W. W. (1996). Friendship and its significance in childhood and adolescence: Introduction and comment. In W. M. Bukowski, A. F. Newcomb, & W. W. Hartup (Eds.), *The company they keep: Friendship in childhood and adolescence* (pp. 1–15). New York: Cambridge University Press.

Calderhead, J. (1996). Teachers: Beliefs and knowledge. In D. C. Berliner & R. C. Calfee (Eds.), *Handbook of educational psychology* (pp. 709–725). New York: Simon & Schuster/ Macmillan.

Chan, J. S. (2000). *The social skills of two elementary students with learning disabilities: A participant observational study across seven school contexts*. Unpublished master's thesis, Queen's University, Kingston, Ontario, Canada.

Conderman, G. (1995). Social status of sixth- and seventh-grade students with learning disabilities. *Learning Disability Quarterly, 18*, 13–24.

Connelly, F. M., & Clandinin, D. J. (1990). Stories of experience and narrative inquiry. *Educational Researcher, 22*, 2–14.

Driver, R., Asoko, H., Leach, J., Mortimer, E., & Scott, P. (1994). Constructing scientific knowledge in the classroom. *Educational Researcher, 23*(7), 5–12.

Dudley-Marling, C., & Dippo, D. (1995). What learning disability does: Sustaining the ideology of schooling. *Journal of Learning Disabilities, 28*, 408–414.

Edwards, K. L. (2000). *They can be successful too!: Inclusive practices of secondary science teachers*. Unpublished master's thesis, Queen's University, Kingston, Ontario, Canada.

Evans, C., & Eder, D. (1989, August). *"No exit": Processes of social isolation in the middle school*. Paper presented at the American Sociology Association Meeting, San Francisco.

Farmer, T. W., van Acker, R. M., Pearl, R., & Rodkin, P. C. (1999). Social networks and peer-assessed problem behavior in elementary classrooms: Students with and without learning disabilities. *Remedial and Special Education, 20*, 244–256.

Freeman, J. G., & Hutchinson, N. L. (1994). An adolescent with learning disabilities. Eric: The perspective of a potential dropout. *Canadian Journal of Special Education, 9*(4), 131–147.

Freeman, J. G., Stoch, S. A., Chan, J. S. N., Hutchinson, N. L., Mann, J. E., & Eady, J. M. (2001, April). *Staying in school: A retrospective study of adults with learning disabilities*. Paper presented at the annual meeting of the American Educational Research Association, Seattle, WA.

Garnier, H. E., Stein, J. A., & Jacobs, J. K. (1997). The process of dropping out of school: A 19-year perspective. *American Educational Research Journal, 34*, 395–419.

Gerber, P. J., Ginsberg, R., & Reiff, H. B. (1992). Identifying alterable patterns of employment success for highly successful adults with learning disabilities. *Journal of Learning Disabilities, 25*, 475–487.

Hamre-Nietupski, S., Hendrickson, J., Nietupski, J., & Shokoohi-Yekta, M. (1994). Regular educators' perceptions of facilitating friendships of students with moderate, severe, or profound disabilities and nondisabled peers. *Education and Training in Mental Retardation and Developmental Disabilities, 29*, 102–117.

Haring, T. G., & Breen, C. (1989). Units of analysis of social interaction outcomes in supported education. *Journal of the Association for Persons with Severe Handicaps, 14*, 255–262.

Hartup, W. W. (1993). Adolescents and their friends. In B. Laursen (Ed.), *Close friendships in adolescence* (Vol. 60, pp. 3–22). San Francisco: Jossey-Bass.

Heshusius, L. (1989). The Newtonian mechanistic paradigm, special education, and contours of alternatives: An overview. *Journal of Learning Disabilities, 22,* 403–415.

Hutchinson, N. L. (1996). Promoting social development and social acceptance in secondary school classrooms. In J. Andrews (Ed.), *Teaching students with diverse needs* (pp. 152–201). Scarborough, ON: ITP Nelson Canada.

Hutchinson, N. L. (2002). *Inclusion of exceptional learners in Canadian schools: A practical handbook for teachers.* Toronto, ON: Prentice Hall Canada.

Hymel, S., Wagner, E., & Butler, L. J. (1990). Reputational bias: View from the peer group. In S. R. Asher & D. J. Coie (Eds.), *Peer rejection in childhood* (pp. 156–186). Cambridge, MA: Cambridge University Press.

Johnson, G. M. (1997). Resilient at-risk students in the inner-city. *McGill Journal of Education, 32,* 35–49.

LaGreca, A. M., & Stone, W. L. (1990). LD status and achievement: Confounding variables in the study of children's social status, self-esteem, and behavioral functioning. *Journal of Learning Disabilities, 23,* 483–490.

Laursen, B. (1996). Closeness and conflict in adolescent peer relsationships: Interdependence with friends and romantic peers. In W. M. Bukowski, A. F. Newcomb, & W. W. Hartup (Eds.), *The company they keep: Friendship in childhood and adolescence* (pp. 186–210). New York: Cambridge University Press.

Lévesque, N. (1997). *Perceptions of friendships and peer groups: The school experiences of two adolescents with learning disabilities.* Unpublished master's thesis, Queen's University, Kingston, Ontario, Canada.

Mastropieri, M. A., Scruggs, T. E., Mantzicopoulos, P., Sturgeon, A., Goodwin, L., & Chung, S. (1998). "A place where living things affect and depend on each other": Qualitative and quantitative outcomes associated with inclusive science teaching. *Science Education, 82,* 163–179.

McMillan, J. H., & Reed, D. F. (1994). At-risk students and resiliency: Factors contributing to academic success. *Clearing House, 67,* 137–140.

McMillan, J. H., & Schumacher, S. (1993). *Research in education: A conceptual introduction* (3rd ed.). New York: HarperCollins.

McPhail, J. C., Pierson, J. M., Freeman, J. G., Goodman, J., & Ayappa, A. (2000). The role of interest in fostering sixth grade students' identities as competent learners. *Curriculum Inquiry, 30,* 43–70.

Monk, M., & Osborne, J. (Eds.). (2000). *Good practice in science teaching: What research has to say.* Buckingham, UK: Open University Press.

O'Connor, M. C. (1996). Managing the intermental: Classroom group discussion and the social context of learning. In D. I. Slobin, J. Gerhardt, A. Kyratzis, & J. Guo (Eds.), *Social interaction, social context, and language: Essays in honor of Susan Ervin-Tripp* (pp. 495–512). Mahwah, NJ: Lawrence Erlbaum Associates.

Pajares, M. F. (1992). Teachers' beliefs and educational research: Cleaning up a messy construct. *Review of Educational Research, 62,* 307–332.

Perlmutter, B. F., Crocker, J., Cordray, D., & Garstecki, D. (1983). Sociometric status and related personality characteristics of mainstreamed learning disabled adolescents. *Learning Disability Quarterly, 6,* 20–30.

Richardson, V. (1996). The role of attitudes and beliefs in learning to teach. In J. Sikula (Ed.), *Handbook of research on teacher education* (2nd ed., pp. 102–119). New York: Macmillan.

Rueda, R., Gallego, M. A., & Moll, L. C. (2000). The least restrictive environment: A place or a context? *Remedial and Special Education, 21,* 70–78.

Sabornie, E. J., & Kauffman, J. M. (1986). Social acceptance of learning disabled adolescents. *Learning Disability Quarterly, 9,* 55–60.

Scruggs, T. E., & Mastropieri, M. A. (1994a). The construction of scientific knowledge by students with mild disabilities. *Journal of Special Education, 28,* 307–321.

Scruggs, T. E., & Mastropieri, M. A. (1994b). Successful mainstreaming in elementary science classes: A qualitative investigation of three reputable cases. *American Educational Research Journal, 31,* 785–811.

Seidman, I. E. (1991). *Interviewing as qualitative research: A guide for researchers in education and the social sciences.* New York: Teachers College Press.

Spradley, J. P. (1979). *The ethnographic interview.* New York: Holt, Rinehart & Winston.

Stake, R. E. (2000). Case studies. In N. K. Denzin & Y. S. Lincoln (Eds.), *Handbook of qualitative research* (2nd ed., pp. 435–454). Thousand Oaks, CA: Sage.

Stiliadis, K., & Wiener, J. (1989). Relationship between social perception and peer status in children with learning disabilities. *Journal of Learning Disabilities, 22,* 624–629.

Stoch, S. A. (2000). *Zak: An adolescent with learning disabilities at home, at camp, and at school.* Unpublished master's thesis, Queen's University, Kingston, Ontario, Canada.

Stone, C. A., & Reid, D. K. (1994). Social and individual forces in learning: Implications for instruction of children with learning difficulties. *Learning Disability Quarterly, 17,* 72–86.

Trent, S. C., Artiles, A. J., & Englert, C. S. (1998). From deficit thinking to social constructivism: A review of theory, research, and practice in special education. *Review of Research in Education, 23,* 277–307.

Vaughn, S., & Elbaum, B. (1999). The self-concept and friendships of students with learning disabilities: A developmental perspective. In R. Gallimore, L. P. Bernheimer, D. L. MacMillan, D. L Speece, & S. Vaughn (Eds.), *Developmental perspectives on children with high-incidence disabilities* (pp. 81–107). Mahwah, NJ: Lawrence Erlbalum Associates.

Vaughn, S., Elbaum, B. E., Schumm, J. S., & Hughes, M. T. (1998). Social outcomes for students with and without learning disabilities in inclusive classrooms. *Journal of Learning Disabilities, 31,* 428–436.

Vaughn, S., & Hogan, A. (1994). The social competence of students with learning disabilities over time: A within-individual examination. *Journal of Learning Disabilities, 27,* 292–303.

Vaughn, S., McIntosh, R., Schumm, J. S., Haager, D., & Callwood, D. (1993). Social status, peer acceptance, and reciprocal friendships revisited. *Learning Disabilities Research and Practice, 8,* 82–88.

Wenz-Gross, M., & Siperstein, G. N. (1997). Importance of social support in the adjustment of children with learning problems. *Exceptional Children, 63,* 183–193.

Wiener, J., Harris, P. J., & Shirer, C. (1990). Achievement and social-behavioral correlates of peer status in LD children. *Learning Disability Quarterly, 13,* 114–127.

Wiener, J., & Sunohara, G. (1998). Parents' perceptions of the quality of friendship of their children with learning disabilities. *Learning Disabilities Research & Practice, 13,* 242–257.

Yeates, K. O., & Selman, R. L. (1989). Social competence in the schools: Toward an integrative developmental model for intervention. *Developmental Review, 9,* 64–100.

Yin, R. K. (1994). *Case study research: Design and methods* (2nd ed.). Thousand Oaks, CA: Sage.

Chapter 11

Models of Longitudinal Research: Implications for the Study of Social Dimensions of Learning Disabilities

Barbara K. Keogh
University of California, Los Angeles

The special education research literature is composed primarily of cross-sectional studies in which selected individuals or groups of individuals are studied at a particular time point in their lives. These studies have yielded rich descriptions of a range of exceptional conditions and problems at various ages, including learning disabilities (LD) and social and adjustment problems. However, cross-sectional studies do not allow firm inferences about the links between time periods, nor do they identify the processes which explain continuities and discontinuities in development. Understanding exceptional conditions requires study of the same individuals over time, as one of the goals of research from a developmental perspective is to specify the causal mechanisms underlying specific disorders, not just to describe particular conditions at a single time point. As well documented in the literature on children with disabilities and those considered "at risk," the developmental paths and the long-term outcomes for individual children within groups differ greatly. Some overcome the odds against them and become well adjusted, competent adults, whereas others have continuing personal, social, and educational problems (Werner & Smith, 1992). Thus, the need for longitudinal studies.

Rutter (1981) considered longitudinal studies to be an "indispensable" research technique, arguing that "There are numerous scientific and policy questions which can only be answered effectively through the availability of longitudinal or follow-up data (p. 336)." Blackorby and Edgar (1992) suggested that longitudinal research is "the single avenue (p. 372)" for understanding long-term outcomes for individuals with disabilities. They note that longitudinal data may be descriptive and explanatory, the former providing information about the status of individuals at particular time points, the latter allowing insights about the processes leading to different outcomes over time. I suggest that both kinds of data are especially critical if we are to understand the development of children with exceptional needs.

Despite the power of longitudinal findings, longitudinal research has a number of conceptual, methodological, and ethical pitfalls, is time and labor intensive, as well as being expensive (see Blackorby & Edgar, 1992; Keogh & Bernheimer, 1998; Rutter, 1981; Wong, 1994). It should not surprise us that, when compared to cross-sectional research, there are relatively few, although important, longitudinal studies of exceptional individuals. Longitudinal studies have been based on large "unselected" samples of individuals, on samples representing known conditions, and, on ambiguous or at-risk conditions. Sampling decisions of course are tied directly to the purposes of studies.

Subject selection is a central question for special education researchers. Some exceptional conditions (e.g., Down syndrome) are well defined and individuals are identified with relative ease. Other conditions (e.g., developmental delay of unknown etiology, learning disabilities) are more ambiguous and the identification of subjects is less sure. Consider the implications of various definitions of children at risk when determining sample selection. Werner (1986) and Keogh (2000) underscored the point that "risk" is a probability statement, and that prediction is not certain, especially for individual children with nonspecific problems.

It is important to note also that "longitudinal" refers to a number of different research strategies which have in common the study of the same individuals at two or more time periods. How many time points, the intervals between time points, and when outcome data are gathered all influence the nature of findings. For example, Werner and Smith (1992) found that the long-term status of individuals in their study differed when the study participants were in their adolescence, 20s, or 30s.

My focus in this chapter is on sampling issues associated with four strategies of longitudinal research described by Michael Rutter (1981): Prospective "real time" studies; Retrospective "follow-back" studies; Prospective "catch-up" studies; and Age-overlapping short-term studies. These strategies all allow inferences about stability and change over time, but have somewhat different implications for sample selection and for interpretation. In this chapter I discuss each strategy and the implications for sampling, and briefly describe illustrative studies.

STRATEGIES IN LONGITUDINAL RESEARCH

Prospective "Real Time" Studies

In this strategy individuals identified at one time point are studied at some future time point(s). This is a common design which is implemented in a variety of ways, as the follow-up may involve two time points only a few months or a year apart, or may involve multiple time points over several years. The special education literature contains many examples of relatively short term follow-up studies. O'Connor, Notari-Syverson, and Vadasy (1998) tested the effects of kindergarten phonological skills training on children with and without disabilities at the end of first grade. Wagner, Torgesen, and Rashotte (1994) assessed a large sample of children on a number of measures of phonological processing and reading when they were kindergartners, first, and second graders. In the Carolina Longitudinal Learning Disabilities Project, McKinney, Osborne, and Schulte (1993) assessed children identified as learning disabled and their nondisabled peers at first and second grades and again when they were in the fifth or sixth grades. This type of follow-up is often found in studies testing the efficacy of specific educational interventions for particular problem conditions and may allow consideration of the length of interventions relative to the timing of assessment of effects (McConaughy, Hay, & Fitzgerald, 2000).

Prospective real-time efforts are not limited to relatively short-term follow-ups, however, as many involve study of the same individuals over long periods of time (see, e.g., Bernheimer & Keogh, 2000; Fergusson, Horwood, Shannon, & Lawton, 1989; Prior, Sanson, & Oberklaid, 1989; Thomas & Chess, 1977). Research conducted in the Hawaiian Island of Kauai by Emmy Werner and her colleagues is an example of a major, ongoing prospective strategy (Werner, Bierman, & French, 1971; Werner & Smith, 1977, 1989, 1992, 2001). Because of the magnitude and length of this research I have summarized it in some detail.

Werner and her colleagues began study of more than 800 children in 1955. The sample was composed of essentially all children born on the island of Kauai that year. Slightly more than half the children and families were considered at risk because of economic conditions; three fourths were of minority ethnicity. Information was gathered from the mothers prior to the birth of the child, and children were seen at birth, infancy, ages 2, 10, 18, 31–32, and in their forties; the project is still ongoing. Five-hundred and five of the original birth cohort participated in the follow-up when they were in their 30s. A wide range of developmental, personal, and social outcomes were assessed at each time period, allowing the researchers to describe differences in development paths and outcomes and to identify continuities and discontinuities in development and adjustment over time.

The study is notable in many ways. Of particular importance is that the sample was not preselected nor exclusionary. The criterion for participation was birth in 1955 in Kauai. The methods involved a number of different professionals, including educators, physicians, and psychologists. A variety of data collection techniques were used (e.g. standardized tests, interviews, record searches). There was a relatively low rate of sample attrition. Findings from this prospective longitudinal study provide insights about biological and social conditions as well as stressful life events and protective and risk factors that are associated with resilience and risk at various time points in the lives of these individuals. The finding also documented the nature and prevalence of exceptional conditions.

The Kauai study, like many other large-scale studies of development, was based on a sample of "unselected" children. That is, all children within broad parameters were included. In contrast, many prospective studies by researchers in special education are focused on selected samples of children with particular characteristics. Some conditions, for example, specific genetic syndromes, are clearly defined and individuals are identifiable. Others, such as children with reading problems or social–behavioral problems are less precisely defined and the operational criteria for identifying individuals for inclusion in research samples vary according to place and time. There are a number of potential sampling problems in such studies and they pose threats to interpretation and generalization of findings. Consider studies of ADHD where subjects are often identified on the basis of teacher referral. Many children who "fit" the sampling criteria may not be selected, and some of the children selected may not be true exemplars of the condition. Thus, the initial samples for longitudinal follow-up may not accurately represent the condition to be studied. This is a serious problem in cross-sectional research but is even more of a threat to validity in longitudinal work as the sample initially selected is the sample for the duration of the study.

A second issue in sample selection in prospective studies has to do with age of subjects. Some problem conditions are recognizable early on, whereas others are less clear and are age-related. Children with Down syndrome or some other specific genetic disorders can be identified in infancy and the long-term effects of early experiences, including interventions, can be assessed over time and outcomes. Problems in learning, in social adjustment and in behavior or emotional disorders are not often identified until children are older, thus, data about prior conditions and experiences, about the timing of earlier events, may be uncertain or unreliable. A closely related sampling issue has to do with gender. Should the initial sample in longitudinal research reflect the prevalence of known gender differences in problem conditions at later ages or should the sample reflect broader population figures? More males than females have acting out, conduct disorders in adolescence, more girls than boys exhibit excessive shyness. It is possible, even likely, that the developmental paths for males and females differ. The longitudinal researcher, thus, is faced with decisions about both sample and subsample representation.

In sum, there are a number of issues in prospective longitudinal research designs that deserve consideration by special education researchers interested in particular problem conditions. Subject selection and the composition of initial samples is critical. Only a relatively small number of members of broadly defined samples will show signs of specific problems later, thus, a prospective strategy can be an expensive research design. Sample attrition is a real problem, especially for long-term studies. The use of clinic or school identified individuals may result in biased samples that are not representative of the conditions under study. Assessment techniques vary in appropriateness and validity for different developmental periods, raising questions of comparability and continuity of measurement. Finally, cohort effects must be considered. Samples selected in one time period may differ from samples selected in another time period because of economic and social/political conditions. See Friedman et al. (1994) for descriptions of more than 40 years of developmental follow-up research, one kind of longitudinal research model.

Retrospective "Follow-Back" Studies

In this strategy individuals are identified at a given time point and data about them are gathered from prior records or from their recall of earlier times. An advantage of this strategy for researchers in special education is that the outcome condition is known. That is, individuals have already been identified as having (or not having) a particular problem, whereas in prospective designs the outcomes are uncertain. An example of this strategy is research by Vogel et al. (1992) who studied college students who self-identified themselves as learning disabled. The researchers then compared those who graduated and those who didn't by examining their prior experiences in school, including the educational interventions they had experienced, their achievements, the supports and help they had received, and the like. Sanson, Prior, and Smart (1996) used a somewhat different retrospective method to study 7- and 8-year-old children with reading or behavior problems and their comparison nonaffected peers. As part of a prospective study, the Australian Temperament Project (Prior et al., 1989), detailed information about the children, including regular assessments and mothers' and teachers' ratings had been collected at intervals from infancy on. Subsamples of children with reading and behavior problems and nonaffected peers were identified when the children were age 7 to 8. The groups were then compared using data collected earlier as part of the ongoing prospective design. The retrospective analyses identified differences in developmental paths relating to gender and to condition. In a similar design, Fergusson and Woodward (2000) identified 18 year-old girls with conduct problems in adolescence and retrospectively analyzed data collected earlier as part of the Christchurch Health and Development Study (Fergusson et al., 1989).

The follow-back design is a useful and efficient way to organize longitudinal data. One of the drawbacks is that there may be inaccuracies or distortions when information about prior events is based on recall. Further, school and clinic records are sometimes unavailable, incomplete, or inaccurate. Because the information is retrospective, it is not easy to assess its validity, nor is it possible to rule out the effects of unknown influences. Such limitations are less likely when the prior data were gathered prospectively, as in the Sanson et al. (1996) and Fergusson and Woodward (2000) studies.

"Catch-Up" Prospective Studies

In this sampling strategy individuals are identified on the basis of their earlier status and followed up contemporaneously. It is a kind of "flip-side" of the retrospective design just described. This design avoids the waiting period between time one and subsequent time points. An example is the research coming from a private school for children with learning disabilities by Spekman, Goldberg, and Herman (1992) and Raskin, Goldberg, Higgins, and Herman (1999). In a 10-year follow-up Spekman et al. reported on the status of 50 individuals (ages 18–25) who were selected because they had been enrolled in a private center for students with learning disabilities 10 years earlier. Twenty-nine were considered successful and 21 were considered unsuccessful as adults. The young adults and their parents were interviewed and case records were examined in order to identify factors related to outcome status. In a second phase of this catch-up study, Raskin et al. identified 41 of the initial 50 individuals who had participated in the first 10-year phase. The mean age of participants in the 20-year follow-up was 32 years. Contemporaneous data were gathered from interviews, case records, and public records in order to document the long-term outcomes for students identified as learning disabled 20 years earlier. See also Richardson and Koller's (1996) study of young adults who had been identified as mentally retarded 22 years earlier.

As with research using a retrospective follow-back design, catch-up studies face problems of completeness and accuracy of records, and of possible bias in recall. Similar to a problem in follow-up prospective designs, they also are affected by subject attrition, as it is frequently difficult, if not impossible, to locate all individuals who were identified at earlier time points.

Overlapping Short-Term Longitudinal Studies

Not as widely used as the designs described earlier, this strategy calls for overlapping short-term longitudinal studies, so that a wide age range can be covered in a relatively short time frame. Project REACH (Keogh & Kopp, 1982) is an example of this design. This prospective research was focused on infant–toddlers and preschool children with developmental delays of unknown etiology. The infant–toddler sample and the preschool sample overlapped in chronological age (1–3 years and 3–5 years) and were similar in demographic characteristics. Thus, it was theoretically possible to gather longitudinal data on various developmental conditions across the age range birth through age 5, but to do this in 3 rather than 5 years. A critical point in this strategy is that the samples must be equivalent, and that is often difficult to achieve with samples of exceptional children. In the REACH work the children and families for both samples were selected using the same criteria. Yet, examination of the samples indicated that they were not comparable in degree of impairment, the infants and toddlers having more serious delays. Nonetheless, this strategy is potentially useful as it allows study of a wide age range in a limited time period. It also minimizes the likelihood of sample attrition.

METHODOLOGICAL ISSUES IN LONGITUDINAL RESEARCH

Schonhaut and Satz (1983) proposed five criteria necessary, if not sufficient, to assess progress over time. These were: Adequate follow-up period, sufficiently large sample size, method of subject selection, comparison group, valid measures. These are all important aspects of longitudinal research, but difficult to achieve. My purpose in this chapter was to call attention to the importance of sample selection and to show how sampling issues are related to longitudinal design strategies. Sampling questions are important for all researchers who study children with problems. They are relevant in both cross-sectional and longitudinal studies, but are critical in longitudinal work as decisions about who to study and the data collected over time cannot be changed retrospectively.

Because it is nearly impossible to study total populations, samples are selected to be representative of the larger population under study (e.g., all children with LD, or all adolescents with social–behavior problems). At least two problems constrain inferences about how representative a sample really is. By definition, longitudinal work requires study over time, thus the sample can represent only the population as defined at a particular time, and definitions change. The possible effects of different cohorts must be taken into account when interpreting longitudinal findings. Consider, for example, the impact of differences in services available to children with disabilities and their families before and after PL 94–142 and PL 99–457. These differences may have contributed to findings at particular time periods. Note that the population of children identified as mentally retarded dropped dramatically after learning disabilities became an accepted diagnostic category (MacMillan, 1989). In addition, change in the IQ cut-off points from one to two standard deviations below the mean resulted in fewer, but more seriously impaired, children identified as mentally retarded. As a consequence, samples of children selected to represent the condition, mental retardation, in 1959 and 1975 were clearly different.

A second sampling constraint is not limited to longitudinal research, but is especially important because the original sample remains the sample over time. I refer to the validity of diagnostic criteria. The problem is clearly apparent in studies of children with LD, where there are broad differences in samples depending on where the children live, where they go to school, and the economic status of their parents. Clinic or school-based samples may not represent a conceptually defined condition such as learning disabilities, but rather may reflect the context or culture of the school or clinic. Many selection factors, including the measures and the criteria used for identification, influence who is selected and who isn't, so that system identified samples may or may not accurately represent the condition under study (Keogh & MacMillan, 1983). Even cursory examination of the research literature documents the heterogeneity of study samples presumably representing learning disabilities, emotional disturbance, or even social–behavioral problems.

Longitudinal researchers are also faced with problems of sample attrition and of nonresponse bias. Families and individuals may move or may choose not to continue in a given study. Few studies over extended periods of time have full data on all sample members at all time points, even when the researchers work hard to ensure continued participation. For example, in a follow-up of children with developmental delays, we found parents of a few of the children did not want them tested at every time period because it was upsetting to the child and to the parents (Keogh & Bernheimer, 1998).

The appropriateness and validity of assessment measures and techniques also contribute to longitudinal results, as measures may not be equivalent over time, especially when different scales are used at different ages (Edelbrock, 1994). Measures may tap different abilities at different time periods (e.g., infant and toddler developmental tests are weighted with items focused on fine and gross motor skills, whereas tests for older children are increasingly language based). Thus, test results may not be comparable over time because of the content of the measures used and also because of possible effects of repeated testing.

Questions of appropriate comparison groups in longitudinal research with exceptional children are also relevant. Given the time and financial demands of longitudinal work, some studies do not use comparison samples except for subsample analyses, and these are often drawn from the primary unselected prospective sample (e.g., Fergusson & Woodward, 2000; Sanson et al., 1996). The issue of comparable comparison groups is especially difficult in studies of exceptional children, as it is questionable if there can be true matches between exceptional and nonexceptional individuals and groups on any but broad demographic variables. Researchers of individuals with mental retardation have used chronological and mental age matches in attempts to achieve comparability, but possible differences between selected groups on many other variables are not controlled. Stoneman (1989) pointed out that when individuals are matched on mental age (MA), a composite score, ". . . there is no assurance that their specific skills and competencies will be similar. . . . it is probable that the skill patterns of two MA-matched individuals would be quite different" (p. 199). Thus the findings may be influenced by a number of untested variables that affect the target samples and their comparison samples differently. Proper comparison groups are essential in experimental designs, but are difficult to define and maintain in longitudinal research. They also strain resources.

Also to be considered are the possible unintended researcher effects on longitudinal findings. The very fact of being part of a longitudinal research study may influence participant behaviors. Having ongoing contact with researchers and the research protocols may change parents' attitudes and child-rearing practices. In our work in Project REACH we found that our relationships with the children and families changed over time. REACH was not an intervention study, but over time the parents increasingly viewed it as such, and the impact of this on the study findings is uncertain (Keogh & Bernheimer, 1998). Finally, the longitudinal researcher using a prospective design faces the practical problem of data management and analysis. Vast amounts of data are common in long-term studies, and analyses are often slow. The researcher may be involved simultaneously in the collection of new data while still processing information already collected. For more detailed discussion of these issues, see Bergman and Magnusson (1990), Egeland (1991), Keogh and Bernheimer (1998), Rutter (1981).

It is important to stress that the power of longitudinal strategies does not minimize the role of cross-sectional research in the study of exceptional individuals. Rutter (1981) noted that "both repeated cross-sectional and longitudinal data are needed to study development. Only in this way can developmental alternations and secular shifts be distinguished" (p. 355). Repeated cross-sectional data, especially if gathered at different time points and with different samples, provide rich descriptions of problem conditions, identify possible cohort effects, and address issues of generalization of findings. The substantive research of Tanis Bryan who is being honored in the volume, is an example. Her cross-sectional studies of children with learning disabilities have identified and replicated a range of characteristics that distinguish them from their peers and which generalize across many samples and many contexts, thus meshing with the findings from longitudinal work. The issue is not whether a longitudinal or a cross-sectional strategy is "better" but which is appropriate for the topic under study.

Despite earlier mentioned concerns about longitudinal methods, the importance of study of the same individuals across time is essential if we are to understand the dynamics of development that are associated with different problems and different outcomes. The potential benefits of longitudinal research are many, both theoretically and practically. Robins (1979) noted that longitudinal data provide information about the duration of problem behaviors and conditions, identify predictors of subsequent disorders, and provide evidence as to the efficacy of treatments and interventions. Documenting the developmental paths of exceptional children which lead to different outcomes is especially important as individual and contextual conditions that contribute to diverse outcomes can be identified. Such information provides insights for developmental theorists, as well as for educators and clinicians who work with exceptional children and their families.

ACKNOWLEDGMENTS

This research was supported in part by grant 5 PO1 HD11944 from the National Institute of Child Health and Human Development. I thank Cindy Bernheimer for her helpful review and suggestions in the preparation of this chapter.

REFERENCES

Bergman, L. R., & Magnusson, D. (1990). General issues about data quality in longitudinal research. In D. Magnusson & L. R. Bergman (Eds.), *Data quality in longitudinal research* (pp. 1–31). Cambridge, England: Cambridge University Press.

Bernheimer, L. P., & Keogh, B. K. (2000). *REACH Follow-up Technical Report.* Department of Psychiary, UCLA.

Blackorby, J., & Edgar, E. (1992). Longitudinal studies in the postschool adjustment of students with disabilities. In F. R. Rusch, L. DeStefano, J. Chadsey-Rusch, L. A. Phelps, & E. Szymanski (Eds.), *Transition from school to adult life* (pp. 371–386). Sycamore, IL: Sycamore Publishing Co.

Edelbrock, C. (1994). Assessing child psychopathology in developmental follow-up studies. In S. L. Friedman & H. C. Haywood (Eds.), *Developmental follow-up, concepts, domains, and methods* (pp. 183–194). San Diego, CA: Academic Press.

Egeland, B. (1991). A longitudinal study of high-risk families: Issues and findings. In R. H. Starr & D. A. Wolfe (Eds.), *The effects of child abuse and neglect: Issues and research* (pp. 33–55). New York: Guilford Press.

Fergusson, D. M., Horwood, L. J., Shannon, F. Y., & Lawton, J. M. (1989). The Christchurch Child Development Study: A review of epidemiological findings. *Paediatric and Perinatal Epidemiology, 3,* 278–301.

Fergusson, D. M., & Woodward, L. J. (2000). Educational, psychosocial, and sexual outcomes of girls with conduct problems in early adolescence. *Journal of Child Psychology and Psychiatry, 41,* 779–792.

Friedman, S. L., Haywood, H. C., & Livesey, K. (1994). From the past to the future of developmental longitudinal research. In S. L. Friedman & H. C. Haywood (Eds.), *Developmental follow-up, concepts, domains, and methods* (pp. 3–26). San Diego: Academic Press.

Keogh, B. K. (2000). Risk, families, and schools. *Focus on Exceptional Children, 33,* 1–10.

Keogh, B. K., & Bernheimer, L. P. (1998). Issues and dilemmas in longitudinal research: A tale of two studies. *Thalamus, 16,* 5–13.

Keogh, B. K., & Kopp, C. B. (1982). *Project REACH Final Report.* Graduate School of Education, University of California, Los Angeles.

Keogh, B. K., & MacMillan, D. L. (1983). The logic of sample selection: Who represents what? *Exceptional Education Quarterly, 4*(3), 84–96.

MacMillan, D. L. (1989). Equality, excellence, and the EMR populations: 1970–1989. *Psychology in Mental Retardation and Developmental Disabilities, 15,* 3–10.

McConaughy. S. H., Kay, P. J., & Fitzgerald, M. (2000). How long is long enough? Outcomes for a school-based prevention program. *Exceptional Children, 67,* 21–34.

McKinney, J. D., Osborne, S. S., & Schulte, A. C. (1993). Academic consequences of learning disability: Longitudinal prediction of outcomes at 11 years of age. *Learning Disabilities Research and Practice, 8,* 19–27.

O'Connor, R. E., Notari-Syverson, A., & Vadasy, P. (1998). First-grade effects of teacher-led phonological activities in kindergarten for children with mild disabilities: A follow-up study. *Learning Disabilities Research and Practice, 13,* 43–52.

Prior, M., Sanson, A. V., & Oberklaid, F. (1989). The Australian temperament project. In G. A. Kohnstamm, J. E. Bates, & M. K. Rothbart (Eds.), *Temperament in childhood* (pp. 537–566) New York: Wiley.

Raskin, M. H., Goldberg, R. J., Higgins, E. L., & Herman, K. L. (1999). Patterns of change and predictors of success in individuals with learning disabilities: Results from a twenty-year longitudinal study. *Learning Disabilities Research and Practice, 14,* 35–49.

Richardson, S. A., & Koller, H. (1996). *Twenty-two years later. Causes and consequences of mental retardation,* Cambridge, MA: Harvard University Press.

Robins, L. N. (1979). Follow-up studies. In H. C. Quay & J. S. Werry (Eds.), *Psychopathological disorders of childhood* (pp. 484–513). New York: Wiley.

Rutter, M. (1981). Longitudinal studies. In S. A. Mednick & A. E. Baert (Eds.), *Prospective longitudinal research: An empirical basis for primary prevention* (pp. 326–336). London: Oxford University Press.

Sanson, A., Prior, M., & Smart, D. (1996). Reading disabilities with and without behavior problems at 7–8 years: Prediction from longitudinal data from infancy to 6 years. *Journal of Child Psychology and Psychiatry, 37,* 529–541.

Schonhaut, S., & Satz, P. (1983). Prognosis of the learning-disabled child: A review of the follow-up studies. In M. Rutter (Ed.), *Developmental neuropsychiatry* (pp. 542–563). New York: Guilford Press.

Spekman, N. J., Goldberg, R. J., & Herman, K. L. (1992). Learning disabled children grow up: A search for factors related to success in the young adult years. *Learning Disabilities Research and Practice, 7,* 161–170.

Stoneman, Z. (1989). Comparison groups in research on families with mentally retarded members: A methodological and conceptual review. *American Journal on Mental Retardation, 94,* 195–215.

Thomas, A., & Chess, S. (1977). *Temperament and development.* New York: Brunner/Mazel.

Vogel, S. A., Hruby, P. J., & Adelman, P. B. (1993). Educational and psychological factors in successful and unsuccessful students with learning disabilities. *Learning Disabilities Research and Practice, 8,* 35–43.

Wagner, R., Torgesen, J. K., & Rashotte, C. A. (1994). Development of reading-related phonological processing abilities: New evidence of bidirectional causality from a latent variable longitudinal study. *Developmental Psychology, 30,* 73–87.

Werner, E. E. (1986). The concept of risk from a developmental perspective. In B. K. Keogh (Ed.), *Advances in special education, Vol. 5. Developmental problems in infancy and the preschool years* (pp. 1–24). Greenwich, CT: JAI Press.

Werner, E. E., Bierman, J. M., & French, F. E. (1971). *The children of Kauai.* Honolulu: University of Hawaii Press.

Werner, E. E., & Smith, R. S. (1977). *Kauai's children come of age.* Honolulu: University of Hawaii Press.

Werner, E. E., & Smith, R. S. (1989). *Vulnerable but invincible. A longitudinal study of resilient children and youth.* New York: Adams, Bannister, and Cos.

Werner, E. E., & Smith, R. S. (1992). *Overcoming the odds: High risk children from birth to adulthood.* New York: Cornell University Press.

Werner, E. E., & Smith, R. S. (2001). *Journeys from childhood to midlife.* Ithaca, NY: Cornell University Press.

Wong, B. Y. L. (1994). The relevance of longitudinal research to learning disabilities. *Journal of Learning Disabilities, 27,* 270–274.

Author Index

Subject Index